1996

1996
A BIOGRAPHY

JON FINKEL

RELIVING THE LEGEND-PACKED, DYNASTY-STACKED, MOST ICONIC SPORTS YEAR EVER

DIVERSION
BOOKS

To 1996

You had me at hello . . . You had me . . . at hello . . .

◘   ◘   ◘

For more information, email info@diversionbooks.com

Diversion Books

A division of Diversion Publishing Corp.

www.diversionbooks.com

First Diversion Books edition, May 2021

Paperback ISBN: 9781635767506

eBook ISBN: 9781635767551

Printed in The United States of America

1 3 5 7 9 10 8 6 4 2

Library of Congress cataloging-in-publication data is available on file

CONTENTS

INTRODUCTION

"NOW LET ME WELCOME EVERYBODY TO THE Wild Wild West, a state that's untouchable like Eliot Ness . . ."

Dr. Dre's lyrics slide out of your white Sony Dream Machine as you flick the rectangle snooze button to cut off your alarm. You might live in the Golden State, but probably not. You love California because of "California Love," and anything is better than the radio stations that won't stop playing "Macarena." You hop out of bed wearing your black Orlando Magic basketball shorts with the stripes dropping from the drawstring and the stars from the logo on the side of each thigh. You probably don't live in Orlando, but no matter. Shaq and Penny's uniforms are dope.

As you open your blinds to let the sun pour in on this fine, early summer morning in 1996, you flip on *SportsCenter* to catch part of last night's "The Big Show" with Dan Patrick and Keith Olbermann, two men whose voices you've heard more the last few years than even your own father's. Hell, throw Stuart Scott and Rich Eisen in the mix and you've listened to these sports anchors speak more than anyone in your whole life. You can recite their catchphrases (en fuego, cool as the other side of the pillow) better than the Pledge of Allegiance.

On your dresser you've got your Right Guard deodorant because Charles Barkley says anything less would be uncivilized. In your closet are a bunch of shirts from the GAP and Abercrombie & Fitch and some oversized Tommy Hilfiger polos, and in the back you've got a vintage

'92 Clyde Drexler USA Basketball Dream Team jersey (too many people had Jordan and Bird and Magic, and you're no sheep).

Hanging on random doorknobs and trophies around your room are a bunch of The Game hats. You've got South Carolina's maroon hat that says "COCKS" on it (insert Beavis's laugh in your head) and a maize and blue one that says "U of M" for Michigan and a nice royal blue one that says "Kentucky." You've never stepped foot in Columbia or Ann Arbor or Lexington, but who cares? The hats are tight.

On your wall is the Bo Jackson poster you've had since grade school. You know the one—Bo, shirtless, wearing his football pads and holding a baseball bat behind his head. You have the yellow-bordered "Sultans of Slam" poster with Jordan, Dominique, Spud Webb, and every other great dunker in the NBA. You have the classic Kid Dynamite Costacos Bros poster of Ken Griffey Jr. with flames behind him. Come to think of it, the only hat you have in your room that isn't The Game is a blue Seattle Mariners hat that you wear backward because of Griffey. If you know, you know.

Between some of your posters you've put up a few *Sports Illustrated* swimsuit issue pictures and covers. Of course, there's Tyra Banks and Cindy Crawford and Kathy Ireland. And yeah, you might have a few of your dad's *Playboys* stashed under the bed with Jenny McCarthy and Pamela Anderson on the front.

As you throw on a white "No Fear" t-shirt with the blue logo and slide on your Nike Air Zoom Flights (because you'd have to mow 4,000 lawns to afford a new pair of Air Jordan VIs), you're excited because tonight is the first game of the 1996 NBA Finals between Jordan and Pippen's Bulls and Shawn Kemp and Gary Payton's Sonics. You can't believe the year is only half over. It feels like New Year's Day was a lifetime ago, when you watched Bobby Bowden's All-NFL Florida State defense, Steve Spurrier's Fun 'N' Gun at Florida, and Tom Osborne's Tommie Frazier-led Nebraska battle it out in bowl games in a race for team of the decade.

Then in quick succession, as if blessed by the sports gods, nearly every major star from every sport had their moment. Troy Aikman, Michael Irvin, Emmitt Smith, Deion Sanders, and the Cowboys capped off their third Super Bowl in four years on January 28, and then two days later Magic Johnson miraculously returned to the NBA after his hiatus due to HIV. The next week, the NBA's past and future collided in the All-Star Game when Shaquille O'Neal, Penny Hardaway, and Grant Hill joined Pippen and Jordan in the East's starting line-up (MJ's first All-Star appearance since his return from baseball).

You then quickly transitioned to college hoops' conference tournaments, where the NCAA's biggest name (and NBA's future icon)—Allen Iverson of Georgetown—scorched his way through the Big East and then March Madness. Immediately after that, Ken Griffey Jr. was ready to put the '95 strike-shortened season behind for all of us and signed a record-breaking baseball contract. Then the WNBA announced its existence to the world with a trifecta of women's hoop pioneers in Rebecca Lobo, Lisa Leslie, and Sheryl Swoopes.

The Bulls then became the best basketball team of all time, finishing 72–10. After the Finals, the Los Angeles Lakers drafted a kid out of high school named Kobe Bryant, after which a seismic shift in the NBA took place when Shaq left the Orlando Magic to join him on July 18. *The very next day*, Muhammad Ali lit the torch to start the 1996 Olympics in Atlanta, with Dream Team III, Michael Johnson burning up the track, Amy Van Dyken owning the pool, the Magnificent Seven taking over gymnastics, and tennis's reformed bad boy Andre Agassi winning Olympic Gold.

Wayne Gretzky got traded to the New York Rangers, a sixteen-year-old Venus Williams faced 8-time Grand Slam Winner Steffi Graf for the first time, and then Tiger Woods said "Hello, world," joined the PGA Tour, won his first tournament, and became *Sports Illustrated*'s coveted "Sportsman of the Year." Derek Jeter made his Yankees post-season debut, Mike Tyson fought three times in nine months, and Brett Favre was about to gun-sling his way to the top of the NFL. It was an embarrassment of sports riches, and every day you woke up, a new generational legend was performing a new sports feat—and you didn't even know how good you had it. Of course, every year has its icons; *but dammit, it felt like 1996 was loaded top-to-bottom with them.*

If you came of age during the '90s, with your *Madden* season saved on your PlayStation and *"boom shakalaka"* from *NBA Jam* ringing in your ears, this was your time. You had *Shaq Fu* and *Rock N' Jock, Space Jam* and *Kazaam, Happy Gilmore* and *Jerry Maguire.*

You had it all.

And in the blink of an eye, two-and-a-half decades have passed.

You grew up.

Hell, we all grew up.

We settled down, got jobs, had kids of our own. Now here we are, all these years later, and we're still enamored with the stars, teams, icons, legends, and dynasties of our youth.

Forget 2021 for a minute.

Forget all your responsibilities.

Close your eyes.

Hear *SportsCenter*'s *da-da-da-da da-da-da* one last time. Listen to Stuart Scott's intro. Mentally throw on your Game hat. Grab a bag of Cool Ranch Doritos and a Citrus Cooler Gatorade and for a couple hundred pages let's go back in time, together, and celebrate the 25th anniversary of the most glorious year of sports' glory years: 1996.

SPURRIER VS. BOWDEN VS. OSBORNE

THE RUN! NINETEEN SECONDS LEFT IN THE third quarter of the Tostitos Fiesta Bowl, and Tommie Frazier takes position under center in the most basic of football formations—the "I"—at his own 20-yard line. No shotgun. No five wide. No motion. Nothing. It's a ham sandwich of an offensive set-up. Frazier takes the snap, ducks his left shoulder, and whips around in time for a millisecond fake handoff to his fullback Brian Schuster.

As Frazier tucks the ball to his chest with both hands, he sidesteps past Florida Gator Defender #1. His running back, Clinton Childs, slides off to his right, ready to take the pitch. Florida's Defender #2 looms in front of Frazier, who gives a *Matrix*-fast pitch-fake that dupes Defender #2 enough for Frazier to skip up-field past him.

Two Gator linebackers (Defenders #3 and #4) converge on Frazier a hair too late and grasp at his jersey. One manages to clutch the bottom of the fabric, and for a flutter of a second Frazier's jersey stretches before he tilts his 205-pound frame forward, jacks up the horsepower, and rips free.

At the 35-yard line, a Florida linebacker, Defender #5, squares up in front of the quarterback and wraps his arms around him. *Frazier's legs keep churning.* Defender #6 collapses on him from behind, and Ben Hanks—Defender #2 again!—rejoins the fight and yanks at the quarterback, slowing him almost to a standstill as a Florida safety, Defender #7, and a Florida corner, Defender #8, shove their way into the scrum. Frazier's legs motor on as he clutches the ball. Chop. Chop. Chop.

Brian Schuster, about ten yards back, stops running alongside his teammate.

The play is over, right?

By the 38-yard line there are FIVE Florida Gator defenders hammering away at Frazier. *Frazier's legs keep churning.* Hanks, who wound up in front of Frazier, tugs at the ball but falls on his back as Frazier pushes forward and somehow gains steam; in a Hulk Smash moment (a Husker Smash, maybe?), three defenders fall off and Defender #6 briefly rides Frazier's back like a jockey before sliding off to the ground.

As Frazier sheds the weight, his momentum rockets him downfield. Defender #9 lunges for his hips, but he might as well be trying to catch a passing speedboat while treading water.

By the 50-yard line, Tommie Frazier is free and flying downfield, a red blur of determination on his way to a 75-yard touchdown. The game, like the run, was an embarrassment for head coach Steve Spurrier and his Gators. Frazier's touchdown put the Cornhuskers up 49–18 on their way to a 62–24 win and a second straight National Championship. It also made a mockery of the media hype leading into the game, which largely focused on whether Nebraska's defense could contain Florida's Fun 'N' Gun offense behind stud quarterback Danny Wuerffel.

At the time, it seemed like a fair point to consider; Wuerffel went through SEC defenses like a kid whose video game opponent had a broken controller. He set the then-NCAA record for passing efficiency and the SEC record for touchdowns with 35 (and only 10 interceptions).

"We had something that was clicking," Wuerffel says. "It was a special group. We seemed to be running through a lot of folks. We had a lot of confidence and we thought we'd move through them. In a way, we were overconfident. Before that, teams like Nebraska and Oklahoma, who had great seasons, ran into trouble in bowl games against speed when they played a Miami or Florida State."

During the 1995 season, Florida's offense was every bit as terrifying as those of the Hurricanes and Seminoles Wuerffel mentioned. They'd hung 62 points on 8th ranked Tennessee, 49 on 7th ranked Auburn, 35 on 6th ranked Florida State, and 63 on South Carolina. When LSU "held" the Gators to 28 (while only scoring 10), it was news.

As the bowl game approached, it was legit—at least to everybody outside of the Cornhuskers' locker room—to wonder if Tom Osborne's undefeated Nebraska defense could stop Spurrier's undefeated offense.

"The truth is, we expected this to happen," Nebraska junior strong safety Mike Minter said about the final score. "All week in public we said the right things. But when we went to our hotel rooms, it was like, 'we're going to blow them out.'"

"They played a very aggressive coverage against us," Wuerffel says. "A lot of press and a lot of man-to-man. We saw a whole lot of zone that year because teams were so afraid [that] they'd back off. Add to that Nebraska's ferocious pass rush and they had a good scheme."

Let's also keep in mind that Nebraska's offense was historically great, as well. They came up a rounding error short of averaging a cheat-code level 400 rushing yards per game (399.8 to be exact), and they averaged over 50 points per game, too. They had Tommie Frazier wielding the offense with Jedi-like mastery and an all-time talented backfield with Ahman Green and Lawrence Phillips. The hedge in Florida's favor was that if Nebraska did run wild, the Gators would be able to pass wild to keep pace.

Or not.

A couple weeks before the game, when *Sports Illustrated* writer Tim Layden spent time in the Cornhuskers' film room for a story on how the team prepared for a national championship, he asked a few linebackers if they were worried about Florida. "They looked at each other," he wrote. "They'd seen the film. One of them said, 'It's not going to be close.'"

This was '90s college football juggernaut-on-juggernaut crime. From 1993 to 1999, Florida State, Florida, and Nebraska won six of seven national championships, twenty conference titles, and played each other or someone else in nearly every important bowl game of the decade. The coaches of these teams were football gods: Spurrier with his signature visor; Bowden with the hat and glasses; and Tom Osborne with his seemingly never-ending parade of red windbreakers. For a brief period, they were college football's single-named superstar singers. The names Steve and Bobby and Tom were totally superfluous. When you were talking college ball, Spurrier and Bowden and Osborne were the only shorthand you needed.

This was rarified air. Perhaps only Joe Paterno at the time could have joined this crew, but he hadn't won squat since 1986. No, there were three coaches who *really mattered* in '96. Three coaches who you dreamed of getting an offer from if you played ball in high school. They were the three titans. You might flirt with a Michigan or Notre Dame or Ohio State for tradition's sake, but if you wanted to be at the epicenter of college football culture, you were headed to Gainesville or Tallahassee or Lincoln.

A few years earlier, in 1993, the best football movie of your young life, *The Program*, hit theaters, and the school in the film—Eastern State University (ESU)—had Florida State's exact uniform colors. Duane Davis, who played star linebacker Alvin Mack in the movie, based his character on a Seminole.

"There was a linebacker on Florida State. I based Alvin Mack on Derrick Brooks," he said.

FSU was the school of uber athletes—of dual sport stars Deion Sanders and Heisman Trophy winner and New York Knicks point guard Charlie Ward. Florida was even the home of your favorite drink, Gatorade. If you were a bandwagon 1996 NFL fan (which was basically half the football-loving country at that point), two of the four biggest stars on the Dallas Cowboys—AKA, "America's Team"—Emmitt Smith and Sanders, repped Florida and Florida State respectively.

These weren't just flash-in-the-pan schools that were good for a handful of years. They were a trio of historically excellent programs who year-after-year found themselves head-butting each other for football supremacy and recruiting against each other for next year's crop of five-star studs.

In Florida, the recruiting competition between the Gators and Seminoles (and Miami) was a 365-day royal rumble. And when players finally committed, they often found themselves on a team with former high school rivals—and were now rivals with former high school teammates. In a little-known twist surrounding the 1996 Fiesta Bowl, the two biggest stars, Wuerffel and Frazier, had known each other since childhood in Florida. Wuerffel went to Fort Walton High and Frazier attended Manatee High in Bradenton.

"You play against some of these guys, or you have established friendships," Frazier said. "But when it comes to university against university, you have so much pride for your school."

"I was a big fan of Tommie Frazier," Wuerffel says. "We grew up together. I knew him from high school and our teammates knew each other." And fun fact: Wuerffel grew up a Nebraska fan. "I lived in Lincoln, Nebraska, as a fourth grader. I was a nine-year-old kid the year

Mike Rozier won the Heisman. I was a big, big Husker fan. But not on the day of the Fiesta Bowl, of course."

Following Florida's devastating Fiesta Bowl loss, the tug of war between the trio of schools for college football's 1996–1997 pre-season top dog was heavily in Nebraska's favor and stayed that way when the polls were posted, naming the Cornhuskers #1, Tennessee (with Peyton Manning) #2, Florida State #3, and Florida #4. Aside from Manning's interloping Volunteers, once again, the top 5 was dominated by Osborne, Bowden, and Spurrier.

As had become the norm, fans immediately looked at the schedule to circle the one date that had served as a de facto play-in game to a national championship for much of the decade: the November 30 match-up between Florida and Florida State. And it was just assumed that Nebraska would end the year undefeated and be in position to win the title, as well.

As *College GameDay*'s Lee Corso would say, "Not so fast, my friends."

In a Week 2 shocker, Arizona State, led by quarterback Jake Plummer and their now-famous Desert Swarm defense with Pat Tillman, shut out the Cornhuskers 19–0. It was a dumbfounding, confounding experience for Osborne's men, many of whom had experienced non-stop Ws while wearing the red and white.

"I've never been on a field when we've lost a game," Nebraska's linebacker Grant Wistrom said. "I've never played in a loss."

"They just whipped us," Osborne said. "We didn't generate a good enough running game. We needed a big play ... but we just didn't convert."

Nebraska plummeted to #8 in the polls. That left Tennessee, Ohio State, Arizona State, Florida, and Florida State as the remaining favorites; but really it was just the Seminoles and the Gators who, week after week on the gridiron, put up basketball scores.

The Gators won games scoring 55, 62, 65, 42, 56, 51, 47, 52, and 45. It was like they were playing a pop-a-shot game in an arcade. The only close games they had on their collision course to Florida State was with #2 Tennessee, who they beat 35–29, and a brain fart of a game against Vanderbilt, who they beat 28–21. Every Saturday night you'd turn on the football highlights to a familiar sight: Wuerffel dropping back, a Florida receiver galloping toward the end zone, then the Head Ball Coach Spurrier grinning on the sideline and the Swamp chanting, "It's great . . . to be . . . a Florida Gaaaator . . . "

Wash. Rinse. Repeat.

Wuerffel, the Heisman Trophy favorite heading into the season, believes the key to their '96 dominance stemmed from the bowl-game beating they took at the hands of Nebraska to start the calendar year.

"Going into my senior year we were really focused," he says. "I made a commitment with myself not to watch TV or read any newspapers or magazines. In my mind, I was focused on practice, making the right read and making the right throw. And Coach Spurrier made sure to not treat me like a star at all. He treated me like the back-up kid in junior high."

Florida also anticipated that other college football teams would try to follow the "Nebraska Blueprint" to slow down the Gators, so they spent the whole off-season getting better at running their routes and throwing against the coverages that they'd had problems against.

Florida State, for their part, tore through the ACC like a bowling ball through tissue paper with their star running back, Warrick Dunn. Most schools recruited Dunn out of high school to be a defensive back, but he believed he could be a featured back at a major program and bet on himself.

"I didn't want to play defensive back in college, but that's what everyone wanted me to do," Dunn says. "When I was getting comfortable with the decision to go to Florida State, I made a deal with Bobby Bowden that I'd start out at running back with the offense. If it didn't work out, I'd go back to DB."

It worked out.

While the Seminoles weren't the offensive tour de force that the Gators were, they still embarrassed nearly every single one of their opponents. They beat their first four teams—Duke, North Carolina State, North Carolina, and Clemson—by a combined score of 142–27. A little later in the season, they'd humiliate Georgia Tech, Wake Forest, Southern Mississippi, and Maryland by a total score of 195–34.

By the last Saturday in November, the country had the match-up they were dying to see: #1 Florida (11–0) against #2 Florida State (11–0).

"We scored forty points or more in four consecutive games before playing the Gators at Doak Campbell Stadium on November 30th," Bowden wrote in his memoir. "Danny Wuerffel . . . was as good as any quarterback I ever saw, and the Gators had great receivers such as Reidel Anthony, Ike Hilliard, and Jacquez Green. Spurrier's Fun 'N' Gun offense was really revolutionizing the way football was played in the SEC. I told our team the night before the game, 'We must stop the run first, but don't let their receivers get behind you. You will never catch them if you do.'"

Sometimes you need a little bit of luck for things to break your way. In this game, the pounding heat and the uneven terrain around Gainesville caused a 20-mile-per hour wind to swirl around Florida's famed Swamp, which sucked the 'fun' out of the Fun 'N' Gun. As per football code, neither team would mention the wind as any kind of factor in the game (although Bowden gives the gusts a nod in his memoir), but Wuerffel threw for a wildly uncharacteristic three interceptions that day, including one to end their first drive, which changed the feel of the game. With the swirling winds affecting both passing games, Florida State fed their star running back Warrick Dunn over and over again, just as they had in previous match-ups. And once again, he ate through Florida's defense like it was dollar-a-plate night at the Golden Corral. In five starts against the Gators, including this game, Dunn rushed for 445 yards and caught passes for another 334.

Still, the game remained close, and with one minute and nineteen seconds left, Wuerffel threw a touchdown to make the score 24–21 with FSU up by a field goal. The Gator faithful filled the Swamp with cheers and chants. *One stop! Three and out!* The noise was deafening, and 70,000 people were all thinking the same thing. *Get Danny the ball back!*

Before going back on the field, Florida State's Captain America, Dunn, pulled his offense in around him. Speaking softly, as he always did, he corralled his teammates and leaned in to get their full attention.

"I was always calm, no matter what the moment," Dunn says. "I remember saying that I need everything you guys have right now. If you have anything left, we can get this first down and that's a wrap; we'll be headed to the Sugar Bowl. It was one of those moments in my career where I knew it was on me to let everyone know that now was the time."

They got the first down.

Florida State won.

"I guess I've had my share of fun against those guys," Dunn said at the time, understating his complete and utter dominance against the Gators. "Me being from Baton Rouge, this was a huge goal for me. It'll be a pretty great way to finish my college football career, playing in the Sugar Bowl, so near my Louisiana hometown for the national championship."

The Seminoles left the Swamp with visions of a national championship dancing in their heads. The Gators left under a cloud of disappointment. They'd spent all off-season preparing for this moment and they had their shot, at home, against the second-ranked team in the country—and they lost.

"We knew coming in it would be a tough game," Spurrier said. "Win, lose, or draw. We'll be ready for Alabama. And we'll try to win four straight SEC Championships. Before the season starts, the SEC Championship game is our biggest game of the year. If we can't get ready for that, we're a bunch of dummies."

Regardless, the SEC Championship was a consolation prize to a national championship, and the way things appeared, they'd be on the outside looking in. All Nebraska had to do was beat a mediocre Texas team in their conference championship game and they'd be playing Florida State in the Sugar Bowl. In order for the Gators to still have a chance, a nearly impossible sequence of events would have to happen, which led to die-hard fans running *War Games*-like scenarios that all started with "if" in their heads.

If we beat Alabama in the SEC Championship game and if Texas upsets Nebraska in the Big XII Championship game, then maybe we'll get another crack at Florida State in the Sugar Bowl. And if Ohio State can somehow beat Arizona State in the Rose Bowl and then we crush Florida State, wouldn't we be national champions?

The short answer to this particular convoluted thinking was "yes," but the reality of it happening as of December 1, 1996, was next to zilch.

And then . . .

Florida smoked Alabama in the SEC Championship game, 45–30.

And then . . .

The unranked, 7–4, Texas Longhorns miraculously beat the 10–1, 3rd ranked Cornhuskers in the Big Twelve title game, 37–27.

Which led to . . .

Florida getting invited to the Sugar Bowl.

And then . . .

On New Year's Day, the 4th ranked Ohio State Buckeyes beat the 2nd ranked Arizona State Sun Devils on the game's final drive, 20–17.

Which meant that . . .

Florida (#3) was playing Florida State (#1) for the National Championship on January 2 in the Sugar Bowl.

"Even talking about it now I have to remind myself that it happened," Wuerffel says. "It's like one of those movies like *Remember the Titans* where some amazing story comes together. I use it in my talks all the time. The thing that I latch on to is that life would be great if you were undefeated all year and won the national title. But sometimes you get crushed, just like in life sometimes you get beat and you think you're out of it. But you have to get up and keep going even if it seems like it isn't going to matter. Because that's when it really does matter." From the moment the clock ticked down to 0:00 in Arizona State's loss to Ohio State, Steve Spurrier's mind turned to revenge against Florida State. The loss to FSU had been burning him up. *We had our chances. We had a lot of yards. We had a lot of mistakes. We missed some field goals. We didn't play well enough to win the game. Wuerffel's three interceptions easily could have been five or six.*

The more film his staff watched, the more the conclusion was obvious: Wuerffel needed space to work. Up to that point, Spurrier avoided the shotgun formation and rarely ran it. Other than a few times during the Alabama game and a couple plays during the FSU game, offensive sets out of the gun sat at the back of his playbook. But when looking at the tape he realized it could buy Wuerffel a little time by keeping Florida State's pass rushers away from him. Like Inigo Montoya in *The Princess Bride*, he basically switched from fighting left-handed to fighting right-handed in one game and surprised the Seminoles by running shotgun the full sixty minutes.

He also engaged in some good old-fashioned media manipulation. In the week leading up to the Sugar Bowl, whenever Spurrier had a camera in his face, he talked about how the Seminoles were dirty, how they tried to hurt Wuerffel on purpose in their first game, and how if you watch the film there were too many late hits to count. His goal was two-fold: he wanted to challenge his offensive line to keep the Seminoles' defenders away from Wuerffel and he wanted to get inside his opponent's head. He wanted to get the FSU defenders thinking about whether the hits were late or not. Maybe they'd hesitate when the time came. Who knows? It was worth a shot.

The best part about all of Spurrier's late-hit bluster in front of the camera was that he was like a kid committing to something while keeping his fingers crossed behind his back. During a pregame dinner on New Year's Eve, he pulled Bowden aside and told him he was only blowing up the late-hit talk to light a fire under his boys. It was all for show. Classic gamesmanship.

It worked.

Florida's offense doubled their previous point total and hung more than half-a-hundred on the Seminoles, winning the game 52–20 and earning the title of consensus national champions. Wuerffel threw three touchdown passes to Ike Hilliard and ran for another one.

"It's a great story of redemption," Wuerffel says. "It was a testimony to our seniors that we regrouped for the Alabama game and didn't tank. We emotionally and tactically rebounded."

Dunn had dreaded playing Florida a second time for reasons that all bore out.

"I didn't want to play them twice," Dunn says. "We were in-state rivals. To get up for that game takes a lot, and you have to get up for it again after you already beat them? I just wasn't excited for that one. You can't go back and bottle up the energy from the first time you played them. The team that loses the first time always has the advantage the next time. But they did their job and sealed the deal."

The win was also a lynchpin title when it came the '90s decade of dominance by Florida, Florida State, and Nebraska. Up until that Sugar Bowl, Florida State won the National Championship in '93 by defeating Nebraska, then Nebraska won it in '94 by beating Miami, then Nebraska won it again in '95 against the Gators. With Florida beating Florida State for the title in '96, the three most dominant teams each had their seat at the head of the table.

"In college, I didn't like Danny because he went to an opposing school. I never rooted for him," Dunn says, laughing. "But I grew to respect him and what he stands for and his goal and mission as a man after school. As for Nebraska and Tommie Frazier, I was a huge fan of what they were doing. Frazier was a guy who didn't get a lot of credit, but he was very successful and very valuable in that offense. He could run a 4.3 and throw and he took them to two championships."

Championships aside, Spurrier's Fun 'N' Gun and the strategies he devised to beat Nebraska and Florida State and other contenders eventually led to the record-setting offenses in today's college game. If SEC quarterbacks were put on a chart like the "evolution of man," Danny Wuerffel in 1996 would be a Homo Sapien and Joe Burrow of Louisiana State in 2019 would be a Homo Sapien Sapien. The offense Burrow quarterbacked was a direct descendant of the one Wuerffel helmed.

"That was a big turning point in the SEC," Wuerffel says. "The conference used to be known for backs like Herschel Walker and Bo Jackson and a cloud of dust. Then Spurrier comes in and balls are flying all over the field. It was a new iteration of football and led to so many things. He put Florida on the map as a powerhouse and it led to Urban Meyer and the Tim Tebow years. I think he's one of the greatest coaches there has ever been. People might argue who might be better, but very few have impacted the game more."

Before the decade was out, Nebraska and Florida State would each tack on another title, making the '95 and '96 seasons the most memorable and most important of the Spurrier vs. Osborne vs. Bowden rivalry that would ultimately send a whopping 60 players to the NFL from only three teams.

"Guys like Bowden and Osborne, they took the time to build great programs," Dunn says. "They were all about practicing and getting things right and having long-term success over instant success. Coaches don't have time to do that anymore. Those were some of the last guys. Times were different."

Different and exceptional.

In a single year, you had one of college football's all-time greatest teams in Nebraska, one of college football's all-time greatest schemes with the Fun 'N' Gun, and one of the all-time greatest decades a team has ever had with Bobby Bowden's Seminoles going 163–13 in a ten-year span.

As a college football fan, you had it all.

And NFL fans, particularly of *this team*, weren't far behind. More on that after the break. (That's a classic, old-school *SportsCenter* tease for the next chapter if you're scoring at home.)

THE TRIPLETS
AND DEION

IT'S APRIL 23, 1989, AT THE MARRIOTT MARQUIS IN
New York City, and Troy Aikman, twenty-two years young, fully embod-
ies the "Iceman" nickname his high school football coach gave him.
He's got the dark suit, the blond hair, the steel blue eyes, and the gold
watch. This is his moment, and he knows that the instant his ten-inch
hand grips the hand of NFL Commissioner Pete Rozelle, he officially
becomes the Dallas Cowboys' number-one overall pick and face of
the franchise.

But these aren't the omnipresent, omni-branded, modern cash-cow
Cowboys you're thinking of. These Cowboys just went 3–13. These
Cowboys are losing one million dollars a month. These Cowboys are
abysmal.

Merely two months before the draft, Bum Bright sold the team
to Jerry Jones for $140 million. The night the sale was announced, an
evening that included the axing of beloved coach Tom Landry, the fans
began referring to the deal as "The Saturday Night Massacre." The
headline in the *Dallas Morning News* the day after the purchase read:

JONES BUYS COWBOYS, FIRES LANDRY; Rozelle: "This is like Lombardi's death."

So, there's Davey O'Brien Trophy-winning quarterback Troy Aikman in the ballroom at the Marriott on the most important day of his young life, shaking the hand of a man who just publicly declared that the team he is joining should be in mourning.

Go get 'em, kid! You're about to be the quarterback of a grade-A shit show!

Aikman is cautiously optimistic. The team's first-round pick from 1988, wide receiver Michael Irvin, is a rocket-fueled concoction of charisma and talk and talent. Along with new coach Jimmy Johnson, the two had just come off one of the most successful runs in college football history at Miami. There was a plan, albeit a murky one that nobody was sure would work.

If Aikman could see twelve months into the future (and mercifully look past the upcoming 1–15 season where he'd be hammered and humbled by nearly every defense in the NFL), he'd know that in 1990 the Cowboys would draft Emmitt Smith, the third piece of a trio that would soon be referred to in NFL lore simply as "The Triplets." Aikman doesn't know this fact, but he has faith. He's already committed to being great. He will put in the work.

Eight hundred miles from Manhattan, former Florida State standout Deion Sanders sits on a couch in his agent's Chicago home, wearing a black Starter track suit, black sunglasses, a one-inch dollar-sign earring, a half-dozen rings spread across two hands, and enough gold chains around his neck to anchor a pontoon boat.

With his family surrounding him, cameras filming him, and reporter Andrea Kramer on hand to interview him, Sanders gets the call that the Atlanta Falcons have selected him as the number-five overall pick in the 1989 NFL Draft.

"It looks like you're wearing your signing bonus here," Kramer comments, to which Deion flashes his soon-to-be-famous smile.

We'll see that same (literal) million-dollar smile in highlight reels for five years in Atlanta, one year in San Francisco, and then in its brightest form in Dallas after he signs a seven-year, $35-million contract to join The Triplets in the fall of '95.

◘   ◘   ◘

Troy Aikman is the closest mortal to God in Dallas—or, the closest mortal to Roger Staubach, the Cowboys' star quarterback in the 1970s who led the team to two Super Bowl victories in four starts. Staubach won the Heisman Trophy at the Naval Academy. He served in the Vietnam War. His nickname was Captain America.

Heading into September of '95, Aikman and Staubach were tied with two Super Bowl wins apiece. Of the hundreds of men who had played quarterback in the NFL up to that point, only six had won multiple Super Bowl championships besides Aikman: Staubach, Bart Starr, Bob Griese, and Jim Plunkett each had two. Joe Montana and Terry Bradshaw both won four. For Aikman to ascend to quarterback immortality, he'd need at least one more title.

Incredibly, the odds were in his favor. Despite Jerry Jones replacing taskmaster Jimmy Johnson with hands-off, easygoing Barry Switzer a year prior, the '95 Cowboys were football's version of the Avengers, featuring fourteen current or former Pro Bowlers every time they suited up. Like the Avengers, they had their breakout characters— Troy, Emmitt, Michael, and Deion—and like a modern Marvel movie, they had a highly anticipated box office opening in New York. Well, a season-starting, Monday Night Football game against the New York Giants at the Meadowlands is close enough.

The high temperature on game day in New Jersey reached 84 degrees and the air had that sticky, heavy feel that sometimes wafted off the Hackensack River and into the stadium at the heart of the summer. Mercifully, the temps dropped into the mid-70s as the game approached, but the warm-ups were humid and the stadium was filled with a heated buzz.

Not only were the Giants hosting Monday Night Football against the hated Cowboys, but the G-Men faithful were jacked up because the team was retiring Phil Simms's jersey at halftime. They had even invited franchise icon Lawrence Taylor to participate and catch a ceremonial pass from Simms. If ever there was a chance for a home team to take advantage of a home-team advantage, this was it. The Giants even got the ball first.

In a truly bizarre twist of fate, legendary NFL running back Herschel Walker returned the opening kick sixteen yards for the Giants. If you're the type to believe in karma, then this is why Walker being on the field that night is significant: Walker was a Pro Bowler for the Cowboys in the late 1980s, and became the headliner in the Cowboys trade to the Vikings in 1989 that ultimately netted them a massive haul of draft picks—one of which they'd use to select Emmitt Smith. Bizarre.

Karma or not, after Walker's decent kickoff return, the Giants went three and out.

As Aikman took the field for the first snap of the season, he was flanked by greatness and a sense that anything less than a Super Bowl win would be a disappointment. In addition to his fellow Triplets, his offensive line was one of the greatest, most formidable trenches ever assembled.

His center, Mark Stepnoski, was a three-time Pro Bowler. His tackle, Erik Williams, made four. Nate Newton was a six-time Pro Bowler, and Larry Allen made a staggering ten Pro Bowls in a row. His tight end, Jay Novacek, was a five-time Pro Bowler, and even the fullback, "Moose" Johnston, made two teams.

This is why the Cowboys felt like a lock for another title run. In some corners, the question wasn't "how could they win the Super Bowl"; rather it was, "how could they NOT win the Super Bowl?"

With those expectations on the team, the weight of the football world pushing down on Aikman's shoulder pads, and 70,000-plus fans rooting against him, he stood behind center, took the first snap of the year, and handed it off to Emmitt Smith . . . who promptly ran straight up the middle for a 60-yard touchdown.

Boom.

Emmitt was just getting started. That run was the first of four touchdowns he'd have that night on his way to 163 yards rushing. Michael Irvin caught seven balls for 109 yards and a touchdown. Aikman's passer rating was 128.7, and the Cowboys crushed the Giants, 35–0.

To say this game was a sign of things to come would be unfair to signs. This wasn't a sign. This was an exact blueprint of how the season would go.

Smith essentially never stopped running from September to January. He led the NFL in rushing touchdowns and total touchdowns (25), points scored (150), rushing yards per game (110), and yards from scrimmage (2,148). Michael Irvin finished in the top five in receptions, receiving yards, and receiving yards per game, as well as top ten in touchdowns by receivers. With Smith running the ball so well (and so much), Aikman's total passing yards were not among the league leaders, but he put on a clinic in terms of efficiency, coming in second in the NFL to Steve Young in both completion percentage and passer rating.

Despite a few hiccups against rivals like the Washington Redskins and the San Francisco 49ers, the Cowboys had their hand on the steering wheel for the entire season, finishing 12–4 and cruising into the playoffs on the shoulders of their stars.

What was becoming apparent to all of us, however, was that these guys were more than stars; they were individual cottage industries the likes of which we'd never seen co-exist on the same team at the same time.

During his peak years with the Cowboys in the mid-'90s, Troy Aikman was on the cover of virtually every national magazine that mattered, back when being on the cover of a national magazine mattered. He was on the cover of *Sports Illustrated* three times, the cover of *TV Guide* three times (and their national football preview twice), the cover of *Texas Monthly, Beckett, The Sporting News,* and every football-centric publication in the universe. The coup de grace was likely his famous cover of *GQ* for their fashion issue, which was headlined: *God's Quarterback.*

He was on the front of a Wheaties box, appeared in a *Simpsons* episode, had his own video game for Super Nintendo (*Troy Aikman NFL Football*), and was a pitchman for Nike, Brut Cologne, Met-Rx, Chief Auto Parts, and Acme Brick. And of course, his book, *Aikman Mind, Body and Soul,* was published to tie it all together.

Not to be outdone, Emmitt Smith also had his own Super Nintendo video game, aptly named *Emmitt Smith Football,* and his own book, *The Emmitt Zone.* He was featured with Aikman on the cover of *TV Guide* and *Texas Monthly* and a host of other football magazines, and while he wouldn't get his own *GQ* cover, he would double Aikman's *Sports Illustrated* cover output with six of his own. He was sponsored by Starter, Right Guard, and Visa, and was the featured athlete to promote Reebok's "Pump" sneakers in football.

Michael Irvin shared many of the magazine covers with Troy and Emmitt, had his own solo *Sports Illustrated* cover, was sponsored by Nike, and added McDonald's to The Triplets' endorsement portfolio at the time. Together, they represented nearly half of the major corporate sponsors for the NFL.

Then, there was Neon Deion—AKA Prime Time; AKA Deion Sanders—one of the most bankable, sound-bytable, perfectly branded sports stars in modern history.

Do you know who was the only non-quarterback NFL star to host *Saturday Night Live* solo between 1979 and 2019?

Deion Sanders.

How about the only NFL player to have commercials with both Denis Leary and Dennis Hopper?

Deion Sanders.

And which Cowboy starred in a national TV campaign for Pizza Hut with the team's owner, Jerry Jones? Not Troy. Not Michael. Not Emmitt.

Deion Sanders.

When it came to show time, there was Prime Time and there was everybody else. Sanders graced five *Sports Illustrated* covers, was the subject of a then-coveted *Playboy Magazine* interview ("Neon Deion: Interview with a Prime Time Prima Donna"), had his own video game for Sega Sports called, of course, *Prime Time,* and was a national pitchman for Burger King, American Express, Nike, Pizza Hut, and Wheaties. You couldn't take your eyes off him if you tried.

So, on the game's biggest stage at Super Bowl XXX, it's no surprise that Americans saw Deion's presence everywhere. Literally.

Kick returns? Deion.

Punt returns? Deion.

Disrupting passes (his specialty)? Deion.

What about commercial breaks? Deion. Don't look down or you'd miss him zoom past Wile E. Coyote starring in his roadrunner role in a Pepsi commercial. Tune back into the game and you see a long, deep ball. Who catches it?

You guessed it. Deion.

These guys weren't just ballers; they were brands and influencers before athletes learned to think of themselves that way. Rather than enter games with one or two storylines to follow, NFL announcers and pregame shows devoted entire segments to the Cowboys. One week the feature interview would be with Aikman, the next with Irvin or Smith or Sanders. Their commercials were ubiquitous during their games and everyone else's. Sundays seemed to be swallowed up by Cowboys, which meant it was up to Aikman to keep everyone's egos in check and the team on track toward their ultimate goal heading into the 1995–96 season: an unprecedented third title in four years.

Nothing short of their collective football legacies were on the line.

     ◘   ◘   ◘

"We had some characters in that locker room," Chad Hennings says, smiling.

He's sitting at the end of a long wooden table in a conference room at his company in Dallas. Through the floor-to-ceiling windows behind him one sees luxury high rises and the interspersed greenery of Turtle Creek Park. After winning the Outland Trophy as a star at the Air Force Academy, Hennings served as a pilot in the Gulf War before joining the Cowboys in 1992 as a twenty-seven-year-old rookie. He was on the team for all three of their championships. He's still every bit of 6'6", weighs a solid 250 pounds, and resembles a real-life Buzz Lightyear.

Troy Aikman is across the table from Hennings. He's come right from the gym and everyone who sees him tells him he looks like he could still suit up, and though they're likely just kissing a little local-hero ass, they're not wrong. He's wearing a Nike warm-up suit and a trendy Travis Matthew golf hat. Aikman and Hennings's playing days are twenty years in their rear-view mirrors, but they've remained buddies. Many of the Cowboys from that era have.

"We had guys like Michael Irvin and Charles Haley always joking around. Big personalities," Hennings says. "You pulled us together."

Hennings is talking to Aikman about a book project he's working on, called *Forces of Character*. He's picking his former quarterback's brain about how he managed to lead The Triplets and Deion and Charles Haley and all the other grown men in that locker room to the Promised Land three times.

"People used to ask me all the time how I got along with Michael," Aikman says. "Michael and I have the most unique relationship of any relationship I have. He and I are about as close as you can be. We never do anything together, but when we see each other, he'll come up and give me a kiss and a hug. We love each other. We're almost like brothers, yet we couldn't be more different. That relationship was born out of the fact that at his core, like me, he just wanted to be great and he put in the work. Charles Haley, as big of a goof as he is, wanted to be great. We came together over that."

Irvin, Haley, and Aikman are all Pro Football Hall of Famers. Four other members of the '90s Cowboys dynasty are also enshrined in Canton: Sanders, Smith, Larry Allen, and Head Coach Jimmy Johnson.

Then there are the next-level Cowboys who weren't quite Hall of Famers, but who made a Pro Bowl or two and were integral parts on one, two, or three titles. Guys like Daryl "Moose" Johnston, Tony Tolbert, and Mark Stepnoski.

"My roommates coming into the league were DJ [Johnston] and Step [Stepnoski]," Aikman says. "We were a lot alike. We all had goals and they were such hard workers."

"What about the guys who weren't naturally hard workers?" Hennings asks. "Guys who had all the talent in the world but don't have that drive? How did you motivate them?"

"I think that for us, Jimmy Johnson was going to make it tough on those guys," Aikman explains. "Jimmy knew a secret. And that was that most people don't mind losing. No one likes to lose, but for most people it doesn't really eat at them or hurt them. They're not that competitive. Jimmy decided that he was going to make life miserable for those guys and they weren't going to want to deal with him after a loss. I've gotten to know Jimmy really well over the years and the guy wants to have more fun than anybody, so he really kind of had to put up that front."

The "front," as Aikman called it, could not have worked better. After taking over the team and going 1–15 in his first season as head coach, Johnson made the Cowboys a juggernaut. In his second season they went 7–9. In year three they were 11–5 and made the playoffs. In years four and five they were 13–3 and 12–4 and won back-to-back championships. Then, with a seemingly endless string of Super Bowls on the horizon, Jimmy Johnson quit, eventually citing his unworkable relationship with owner Jerry Jones, who turned to longtime Oklahoma head coach Barry Switzer to replace Johnson.

"When Barry Switzer came in, things got harder for me because I felt like rather than playing good cop to Jimmy's bad cop, I had to absorb the Jimmy role even more because nobody else would do it," Aikman says.

"You spent a lot of time managing personalities," Hennings says. "But at some point individuals have to take ownership of their trajectory."

The Cowboys' back-up quarterback at the time, Jason Garrett, agreed with Aikman's assessment about how the team changed once Johnson left.

"Jimmy Johnson was fantastic at building connections between players," he said. "He pushed us and I think he developed the right relationships. He created the right environment and he instilled confidence in everybody. I thought he was amazing."

To the outside world, the Barry Switzer Cowboys were *also* amazing. They went 12–4 in his first year and lost in the NFC Championship Game, and then in the '95–'96 season, they went 12–4 again and won the Super Bowl, although the difference between the Switzer environment and the Johnson environment that Garrett mentioned was palpable. One was sustainable and the other was not.

The turmoil and strain between Switzer's coaching staff and some of the star players corroded the team from the inside out. Week-to-week it seemed that bad cop Aikman had to press different players' buttons to get the best out of them and keep them working together. It was like the Cowboys had become *Ocean's Eleven,* and Aikman, playing the George Clooney role, constantly assessed who was in and who was out. In this analogy, Barry Switzer was in the role of Terry Benedict, meaning that Aikman had to work against his own coach. It took its toll.

When it came to Super Bowl XXX itself, Aikman prided himself on his preparation and focus. He was not going to be out-worked or out-smarted on his sport's biggest stage. Switzer, for his part, was a study in contrast, to put it politely. He was far more relaxed. Longtime Cowboys PR man Richard Dalrymple put it this way while commentating NFL Films' official recap of the game: "He [Switzer] kind of enjoyed the circus atmosphere of it and didn't take it too seriously. I think for him it was like a big bowl game."

For Aikman, it wasn't a big bowl game. It was the biggest game of his career. A third Lombardi Trophy would raise him above the two-Super Bowl-wins club for quarterbacks, leaving only Montana and Bradshaw above him (each with four). A win would also put the Cowboys in a tie for most Super Bowl victories by a franchise in NFL history (5, tied with the 49ers). As the quarterback, those feats mattered. Switzer's chill approach to all of it was a tough pill to swallow, which is why Aikman couldn't wait until kickoff. At least then he'd have the ball in his hands and he could control the outcome of "The Duel in the Desert" (the NFL's promo tag line for the game) against the Pittsburgh Steelers.

From the initial snap that night of January 28, 1996, Aikman was determined to get his big guns involved; the first offensive series featured a 20-yard pass to Michael Irvin and a 23-yard run by Emmitt Smith to set up an opening drive field goal.

After the Cowboys' defense forced a quick three-and-out, Aikman went back to his guys, handing off twice to Smith, throwing once to Irvin for 11 yards and then, in a moment Dallas fans had been anticipating since September, he hit Sanders on the aforementioned 47-yard pass, lighting up the stadium in Tempe.

A few plays after Sanders's catch, Aikman hit Jay Novacek for the game's first touchdown and a 10–0 lead. Fans around the country braced themselves for what was beginning to look like a slaughter. On defense, Charles Haley was hulking out. He got sacks. He got pressures. He was a problem. Sanders and the secondary were also suffocating Pittsburgh's wide receivers, making Steelers quarterback Neil O'Donnell look slow and lost.

Incredibly, even with all the momentum on their side, the Cowboys entered what Daryl Johnston described in the post-game interview as a "lull" and the Steelers began to move the ball. They scored a touchdown before the half but then early in the third quarter, a Larry Brown interception for the Cowboys stopped another Steelers drive that felt like it was headed for a score. Aikman quickly capitalized on the turnover with a pass to Irvin and a handoff to Smith for a touchdown.

This put the Cowboys ahead 20–7. It was almost the end of the third quarter and the game, finally, seemed in hand. There would be no embarrassing disaster. No inexplicable meltdown. They would fulfill their destiny.

Wellll . . . Not yet.

The Steelers opened the fourth quarter with a 60-yard drive that ended in a field goal.

Score: Cowboys 20–Steelers 10

Then . . .

Pittsburgh shocked Dallas by going for an onside kick and amazingly, astonishingly, recovered the ball.

O'Donnell then channeled his inner Ginsu knife and carved up the Cowboys' defense: two passes to Andre Hastings, one pass to Ernie Mills, a handoff to Bam Morris, a pass to Bam Morris, and ultimately a handoff to Morris from the 1-yard line that he'd take into the end zone.

Score: Cowboys 20 – Steelers 17

Was this really happening? Could the Cowboys lose?

In a word: yes.

Dallas struggled on the next drive and after Levon Kirkland sacked Aikman, they were forced to give the ball back to a surging Steelers offense on their own 32-yard line with 4:15 left in the game.

Aikman was anchored to the sideline. He couldn't hand the ball to Smith or throw to Irvin. He couldn't hit Novacek on an out route. He couldn't do anything. All he had worked for and all the team had worked for that whole season was up in the air and the famous Triplets were helpless to do anything about it.

Fortunately, it was prime time and they still had Prime Time and his secondary on the field. Like most quarterbacks who faced Deion Sanders on defense, O'Donnell had shied away from throwing near Sanders all day. As Sanders had done his whole career, he effectively cut the field in half for the opposing offense. Quarterbacks rarely even looked his way, which would soon prove invaluable.

On the second play of the drive, the Cowboys' defense brought an all-out blitz that forced O'Donnell to get rid of the ball quickly. With nobody open on Sanders's side of the field, he threw it into the flat to the strong side where he later said he expected a receiver to be. Alas, the only person there was Cowboys cornerback Larry Brown, who picked off O'Donnell for a second time that day.

"We were blitzing and I beat the receiver to the spot," Brown said of the interception.

Two plays later, on offense, Emmitt Smith made a lightning quick cutback after a handoff to score a touchdown with 3:43 left in the game.

Score: Cowboys 27 – Steelers 17

The relief on the sideline was felt throughout the stadium. As if unscrewing a safety valve to release the pressure, Sanders found Brown near the Cowboys' bench and joked with him.

"You get one more [interception] you can run for mayor of Dallas, straight up," Sanders said. "I'll vote for you, dog. As long as you give me a job."

The touchdown by Smith was the final score of the game and it gave the Cowboys an unprecedented third Super Bowl in four years.

They did it.

Aikman got his third title, Smith became the fifth player to have a touchdown in three Super Bowls, Irvin had five catches for 76 yards, Deion caught the game's most exciting catch, and Chad Hennings had two of the team's four sacks.

They all should have been ecstatic.

They weren't.

"The joy just wasn't there. It was not the same," Cowboys safety Darren Woodson said in a retrospective on the game. "It was . . . thank God the season is over with."

Echoing Woodson's sentiments, rather than feeling elation after winning their third Super Bowl in four years, many of the players simply felt relief. Aikman even considered retirement. The following year the team was 10–6. Then 6–10. Then Switzer was fired and shortly thereafter Aikman and Irvin retired, and Deion and Emmitt moved on.

The four of them had no way of knowing that standing victorious on the field of Sun Devil Stadium after Super Bowl XXX would be the apex of their Hall of Fame careers.

Yes, they each still had plenty of individual bright spots. Sanders entered the 1996 season attempting to do something no modern-day NFL player had done successfully in decades: play both ways every game.

"He's not going to make anybody forget about Michael Irvin," Aikman said before the season. "But he gives us the ability to make some big plays down field."

"One of my goals has been to play wide receiver," Sanders said. "I love the challenge."

The "challenge," while not the start of a cornerback/wide receiver revolution, was still must-see TV and worked out reasonably well. Sanders hauled in 36 catches, one touchdown, and nearly 500 receiving yards on the season, which may not seem like much, but was still 500 more yards than any other cornerback caught that year. And yes, Emmitt Smith would go on to break Walter Payton's record and become the league's all-time leading rusher in 2002.

All of that notwithstanding, 1996 was the zenith for The Triplets and Deion's on-field popularity, though it would not be their final act in football. Far from it.

◘   ◘   ◘

There's a general roadmap that legendary sports teams follow when their members retire. Typically, the one big star gets a national broadcasting deal or perhaps joins the franchise as an executive in some capacity, while the mid-level, glory-year stars get local sports jobs, slap their names on restaurants and car dealerships, speak at city events, attend signings, and, if they're lucky, end up either in the Pro Football Hall of Fame or their team's ring of honor.

Realistically, a handful of members of the team remain actively involved in the national sports conversation a decade after the dynasty's final snap. Two decades later, that number may have dwindled down to one. Or none. It's just the way things go. Time passes. New heroes emerge. People move on.

Unless you're talking about the 1996 Dallas Cowboys who, by all counts, became a feeder system for the modern football media machine.

Troy Aikman has manned Fox Sports' number one football booth for over a decade with Joe Buck and has broadcast six Super Bowls, remaining one of the biggest names in the sport. Emmitt Smith was a panelist at both the NFL Network and ESPN before moving on to become a real estate developer. Michael Irvin began his broadcasting career on the famous *ESPN Sunday Night NFL Countdown* show and then moved on to work as a panelist on a variety of shows at the NFL Network. Deion Sanders worked for CBS Sports and the NFL Network, and then signed a cutting-edge deal with Barstool Sports before becoming the head coach at Jackson State. Jimmy Johnson is one of the stars of Fox NFL Sunday. And the list goes on. Daryl Johnston is a broadcaster for one of Fox's top teams along with Chris Myers, and Darren Woodson worked as a broadcaster for ESPN for a decade and a half.

If you're keeping tabs, this means that on the 25th anniversary of The Triplets and Deion Sanders's last Super Bowl victory, the team's biggest stars and best players are still front and center on television screens, laptops, and apps across America and still swallowing up Sundays—calling games, starring in commercials, giving commentary, and, for lack of a better term, keeping themselves in prime time. It's the dynasty that never ends.

3

MAGIC'S KINGDOM

LARRY BIRD SAT IN THE STANDS AT THE FLEET Center in Boston, dressed in street clothes, watching the Celtics get beat. Again. He'd had it with this '95–'96 Bizarro World version of his once-proud franchise. Long gone were the Big Three—Bird with Kevin McHale and Robert Parish—and the yearly banner ceremonies. This team stunk. Period.

35 wins in 1995.

32 in 1994.

67 wins over two seasons? Holy hell, he'd led the '85–'86 squad to 67 wins that year alone.

Pathetic.

He could barely stomach watching these guys.

Especially Reebok Pump-wearing, closed-eyes dunking, trade-demanding Dee Brown.

"I'm not too happy with Dee right now," Bird said to the media at the time. "He's the leader of the team, and he wants to be traded. He's getting paid a lot of money to do what he does. He's been inconsistent.

Some nights he comes to play, and some nights he doesn't. When Reggie Lewis left us a couple years ago, I thought he was going to step it up. When he didn't, I knew he wasn't going to be any better than he already was."

Damn, a legendary takedown from Larry Legend.

Then . . .

As he sits in the stands, watching his team get beat, he overhears a few fans talking nearby. One turns to the other and says, "If only Larry Bird were in the game."

Record scratch.

The crowd goes silent.

I've had enough of this shit.

Summoning Superman in a phone booth, Larry Bird stands up just as a spotlight from the arena finds him. He tears off his suit to reveal a uniform and steps on the famous parquet floor. The Boston faithful go bonkers.

Larry! Larry! Larry!

In short order he hits a three, he dunks, and then he hits a reverse lay-up to win the game.

Finally, somebody showed those bums how to play.

. . . If only the basketball comeback were real. All of the above took place four years after Bird's retirement, while filming a Miller Lite commercial on Monday, January 29, 1996.

Bird, who had a front office position with the Celtics at the time, was still so revered in NBA circles that a gaggle of reporters covered him playing in a fake game while wearing an atrocious, white and blue, we-don't-want-to-pay-an-NBA-license-fee uniform on behalf of a beer company. But it was a good thing the media were there.

At nearly the exact moment that Bird was peeling off a tear-away sports jacket and tie in Boston, three thousand miles away in Los Angeles, Magic Johnson was announcing his for-real comeback, upstaging

Bird's faux attempt. In fact, it was announced in time for the media to get Bird's on-the-spot reaction.*

"I have *no* desire to come back," Bird said when informed that Johnson's NBA return was official. "Once I was done playing, that was it. I made up my mind to retire. Magic should do what makes him happy. I don't think he'll be at the form he was when he was 28 or 29. But I still think he'll be a very good player for them."

Judging from his measured response, Bird was not entirely caught off guard by the news. None of us were. Magic's NBA return had been rumored on-and-off for years, and he kept his desire to play again about as secret as a kid with ice cream on his shirt *swearing* he didn't sneak any rocky road.

In the four years since Johnson's staggering announcement that he had to retire from playing NBA basketball due to HIV, he had somehow managed to play *more basketball.* He famously played in the 1992 NBA All-Star Game (won the MVP) and on the 1992 Dream Team (won gold), and had a brief NBA comeback that ended before the '92 season started (too controversial), but those are the signature moments of his post-Lakers career we all knew about; after the aborted "official" comeback, he unofficially never stopped playing.

It started with near-daily pick-up games with his ex-NBA buddies all over Los Angeles (he dominated), and then morphed into the Magic Johnson All-Stars, a worldwide, barnstorming squad he assembled whose sole purpose was to slake his unquenchable thirst for competitive basketball.** He hand-picked his team of past pros: Reggie Theus, Jim Farmer, Lester Conner, John Long, Mark Aguirre,

---

* What are the odds of this happening, by the way? Magic could have come back at any time. Bird shot dozens of commercials with all kinds of concepts during his career and retirement. For these two icons, on this day, to be in front of cameras talking about a real comeback and a fake one, merely hours apart, it has to be a zillion to one.

** Well, it wasn't the *sole* purpose. Between appearance fees and corporate sponsors, Magic made over $300,000 per game. So yes, it quenched his desire for hoops and money.

and a few others. Together, they traveled the world in the name of hoops.

Japan. South America. Israel. Europe. New Zealand. Australia.

The Magic Johnson All-Stars circled the globe, racking up a 55–0 record, which included a five-game series in the United States against teams in the Continental Basketball Association. Much like the Apollo Creed versus Ivan Drago fight (cue your Duke voice with spittle coming out of your mouth), the games were *supposed to be an exhibition!*

Magic didn't care.

"Whether it be a pick-up game or playing against Larry and the Celtics in a Game 7 situation . . . I'm playing to win," Johnson said in February of '94, prior to his All-Stars' game against the CBA's Quad City Thunder. "Basketball for me has always been fun. But I have always played to win. You'll see on the court that the desire is still there."

The star forward of the Thunder, 6'9" 235 lb. Bobby Martin, who was a college star at Pitt, laughably warned that Magic was on "QC turf" and the game wasn't going to be a picnic.

"We all got a little something for Magic," Martin said. "I have respect for him as one of the greatest players the game has ever known. But he's in our house now and he's got to get some. We have to show him."

Well.

Magic got some.

In front of 6,104 fans in a game locally billed as "Showtime" at The Mark (the Quad Cities' home court), Johnson dropped 28 points, 11 rebounds, and 17 assists on the way to a 133–109 slaughter. The only thing missing was Magic saying, "If he dies, he dies."

As the team traveled the world, the triple-doubles and wins piled up— as did the nagging sense in Magic's mind that he had unfinished business in the NBA. He was in his mid-30s, he felt great, the HIV was under control, and like a cartoon character sniffing the wafting scent of a freshly made apple pie out of the oven, the game was a constant temptation.

In the spring of 1994, after the Lakers fired head coach Randy Pfund, Jerry Buss convinced Magic to take over the coaching duties. Before he drew up a single X or one O, he was immediately asked about a comeback.

Magic, how do you feel about coaching—but really, are you going to play again?

"I'm retired. Let's leave it at that," Johnson said when asked about whether he'd suit up any time soon. "I've always had the desire to coach in the back of my mind. I'm doing it for him [Buss]."

As you can expect, clipboard-carrying Magic didn't have the same energy and excitement for the fans as baby jump hook-shooting Magic. The experiment was a dud in every conceivable way. The team was bad (5–11), Johnson didn't enjoy himself, and fortunately the entire saga lasted all of five weeks. The only part Magic *did like* was when he'd cobble together a few members of his coaching staff and scrimmage against the actual Los Angeles Lakers . . . and win.

Still, there was no comeback in 1994.

In 1995, he was so close to coming back after his Maui fantasy camp that he talked about which uniform he would wear, and he spent much of his flight home to Los Angeles in conversation with Los Angeles Lakers legendary announcer Chick Hearn about what his return to the game would look like.

"We came back on a Sunday," Hearn said in a *Los Angeles Times* piece. "And I was convinced he would call on Tuesday to tell me he was doing it."

Didn't happen. Of course, this didn't mean that Magic was not playing basketball. *He was playing.*

All. The. Time.

He had a regular run at UCLA that on any given day could include international pros, college stars, ex-teammates, or current NBA legends like Hakeem Olajuwon. He worked out as if he were still on a twelve-man roster, banging out hundreds of sit-ups a day, spending hours in the weight room, jacking up his bench press (going from 135 pounds up to 300 pounds), and even setting up an entire gym on his yacht in the Mediterranean so he could stay in shape on vacation. He was like a retired chef who spent all of his time in the kitchen, experimenting with recipes, trying new ingredients, and hanging out with other chefs. For a guy who said he was done making food, the man was doing one hell of a lot of cooking.

And then Michael Jordan came to his hometown to film *Space Jam* and things changed. A little. For a brief period of time in August and September of 1995, most of the world's best basketball players weren't scattered in different cities throughout the United States. They were right there in Los Angeles in Magic's backyard playing nightly pick-up games on a makeshift court under a tent on the Warner Bros. lot, specifically built for Jordan.

Not only were some of Jordan's film co-stars—like Patrick Ewing, Larry Johnson, and Charles Barkley—in the area; but the players who lived in Los Angeles (or traveled there) all stopped by for a run. Guys like Juwan Howard, Pooh Richardson, Grant Hill, Dennis Rodman, Cedric Ceballos, and more. When basketball historian Brandon "Scoop B" Robinson sat down with Barkley for an interview and the subject of the famous *Space Jam* tent came up, Sir Charles's eyes lit up.

"Charles said it was legitimately a who's who of basketball stars," Robinson says. "He said Chris Webber was there and Reggie Miller was there and that the duels that Jordan and Miller had were serious. He said guys competed and got better under that tent. Even Dennis Rodman was there playing hard."

For most of the *Space Jam* shoot schedule, Magic wasn't able to play because he had acquired a 5 percent ownership in the Lakers, and due to a collective bargaining issue, he couldn't be seen with active players. As fate would have it, the impasse ended right before Jordan's last night in town. That's when Magic got a phone call from his buddy Lester Conner.

The rest of this story is told masterfully in Gary Smith's legendary *Sports Illustrated* piece on Magic's return:

"You playing?" asked Conner. "Can't," said Earvin. "Cookie and I are going out." Then came a long pause. Everything you needed to know about Earvin and the NBA, you had time to figure out during that pause. In no time, he wrangled a rain check from Cookie, slipped into his sweats and sneakers and slid out into the night. He entered Jordan's tent. The joint went silent. All the NBA studs, all the Warner Bros. producers and directors, just stared.

Rodman, on the NBA all-defense team five times, covered Magic. Magic spooned it all out that night—all the no-look passes and junior skyhooks and post-up power moves; the sorcerer come back to life with a blacksmith's body. When Jordan had watched enough, he playfully motioned Rodman aside and elected himself to cover Magic. "MJ," said Magic, "I'm not the regular guy I used to be. I'm six-nine, 250 pounds. Why don't you cover one of the guards and send a big man over to me?"

Grinning, Michael regarded Earvin for a moment and then said, "Guess you're right." And then Earvin, having had a little more fun, having won again, grabbed his sweats to head home, shining like a Sunday morning and shrugging it off as the players kept asking, "Damn, why aren't you still playing?"

□　　□　　□

In the end, maybe Magic simply ran out of excuses not to play. Or he wanted to go out on his own terms. At various times when asked about his comeback he's said all of the above and more—but pinpointing the exact reason doesn't matter. Not really.

What matters is that throughout the history of American sports up to that point, maybe a dozen athletes ever reached the height of fame that Magic Johnson had reached in the early '90s before he had to quit at the peak of his powers.

Babe Ruth, Jackie Robinson, Muhammad Ali, and Jordan for sure.

Mickey Mantle, Joe DiMaggio, Ted Williams, and Willie Mays, perhaps.

Jim Brown and Joe Montana maybe.

Jack Nicklaus and Mike Tyson, again, maybe.

And whomever you're probably thinking about right now, add them in, too. Magic was an athlete, a celebrity, a brand, a feeling, an entertainer, an influencer, a vibe, a mood . . . all of it. During the fifty-or-so years from the mid-1950s to the mid-2000s—when the cover of *Sports Illustrated* wasn't just a signal of what was happening in sports, but a barometer of which athletes were at the center of the sports universe—Jordan was on the cover the most times, with 49 appearances; Ali was second, with 37; and Magic was third, with 23. Kareem Abdul-Jabbar and Nicklaus were tied for fourth.

"The purple and gold brand of the Lakers, at that time, was almost presidential," Robinson says. "When you add in Magic's magnetic personality, his ability on the court, that he played in Los Angeles and that he was so likeable, that sealed the deal."

Starting with his 1979 NCAA Championship win at Michigan State (and his Most Outstanding Player Award) and continuing through his five titles with the Lakers and his Olympic Gold medal, Magic's stardom had grown across the '70s, '80s, and the '90s. If you were under thirty years old, you likely didn't remember a time when Magic wasn't a household name. You also knew exactly where you were when you heard the news that he had HIV, and you most certainly stayed up late the next night to watch Magic talk about his retirement on *The Arsenio Hall Show*. You watched in the hopes that Magic would reassure you that he'd be okay, but your understanding of HIV was primitive, as was everybody else's, and deep down you feared he would be dead soon.

But he didn't die. He didn't get sick, even. You never saw the pictures you dreaded; of the great Magic Johnson skinny, ill, and withering away before your eyes. In fact, you saw the opposite. Magic smiling. Magic playing ball. Magic gaining muscle. You saw him on talk shows and in commercials and opening businesses and on the sidelines coaching—everywhere, it seemed, but the one place you truly longed to see him: in an NBA uniform.

There was something unfinished about that. Something off . . . It felt like we had all collectively watched an amazing three-hour movie and then with fifteen minutes to go, at the apex of the action, the power went out and we were never allowed to know what happened.

In a word, we needed closure. Magic did, too.

Two weeks before the official announcement of his return, Magic was 90 percent sure he was coming back. Well, maybe 80 percent. Or maybe 50 percent of the time he wanted to come back all the time. Truthfully, he didn't know; and rather than look for a sign from the basketball gods, he decided to force the issue and start attending Lakers practices to feel things out. Would he fit in? Would he be a distraction? Would he still have an impact? Would he make the team better? Would he, you know, like it?

He lasted two days.

"I just don't think I can do this," Johnson said.

"At that point, I didn't think he would do it," his agent, Lon Rosen, stated.

Then his phone rang. And rang. And rang. First it was Lakers Coach Del Harris. Then Lakers All-Star Nick Van Exel, Cedric Ceballos, Lakers Executive Vice President Jerry West, and General Manager Mitch Kupchak. They all gave their individual pitches to the legend that boiled down to two words: come back.

In a perfectly 1996 moment, Johnson made his final decision to return not in Los Angeles, but in Phoenix, during the Cowboys–Steelers Super Bowl week. While there, he rented out a gym and practiced with a few of his Magic Johnson's All-Star teammates, Lester Conner and Marchell Henry; but rather than scrimmage, he worked on his defense and in Conner's words, "the kinds of things you work on in training camp." By the end of the week, he was so ready to get his NBA career going again that, in an all-time this-is-how-committed-I-am move, he bailed on his 50-yard line seats at the Super Bowl to work out in Los Angeles that Sunday with Kurt Rambis. A startled Rambis said, "You ditched 50-yard-line Super Bowl seats to play H.O.R.S.E. with me?"*

At 9:00 on Monday morning, having just passed a physical that confirmed he'd put on 30 pounds of muscle since he last donned the purple and gold, Johnson perused one of the more unique contracts in NBA history. There were two key documents. The first sold back his 5 percent stake in the Lakers to Jerry Buss, and the second was a contract to finish out the season for $2.5 million. As the entire Lakers brass looked on, Johnson, never one to miss out on a good joke, said, "Aw, forget it. I'm leaving."

Ha. Ha.

Then, he signed on the dotted line.

Wrote Scott Howard-Cooper of the *Los Angeles Times*, "The blue ink on the white paper made Magic Johnson, the player turned coach owner/vice president, a player again. It had been 4½ seasons since he first retired on Nov. 7, 1991, after testing HIV-positive, 3½ seasons since his first comeback ended before the end of training camp and about two weeks since another return was considered and finally rejected. But now it was official. Finally. Magic Johnson had become a Laker again."

The press conference held after practice later that day at Loyola Marymount University was standing room only as Johnson, wearing a gold Lakers workout jersey over a black t-shirt, fielded questions and

---

*   Rambis didn't say this.

flashed his smile, and in no uncertain terms put this comeback on his own personal Mt. Rushmore of life events.

"It's definitely a happy time," he said to the dozens of reporters and seventeen cameras. "Probably rates right up there with getting married to having my kids to winning all those championships, the Olympics. It ranks right up there."

Asked if he had any regrets, he said he had one: not getting back on the court sooner.

"I think I've been kicking myself too long. I should have been back a long time ago, but I think the time is right. The Lakers are playing well right now. I think they are doing a tremendous job . . . I've probably been disappointed, frustrated, and the whole thing that I didn't do it before . . . So this is like relief, in a sense, for my own mind. You sit in bed at night and watch all these games, I go to every Laker home game and sit there, and you struggle, and you struggle, and you struggle with it. So now I'm just happy it's over with and I'm back and now I'm doing what I love to do."

◘   ◘   ◘

Prior to Magic's comeback announcement, the 1995–96 Lakers' attendance hovered in mid-market, middle America territory, mingling with Milwaukee and Indianapolis and other teams in the bottom third of seats sold. Gone were the '80s glory days where every Lakers game had the feel of a big-time Westwood movie premiere. In the winter of 1996, Lakers games felt more like an indie movie showing at an art house in Tarzana. All that changed after The Announcement.

The morning of Johnson's press conference there were still 2,300 seats available for the next night's game against the Warriors. Five hours later (pre-internet, pre-Stub Hub app or anything like it), the tickets were gone. Upper-deck seats that were normally $20 to $40 were now $100 to $300. The ripple effects were even felt in Denver, where Johnson's first road game would be played.

"Since the rumor started on Friday, we have sold 683 tickets, and it's only 1 o'clock," Kirk Dyer, director of ticket operations for the Nuggets, said at the time. "Saturday we sold about 350 tickets alone. As a comparison, last Saturday we sold a total of 18 tickets."

The same story played itself out in box offices throughout the NBA. Johnson's comeback was single-handedly raising attendance for nearly the entire Western Conference. He was a walking moneymaker.

On television, TNT immediately added Johnson's return to their Tuesday night schedule. Out of thin air, only 48 hours after the Cowboys won their third Super Bowl, American sports fans had another must-watch event. Adding to the drama, the Lakers announced that Johnson would be coming off the bench, meaning that as a record-breaking television audience (for a late January NBA game) tuned in for tip-off, they were greeted with an 18–25 Warriors squad headed up by Latrell "Spree" Sprewell and Joe Smith (with Tim Hardaway and Chris Mullin coming off the bench) and a Lakers starting five of Elden Campbell, Cedric Ceballos, Vlade Divac, Eddie Jones, and Nick Van Exel.

A decent group, but hardly a *Friends*-to-*Seinfeld* can't-miss night of television.

Thankfully, Lakers coach Del Harris didn't want to be remembered as the guy who finally got Magic Johnson back but then benched him for the whole first quarter, so after a foul barely two minutes into the game, Harris motioned to Johnson to check in. As he rose from his seat, the Great Western Forum's Zima-sponsored Jumbotron zoomed in on him and all 17,505 fans jumped up to applaud the return of their hero, giving him a full fifteen-second standing ovation as he stripped off his warm-ups and stepped onto the floor. On his first possession, Magic inbounded the ball, raced up the court, and got himself in isolation on the block against Joe Smith. Every dribble he took ratcheted up the crowd to a higher level of anticipation.

Dribble.

Ahhhhhhhh!

Dribble.

Yeahhhhhh!!!!

Dribble.

Let's goooooooo!!!!!

The Forum was in a frenzy as Magic found his spot on the floor and . . . missed a turnaround hook shot.

Ohhhhhhhhh.

For the moment, the roof of the Forum was intact. Two possessions later, a no-look pass by Johnson gave the fans a flutter of excitement, but not the exact thing they were looking for to fully explode. With about two minutes left in the quarter, Johnson dribbled the ball up the floor and when he got to half-court he saw a seam, picked up speed like an 18-wheeler going downhill, and drove to the basket, hitting a running lay-up that gave the fans an excuse to keep screaming.

Still, it wasn't a quintessential Magic moment.

It wasn't "Showtime."

A minute later he hit a left-handed hook shot in the paint.

Closer.

Then, it happened.

After missing a three, Johnson got the ball on the right side of the paint and as Sprewell approached to defend him, Magic hit him with a classic head, shoulder, and ball fake combo that had Spree defending a ghost. With Spree swiping at air and looking out of bounds, Magic laid the ball in and the crowd finally took the roof off the place.

Magic bound down to the other end of the court, soaking it in.

Are you not entertained?!!

On the local game call, Chick Hearn said that Sprewell "went for it like a carp going after a worm." After the game, all Sprewell could say was, "Hey, he got me. That was a sweet move."

Johnson played 27 minutes and scored 19 points on 7–14 field goals, while dishing out ten assists and grabbing eight boards, only two short of a triple-double after a 55-month layoff from NBA basketball.

The reaction around the league was all in one direction: positive.

"I think he does have a lot left in him," his one-time coach Pat Riley said.

"I'm glad to have him back," Jordan said. "I haven't talked with him since last summer when he played with me for a week in Hollywood. He was bigger than ever, but he's still able to play."

"I'm happy to see him back," Charles Barkley said. "I don't think he should have retired in the first place."

Happiest of all was Magic himself, who said in the postgame press conference, "I can't even begin to tell you how I feel. It's one of the most exciting days of my life, ever. You wait for this day for a long time and you're finally here and you go out there and you say, 'oooh, man.'"

The Lakers would go on to a 29–11 record with Magic on the team, ultimately losing in the first round of the playoffs in four games to the Houston Rockets. There would be no sixth ring for Magic, no sterling retirement to replace the sudden first one. And despite Ceballos and Van Exel and company saying all the right things, the team quickly devolved into dysfunction behind the scenes. There was resentment, frustration, confusion, and a heavy dose of Magic fatigue. Yes, these were the Lakers. But these weren't his guys. As Jeff Pearlman writes in his excellent book on the 1996 to 2004 Lakers, *Three-Ring Circus*, " . . . while Kareem Abdul-Jabbar and James Worthy were always willing to overlook/accept Johnson's propensity for the spotlight, now Magic seemed to be more obnoxious uncle than peer."

Ouch.

Twenty-five years later, it's clear that the actual night Magic came back, on January 30, 1996, was the best night of his entire comeback. It was the game we remember. It was the moment that mattered most, because for one more night, Magic was magic.

He needed that. We all did.

GRIFFEY IN '96

KEN GRIFFEY JR.
A LEGEND IN FIVE PARTS

Part I: The Swing

"Everybody says I have an uppercut swing. I don't have an uppercut swing. It's just my follow-through is up . . . I was taught to keep the bat in the zone as long as I can and that's what I try to do. The longer it's in the zone, the better chance you've got of making contact."

—Ken Griffey Jr.

□   □   □

If you bring a man who grew up loving baseball in the '80s and '90s to the Museum of Modern Art and ask him to describe a masterpiece by Van Gogh, Monet, or Pollock, you'll likely get a shrug and an answer somewhere along the lines of, "eh, it's just paint."

You ask that same man to describe Ken Griffey Junior's swing, and there's a damn good chance he might get a tear in his eye while he runs out of adjectives.

Beautiful. Pretty. Gorgeous. Sweet. Perfect. A work of art. Majestic. Graceful. Poetic. Breathtaking. Mesmerizing. Spectacular. Belongs in the Louvre. Magnificent. Spellbinding.

A man might not describe his own wife or daughter this way, but get him going on Griffey's swing and he's a cross between a thesaurus and Don Quixote. Such is the power of the most effortless, efficient, exquisite (see, I'm doing it now) baseball swing in the history of man.

George Kenneth Griffey Jr. was born on November 21, 1969, in Donora, Pennsylvania, incredibly sharing a birthday with another baseball Hall of Famer from Donora—Stan Musial. His father, Ken Griffey Sr., was a three-time Major League Baseball All-Star and two-time World Series champion with the Cincinnati Reds. As a kid, Junior was an exceptional all-around athlete who starred in several sports at Archbishop Moeller High School. On the football team, he was a standout wide receiver who got offers from Michigan and Oklahoma.

"I'd have probably gone to Michigan," he once said on *The Dan Patrick Show*. "Only because one of my friends, Vada Murray, who passed away, went to Michigan and as a freshman and sophomore he was my big brother at Moeller."

Had he chosen to become a Wolverine, quarterback Elvis Grbac might have had a receiving corps that featured Heisman Trophy winner Desmond Howard at split end and Ken Griffey Jr. at flanker. But having Bo Schembechler's and Barry Switzer's recruiters in the bleachers of his football games was nothing compared to the traveling circus of MLB scouts that followed his every move on the diamond.

"The average game, at times there would be 20 or 30 of them," Mike Cameron, Griffey's head baseball coach in high school, said. "Bobby

Cox was general manager of the Atlanta Braves then, and he came out. You just don't see general managers at high school games. As it became more and more clear that maybe only the first five teams in order of the draft would have a shot at him, they dropped off a little bit."

Cameron goes on to explain that whenever Griffey came to the plate, everything around the field stopped, and there would be silence, with all eyes on Junior, waiting for him to uncork that pure-as-Michelangelo's-David swing.

"I can remember throwing batting practice to him. You could just see his hands, how quick they were. And once he got his bat going, the bat speed. I just kind of marveled at it," Cameron said. "I found myself looking and saying, 'oh my gosh.' You knew he was so much different than the other players. He was a player that could have played in any era and been a star."

Ratcheting up the pressure was the fact that Junior's reputation preceded him every single time he stepped to the plate. Not wanting to give up home runs and be embarrassed, most pitchers delivered him more junk than a burner Gmail account.

"They wouldn't pitch to him," Cameron says. "Then you would see a high school pitcher say, 'you know what, I'm going to challenge him so I could say I struck out Ken Griffey' . . . He would hit balls so high, so majestic. We were playing Norwood down on their field, it was called Millcrest. He hit one over the fence, over the trees, and then it went over this building. I mean, it just kept going."

Even though the Ohio high school prep season was short due to the weather, Griffey hit .478 and belted 17 home runs during his junior and senior years, making his decision to enter the Major League Baseball Draft an easy one. On June 2, 1987, the Seattle Mariners selected him as the number-one overall pick and gave him a signing bonus of $160,000. He spent one short season with the Single A Bellingham Mariners (led the team with 40 home runs, 13 steals, and 40 RBIs), played with the

Class A-Advanced San Bernardino Spirit and then the AA Vermont Mariners in 1988, and then on April 3, 1989, he made his Major League debut while he was still nineteen years old.

Success came fast.

He hit a double off the Oakland A's ace, Dave Stewart, in his first at bat.

He hit a home run in his first swing at Seattle's Kingdome.

Less than one month later he won the American League Player of the Week.

By June he had an eleven-game hitting streak going and five of his eleven home runs won games for the Mariners. He'd also sold over 500,000 of his namesake Ken Griffey Jr. milk chocolate bars (he got a nickel for every bar). In 127 games that season he hit .264 with 16 home runs and 61 RBIs, but finished third in the 1989 Rookie of the Year Award voting. (Pop Quiz: Which two players finished ahead of Griffey in the voting?*)

"We knew he was going to be a star just by watching that swing," Mike Jackson, a Mariners relief pitcher with the club in 1989, said. "That natural swing."

Steve Rushin, longtime *Sports Illustrated* writer and author of the memoirs *Sting-Ray Afternoons* and *Nights in White Castle*, covered baseball for *SI* in the '90s (among other things). His take on Griffey Jr.? "Barry Bonds before steroids was the greatest player I ever covered, but with the benefit of hindsight, Griffey was the best of his generation. Certainly in my mind's eye I can still see that follow through on his home run swing."

The swing, the swing, the swing.

"His swing was perfection," Mariners catcher Chris Iannetta said.

"It was perfect," Kyle Seager, Mariners third baseman, said.

---

* Go treat yourself to a thirty-year-old Ken Griffey Jr. milk chocolate bar if you guessed pitchers Gregg Olson of the Orioles and Tom Gordon of the Royals.

"The smoothest swing ever," Robinson Cano, Mariners second baseman, said.

Major League Baseball reporter Jon Tayler described it like this: "It was fluid; there was no wasted motion; the follow-through was textbook. His stance was impeccable, his stride was flawless, his head somehow never moved despite the incredible violence he applied to a baseball. It was a swing designed by some higher being, given to a man with limitless gifts for the sole purpose of hitting home runs. It was, to put it bluntly, fucking incredible."

From 1990 through 2000, Griffey's swing helped him make eleven straight All-Star games, win seven Silver Slugger Awards, lead the American League in home runs four times (hitting over 40 seven times), drive in over 100 runs seven times, and have a slugging percentage of at least .600 five times. It was the swing every single kid in America playing little league in the '90s emulated—the slightly pigeon-toed stance, the hip twist, the bat wiggle, the staring down of a bomb, all of it. By '96, the swing had been reengineered in *Ken Griffey Jr. Presents Major League Baseball* for Super NES and *Ken Griffey Jr.'s Winning Run*, also for Super NES, meaning you could pretend to be Junior in real life and then play as a 32-bit junior Junior on your television screen.

However.

As famous and fantastic as Griffey's swing was, it wasn't nearly as copied as his other signature move: the backwards hat.

Part II: The Backwards Hat
Thor had his winged helmet.

Batman had his cowl.

Ken Griffey Jr. had his backwards hat.

The biggest difference between these three men and their number one accessory is that millions of high school and college twenty-something dudes weren't walking around in 1996 with wings and pointy-eared masks, but dammit if half the country's men under the age of 30 didn't wear backwards hats.

It was iconic. It was rebellious. It was 100 percent Griffey.

"Baseball has unwritten rules and was conservative and old school," Rushin says. "All these adjectives that don't sound like a lot of fun. But Griffey was definitely the coolest star in the game. He had the backwards hat. Some thought it was bush league, but anyone under 30 at the time thought it was refreshing. His style brought a generation of young people into baseball."

As often happens with trendsetters, they don't set out to set trends; rather, they happen organically. Griffey started wearing his hat backwards for a reason that many boys can relate to: he wanted to be like his dad.

"I wear my hat backwards because my dad had a 'fro and I wanted to wear his hat. If I put his hat on at age six, and he's got an eight-and-a-half hat size and I got like a little five, it's not really gonna stay on my head. It was too big and slid down over my eyes. So I just turned it around because I just wanted to wear my dad's hat," Griffey said in an interview with Sports Business Radio.

Translation: tens of millions of dudes in the 1990s wore their hats backwards because a kindergarten-aged Ken Griffey Jr. in the 1970s wanted to wear his dad's hat and it didn't fit. How's that for a ripple effect?

But still . . .

The trend wouldn't have started if Griffey gave it up as a kid, if he looked like a dork, if he had a swing like a broken lawn chair, or if it came off as a try-hard move. It could have backfired for any number of reasons, like most trends do. Just ask Kris Kross how the whole "wearing clothes backwards" thing worked out for them in the long run. But much like James Bond's tailored suits, Frank Sinatra's fedoras, and LL Cool J's Kangols, Griffey's backwards hat is a timeless statement of cool.

And like most things that are young and cool, they piss off the old and lame. Back in 1994, crotchety Buck Showalter took issue with Griffey and how he comes on the field with his "hat on backwards, and his shirttail hanging out," saying that to him, "that's a lack of respect to the game." In other words, *I'm a grumpy old man!*

Griffey responded as only he could, saying Showalter was just jealous because on his Yankees roster "he doesn't have a twenty-four-year-old who can carry my jock."

Even to this day, the backwards hat as point of style offends the stodgy. Not just for regular guys whose wives frown upon the backwards hat as a "college thing" but even for Griffey himself, whose own country club recently had the audacity, nee, the gall, to ask Mr. Backwards Hat himself if he would politely wear his hats forward. Griffey told them to shove it.

"You talk about being defiant," Griffey said of the incident. "I belong to a country club . . . and I got a letter in the mail that says . . . 'Keep Forward,' meaning your hat bill facing forward. So, I built hats and it said 'Keep Forward' on the back of it so when I turned it around it said 'Keep Forward.' And I wore it. That's who I am. You're not gonna let me wear my hat backwards? It's not like I'm a slob. It's not like my shirt is untucked. This is who I am."

Amen.

The hat was such a symbol of Griffey and his joy for the game that when he was inducted into the Major League Baseball Hall of Fame in 2016, after the final words of his speech, where he said, "I want to thank my family, my friends, the fans, the Reds, the White Sox, and the Mariners for making this kid's dream come true," he reached down into the dais, pulled out a Cooperstown Hall of Fame hat, and put it on . . . backwards.

The ultimate Junior mic drop.

Part III: The Catches

Bottom of the third.

One out.

The Seattle Mariners are leading the Detroit Tigers 1–0 on the road in a midsummer day game. Luis Gonzalez is at the plate. He's 0–1 on the day so far. The playoffs are still a ways out. There is nothing exceptional about the game or remarkable about the performances. It's a boring game in a boring moment, about as memorable as filling up your gas tank. Then . . .

Craaaaaack.

Gonzalez catches a slider away on the fat part of the bat—not perfectly, but good enough. The ball sails high into the gap between center and right. The center fielder, Ken Griffey Jr., had been playing Gonzalez straight away and at the moment of contact, he's roughly an entire bus stop from where it looks like the ball is going to land.

Some Tigers fans in the stadium stand because it might be a home run.

The few Mariners fans stand because they're used to having Ken Griffey Jr. as their center fielder and they know that a close ball doesn't leave the ballpark unless Junior gives it permission. As the ball hits its peak and starts to come down on its long arc, it is clear to everyone that it's a homer.

Everyone, that is, except Griffey, who had been sprinting at Mach 2 from the instant the ball left Gonzalez's bat. When Griffey's feet hit the warning track, the ball is all but in the official scorecard as a run.

But Griffey dashes and plants and leaps and raises his glove . . .

Up . . .

Up . . .

Up . . .

Griffey rises until the fence is below his chest and with his glove seemingly twelve feet off the ground he dips his body over the rail, snags the ball before it hits the front row of the bleachers, and then wheels around to fire it to second base to keep the runner on first. Your eyes tell you the ball had to have been a home run. It had to be. The ball was out. No human could reach it. But Griffey did. And the visiting team's announcer, the legendary Ernie Harwell, is calling it one of the all-time greatest catches with this call:

"Junior going back . . . to the track . . . the wall!!!...makes the leap . . . and the catch!!! Amazing catch by Junior as he takes a home run away from Luis Gonzalez! My oh my!! Perfect timing and Junior receiving a standing ovation from these Tigers fans! Look at his timing as he scales the wall . . . jumps as high as he can and at the apex of his leap, takes that home run away!!!"

You know how many other outfielders routinely got standing ovations in ballparks that weren't their own in the '90s (or ever)? I'll save you the Googling. Zero. The answer is zero. There's Griffey and then there's everyone else.

After one catch he made racing into the deep left center alcove at Fenway Park he hit the wall so hard it looked like his soul left his body (he held onto the ball).

On another catch he made, he ran head-on into the wall and hit it with such force the padded cushion next to the pad he hit crashed to the ground (he held onto the ball).

On a nightly basis, Griffey was a one-man sizzle reel for the entire sport of baseball. He was the only player who gave you legitimate FOMO if you didn't catch him playing defense that day. And this was long before your kids would explain to you what the hell FOMO was.

"Mookie Betts is remarkable in the outfield, but Griffey is still the measuring stick," longtime *Boston Globe* sports media columnist Chad Finn says. "Nobody has the on-field flair. You'd go to watch him on the road because you never knew what you'd see. And you never knew if you'd see a player like him ever again. He played center field with a grace that your dad told you Willie Mays played with. But Griffey felt like he was yours."

Part IV: The Charisma

Ken Griffey Jr. sat near his locker at the 1993 MLB All-Star Game at Baltimore's Camden Yards fielding questions and signing bats, mitts, balls, hats, and whatever else was thrown in front of him. Video cameras rolled, photographers flashed pictures, and media members jammed recorders into the twenty-three-year-old's face.

Can you sign this for my son?

How do you like Camden?

What do you think of Cal Ripken Jr.?

Then . . . a voice.

"Where's Ken Griffey Jr. at?" the voice booms through the locker room.

It's a deep and familiar voice to sports fans the world over.

"Excuse me, excuse me," the voice says.

Then a 6'6" figure appears, wearing a white and black pinstriped uniform, cutting through the crowd, holding a black Louisville Slugger bat with a silver signing pen in hand.

Griffey looks up and gives a smirk that appropriately says, holy shit, it's Michael Jordan.

"Turn this off," Jordan says to a cameraman, jokingly, as he makes room to hand Griffey his bat. "Let me get my autograph."

Griffey grabs the bat and signs.

"I'm gonna leave my number. Call me, man," Jordan says, grabbing the bat and walking away. After Griffey's scrum is over, he catches up with Jordan and while the two talk, Griffey asks about getting one of MJ's Chicago White Sox jerseys and right there, on the spot, Jordan takes the shirt off his back, signs it, and gives it to The Kid, who puts it on just as a regular kid would. Such was the sheer magnetism and popularity that Griffey had heading into the mid-1990s.

"When Griffey came along in 1989, he was instantly the most charismatic player in the sport," Finn says. "Fans were automatically drawn to him the way they were drawn to Jordan. The charisma, the personality, the smile, the leaping catches and home runs. He was the coolest player to come along in our lifetime."

Along with the cool came the cash. By 1993, Junior was the most popular player in baseball. By 1996, when he signed a four-year, $34 million contract to make him the highest paid player in baseball, he was a household name, a national brand, and a candidate for president of the United States. While Bill Clinton and Bob Dole tried to convince voters that their platform was best for America's future, Griffey saw an opening and made this appeal to the American people, via an ad with patriotic music, the American flag waving and yes, excellent Griffey highlights:

"We need a man in the White House who knows the difference between a forkball and screwball. We need a man in the White House who can hit five home runs in a five-game playoff series and who isn't Reggie Jackson. We need a man in the White House who knows an ERA is more than just an amendment. We need a man in the White House with his own candy bar and who isn't Reggie Jackson. We need a man in the White House who will remember to take his spikes off before entering the White House. That man is Ken Griffey Jr . . . Paid for by Nike."

The "Griffey in '96" ad campaign/faux presidential campaign was one of Nike's most famous and omnipresent ads of the '90s. Pairing Griffey Jr. with his running mate, Mariner Moose, Nike blasted the ads all summer and printed a boatload of accompanying pins, buttons, bumper stickers, shirts, hats, and more. The mock campaign featured James Carville and even George "Funkadelic" Clinton, instead of

William Jefferson. In another shot at Bill, the ads spoofed the President's famous response about trying marijuana (he did but he didn't inhale) with Griffey saying he tried chewing tobacco, but didn't spit.

The copywriter who created the "Griffey in '96" ad campaign, Hank Perlman, said at the time that the commercials were created to make Griffey's profile more Jordanesque. "I think we wanted to put a lot of effort in Ken Griffey Jr. and try to make him one of the biggest guys," says Perlman, whose firm, Wieden & Kennedy of Portland, Oregon, worked on the Griffey commercials. "Griffey has the potential. Kids love Griffey. Everyone loves Ken Griffey. His personality is awesome. He's an amazing baseball player."

And like Jordan, he sold the hell out of shoes. To coincide with the "Griffey in '96" campaign, Nike released the Air Griffey Max 1, which was baseball's answer to the Air Jordan line. He also appeared on a box of Frosted Flakes with Tony the Tiger, a box of Wheaties solo, and did commercials for Foot Locker, Nike, Pepsi, and more. And he made a slew of appearances in TV shows and movies, including playing himself in an episode of *The Fresh Prince of Bel-Air*, HBO's *Arli$$*, and the TV spinoff of *Harry and the Hendersons*. He even played himself in the movie *Little Big League*. He was also probably the greatest MTV Rock N' Jock softball player of all time, ripping hits off of everyone from rock stars to supermodels.

"Griffey's charm and exuberance were so authentic," Finn says. "He was relatable on such a human level."

He was relatable in non-human form as well, including 64-bit form and cartoon form. On the video game side, Griffey was the star of four products, beginning with the aforementioned Ken Griffey Jr. Presents Major League Baseball in 1994 and culminating in the super popular Ken Griffey Jr.'s Slugfest in 1999. On the cartoon side, Griffey was one of nine Major Leaguers who appeared in the famous *Simpsons* episode "Homer at the Bat."

"There hasn't been a player since who young people flocked to see like they did with Griffey," Rushin says. "He was the coolest star in baseball."

Part V: The Cards

It would be author malpractice to write a chapter on Ken Griffey Jr.'s popularity in 1996 and not include a short section on how he changed the baseball card market forever. Beginning in 1989, when Griffey was chosen to be card #1 in Upper Deck's very first baseball card set, he became a unique force in the trading card world, setting off a scramble for his cardboard that we hadn't seen before and have not seen since.

Steve Grad, one of the world's foremost autograph and sports memorabilia authenticators and a star of *Pawn Stars*, recalls the impact Griffey had on the hobby in his early collecting days. In the late '80s and early '90s, Grad was living in Chicago at the height of his autograph hunting and the number-one target then, obviously, was Michael Jordan. Back then, the Bulls flew commercial and Grad went so far as to track the flights to meet the team at the United Airlines terminal to score autographs.

"It would be like a Saturday morning at the airport and the Bulls would arrive at the terminal and we'd have the cards ready to sign," Grad says. "But even then the players knew the value. I remember once a friend gave Jordan a rookie card to sign and he said, 'You don't want me to sign that, it's my rookie.'"

At the time, there weren't more than a handful of players across all of sports whose cards you'd have treated that way, but that rarified air was occupied by two icons.

"From an autograph perspective, Griffey was like Jordan," Grad says. "You just didn't get his cards signed. They were the nicest looking cards. But I've probably authenticated 2,000 or 3,000 of those cards in my lifetime."

In total, Griffey has an estimated 138 rookie cards across Fleer, Donruss, Upper Deck, Topps, and dozens of other brands. And you, like everyone else, probably had a handful or more of the most popular—and you also probably thought right now you'd be reading this in your ocean-front mansion in Malibu after you sold your collection.

Sorry.

Riding Griffey's popularity, the trading card industry reached a peak of $1.2 billion in card sales in 1991. By 2000, the number was down to $400 million and dropping due to a complete oversaturation of product and printing and card sets.

The industry has seen a massive uptick since 2015, as manufacturers like Topps and Panini have wised up (they only print a certain number of cards per set, sometimes even just a single card) and gotten creative, adding a host of variations with increasing rarity, as well as increasing the appeal of certain card sets by adding uniform patches, autographs, equipment slices, and more. The basketball card market, in particular, has gone through the roof, with LeBron James rookies going for over one million dollars and rare variations of young stars like Giannis Antetokounmpo and Luka Doncic reaching high five figures. But while their cards may be more valuable, their impact still pales in comparison to Griffey's.

"From a collection and hobby standpoint, Griffey is the standard," Grad says. "There is no other player who has transcended like him."

HAPPY GILMORE

FORTY-EIGHT HOURS AFTER VALENTINE'S DAY IN 1996, a love story for all time—cloaked as a sports movie—hit theaters. It was about a young man grappling with a series of obstacles: his girlfriend left him because he wouldn't give up his dream; his grandmother had her house repossessed by the IRS; he was broke.

By sheer happenstance, he discovers that he can absolutely hit the shit out of a golf ball and his prospects instantly start looking up. He meets a golf pro, Chubbs, who agrees to train him for the PGA Tour. But he quickly gets on the wrong side of the tour's best player, Shooter McGavin. As he struggles with his newfound professional talent and his rivalry with McGavin, he meets the PGA's beautiful head of public relations, Virginia Venit. Venit goes from handler to confidante as the young man battles his demons, his temper, and the other golf pros to earn enough money to save his grandmother's house. Defying all odds, the young man hits an impossible shot to win the tournament, the girl, and the keys to his grandmother's home.

That young man was Happy Gilmore.

Are you crying? It's okay if you are. It's a beautiful story of redemption. When you really think about where Gilmore was at the start of the film—dumped, jobless, and dealing with a dispossessed grandmother—to where he ends up—a pro athlete in a relationship with a gorgeous career woman—one can only admire Gilmore's gumption as he turned his life around.

Adam Sandler, who wrote the movie along with *Saturday Night Live* writer Tim Herlihy, based the film very loosely on his childhood friend Kyle, a hothead hockey player who also golfed with Sandler and his dad. He apparently outdrove Sandler all the time and the Sandman attributed that to Kyle's hockey skills. From that little nugget, Sandler and Herlihy created the entire *Happy Gilmore* storyline.

Prior to Happy, the only other golf movie to break into the mainstream was the legendary comedy *Caddyshack* in 1980, but an entire generation of kids grew up and got their driver's licenses between the two films. By 1996, millions of teenagers were so sick of their dads saying "be the ball" and "so I got that going for me, which is nice" and "the world needs ditch diggers too" and "you'll get nothing and like it" that Sandler took it upon himself to give '90s kids a golf movie that they could quote endlessly and call their own.

Thanks to Sandler, when someone says to you, "I eat pieces of shit like you for breakfast," you can respond with, "You eat pieces of shit for breakfast?"

Whenever you swat your friend on a basketball court or have a mic drop moment, you always have, "The price is wrong, bitch," at the ready.

See a friend or stranger in a weird outfit? Sandler's got you covered: "If I saw myself in clothes like that I'd have to kick my own ass."

Anytime you're out on the golf course and you see someone working on their swing, you can't help yourself from saying, "It's all in the hips," and if a putt comes up short, it's perfectly acceptable to shout,

"Why don't you just go home! Go to your home!" Your boys that you're playing with will nod in approval. You're all in on the joke.

And the coup de grace is for Gilmore fans who are now parents: when your sweet little offspring looks up to you with loving eyes, after you've put them back to bed for the hundredth time, and they ask, "Can you get me a warm glass of milk?" the Sandman gave you the single greatest response a parent can give, as you paraphrase and say:

"I can get you a warm glass of shut the hell up!"[*]

---

[*] I have never actually said this line to my kids . . . I've only thought it about four million times. But it would feel good to say it. Just once.

6

THE ANSWER

GEORGETOWN FORWARD BOUBACAR AW CROSSED the three-point line and was met by nobody. No switches. No rotations. No defensive collapses. Nothing but air and opportunity. All four Texas Tech Red Raiders hung back, feet planted on the baseline as Aw shifted into fourth gear with a clean, uninterrupted runway to the rim.

The lay-up line in warm-ups wasn't this open.

As Aw strode over the foul line, confident of an easy bucket, his teammate, sophomore Allen Iverson, was so far away from the play he might as well have been grabbing Twizzlers and a Sprite at the concession stand.

And yet, he felt something.

Like a hawk catching a twitch in the grass from three hundred feet in the air, Iverson's senses heightened. Maybe it was Aw's clunky first step; maybe it was that two of the defenders moved imperceptibly to Aw's strong side; maybe it was a legitimate Spidey-sense the great ones have; but while 70,149 spectators were certain Aw had a gimme bucket, *Iverson wasn't buying it.*

The rest of the sequence happens in roughly three-tenths of a second.

Aw picks up his dribble and jumps off one foot just as Iverson slides across the three-point line. When Aw is at the basket, Iverson still isn't in the paint. After Aw's release, the ball rolls off the left side of the backboard as Iverson teleports into trail position. In the instant that Aw falls out of bounds and looks up at his muffed lay-up in disbelief, Iverson plants both feet and pogo-sticks about 40" off the hardwood for a two-handed, where-did-he-come-from, holy shit put-back dunk over two Red Raiders.

Kaaaaboooom.

The crowd erupts, and with fifteen minutes and fourteen seconds left in the Sweet Sixteen round of the 1996 NCAA Tournament, Allen Iverson turned the Georgia Dome in Atlanta into the Georgetown Dome.

When his feet finally touched the ground after the slam, the Hoyas trailed the Red Raiders 55–60. Iverson dished it all out for Texas Tech after that: steals, no-look passes, slicing drives, tear drops, and jumpers. Georgetown quickly took the lead and went on to win 98–90. Iverson had 32 points, 5 steals, and 5 assists. Darvin Ham, who was Texas Tech's leading scorer in the game, could only marvel at the 6', 160-pound point guard, saying he was "extremely quick and knows how to get other players involved. He orchestrated it all. He's something special."

Iverson now had 88 points through just three games of March Madness (31 against Mississippi Valley State in the first round and 25 against New Mexico in the second round). Up next, #1 seed UMass in the Elite Eight with their own unstoppable All-American, 6' 11" Marcus Camby.

With the score of the game 3–4 early in the first quarter, Iverson was isolated one-on-one with Carmelo Travieso out near the three-point line, a Bugatti matched up with a minivan. Iverson dipped his shoulder and crossed Travieso, flashed into the paint, and took a beeline for

Marcus Camby who recognized what was happening a beat too late. Camby lunged to the hoop just as Iverson buzzed his tower and banged a two-handed jam directly in his face.

Thwaaaaaap.

The announcers, the crowd, both benches . . . they all went apoplectic. Dudes Iverson's size don't do that. Not in practice, not in games, and certainly not on near-seven-foot All-Americans. It was more than a slam. It was a statement.

The Hoyas lost the game, but it was the signature play of the night and the one we all talked about at lunch the next day. There was no "Hey, what's up?" or "Yo, bro, can I have some of your Funyuns?" Only, "Did you see Iverson smash on Camby?!"

It was one of those plays.

Even though Georgetown got knocked out, Iverson poured in another 23, giving him 111 points in a single tournament. It was a mind-boggling scoring tear he started nearly four months earlier in the Preseason NIT Tournament, where he served more buckets than a Kentucky Fried Chicken drive-through.

24 points against Temple.

23 points against 25th ranked Georgia Tech.

40 points in the final against 19th-ranked Arizona.

"I've been through three calf shows, nine horse ropings, and I saw Elvis once," Arkansas coach Nolan Richardson said. "But I've never seen anything like that Iverson boy."

Stephon Marbury, Georgia Tech's own star point guard, said that Iverson's scoring wasn't even the most exciting part of his game.

"People always say how Allen is a scoring point guard, which is true," he said. "But he's also a great passer. I mean he's thrown some no-look passes even I have never seen before."

Throughout that 1995–1996 season, Iverson led the nation in the "doing things nobody had ever seen before" category. He even kicked off 1996 on the cover of *Slam Magazine*, a rare honor for a college kid. On a game-to-game basis he was the most uniquely dynamic and dazzling performer the college hoops scene had witnessed in years. He had swagger before it had a name. He had his own style to rival Michigan's Fab Five, rocking the smog gray #3 Georgetown uniform, matching sleeveless t-shirt underneath, and black Air Jordan XI Concords.

He was an entertainer and a showman and had been his whole life. Dating all the way back to middle school, Iverson's athleticism seemed to have its own gravitational pull, his feats being the Jupiter of whatever sports solar system he existed in at the time. In eighth grade, standing at only 5'6" and not even weighing a buck fifty, hundreds of people would show up to his football games to watch him play. For a time, football was arguably his best sport.

Gary Moore, Iverson's coach at Aberdeen Elementary School, said, "From day one, he actually wanted to jump right in and play. He wanted to be my star player. That aggression and that enthusiasm is what I admired most about him. When I saw him dance and move, completely reverse his field all the way back around and not allow any of those kids to touch him, that's when I really said, 'Wow, this boy's something.'"

As a freshman in high school Iverson started on the varsity football team at wide receiver and safety. As a sophomore, he moved to quarterback and defensive back, once intercepting five passes in a single game. Junior year he led the team to a Virginia high school championship, returning a punt for a touchdown, rushing for a touchdown, and throwing for 200 yards while grabbing two interceptions in the title game. He'd go on to win Virginia's high school football player of the year award and field recruiting offers from most of the major football programs on the East Coast.

In particular, Florida State, who had recently won the National Championship with Heisman Trophy winner/starting point guard

Charlie Ward as their quarterback, thought Iverson might be their next multi-sport star.

"We were on him hard," former Florida State assistant head coach Chuck Amato once told *VICE Sports*. "He was just a great athlete and a competitor. He would've been the first Michael Vick."

Or the next Charlie Ward.

Either way, it never happened. After winning Virginia's high school state basketball player of the year in the winter of 1993 (averaging over 30 points per game), Iverson famously ran into legal trouble following a controversial brawl in a bowling alley in Hampton, Virginia. The entire situation was a racially charged embarrassment to the legal system that led to all the black kids involved in the brawl (Iverson and his friends) getting arrested while all the white kids got off. After getting charged with three felony accounts and sentenced to five years in prison, Iverson served four months at a minimum-security jail before he was granted conditional clemency by Virginia's governor, Douglas Wilder. He was allowed to finish high school, but not allowed to play sports.

During this time, Iverson's mom made a hall-of-fame parenting road trip to Washington, DC, on behalf of her son, to ask John Thompson if he would personally let Allen play for Georgetown, since the legal issues had scared off nearly every other school. Thompson agreed, but made it clear that Iverson was there to play basketball, not football. Still, Iverson couldn't quite let his pigskin dreams die, so he decided to broach the subject with Big John early in his freshman year. In an interview for *Slam Magazine* in 2012, Iverson said that the conversation went about as well as telling your dad you totaled his newly restored 1974 Pontiac Trans Am.

"He said, 'I'll tell you what I think about you playing football. If you don't get your skinny black ass the eff out of my face...you better,'"

Iverson said. "Just like that. I never thought about playing football again after that. I mean, he made it clear that this is not why I was here."

Right.

Iverson wasn't on Georgetown's campus to bang helmets with Eddie Coblentz on the football practice field or to square off against Bucknell in a Patriot League playoff game. He was there to do battle; to help Thompson wrestle control of the old Big East from UConn, Syracuse, Villanova, and the other hated conference rivals. That was the singular goal. And Iverson performed brilliantly.

As a freshman, he averaged 20 points, 4.5 assists, and 3 steals per game, leading the Hoyas to a 21–10 record and a Sweet Sixteen appearance in the 1995 NCAA Tournament. His sophomore year was even better as Georgetown finished with a 29–8 record, a top AP ranking of #4 in the country, a regular season Big East 7 division title, an appearance in the Big East Tournament Finals, and the NCAA tournament Elite Eight. Individually, he was a first team All-American, a first team All Big East selection, and a two-time Big East Defensive Player of the Year.

Thompson's gamble on Ann Iverson's kid twenty-four months prior had paid off, but it would only be a two-year on-court partnership. Despite Thompson having a near 100 percent graduation rate during his two-decade tenure at Georgetown, Iverson had extenuating circumstances that made turning pro necessary (he had a younger sister who suffered from seizures and a daughter who needed financial support).

"My family needs me right now," Iverson said at the press conference announcing his decision to enter the NBA Draft. "I didn't like the things going on back in Hampton with my mom and my sisters' living situation. I think that really pushed me out. I have an opportunity to take care of them."

He also had an opportunity to become a legend.

No less than uber-agent David Falk, who represented previous Georgetown stars Patrick Ewing, Dikembe Mutombo, and Alonzo

Mourning, as well as Michael Jordan, took on Iverson as a client. Within hours of his announcement, he was projected as a top-five NBA Draft pick and a shoe-in for a major sneaker deal; step one in turning Iverson the athlete into Iverson the icon.

◘   ◘   ◘

Iverson was a lock to sign with Nike.

This was the presumed wisdom among every shoe company in existence. Iverson had been wearing Nikes since his days of slamming Capri Suns and eating Fruit-by-the-Foot. His high school team, Bethel, was a Nike high school. All the camps he'd gone to were Nike camps, and it was a well-known secret that Nike had flown him to these camps. Georgetown was an elite Nike school, and his coach/mentor John Thompson was on the board of Nike and was personal friends with Phil Knight. You didn't need to be Jimmy McNulty and Bunk Moreland to crack the mysterious case of where Iverson was likely headed.

But, a couple young guys at Reebok in the spring of 1996 had the foresight to understand Iverson wasn't just a player you sign—he was a brand you build a company around. Fittingly, this belief took root with that classic Iverson slam on Marcus Camby in the NCAA tournament.

Que Gaskins, who was then on his way to becoming the Global Vice President of Reebok, recalled his thoughts the moment after the dunk in an oral history for Nice Kicks. "I just remember saying to myself, 'Oh my god, we gotta get this kid! That's the one!'"

His colleague, Todd Krinsky, who is now a Senior Vice President at Reebok, watched the same game and had the exact same reaction. "At that point, he had arrived, and we felt right then that he was what we needed. That play on Camby, he had arrived on the national landscape in the NCAA tournament. We had already been talking about him, but that was the moment where we went, 'Yeah. He's the guy.' Before that, he had the swagger and we knew he was a great player, and he was exciting and had no fear, but that next day, we moved the conversation from 20 miles an hour to 80 miles an hour. Right after that, we started to develop the Question." If your sneaker game is a little fuzzy, in the late '90s, "The Question" would become Reebok's Whopper to Nike's Big Mac—but we're not there yet.

Heading into 1996, Nike owned most of the sneakers on that decade's Mount Olympus of kicks. The Air Jordan line was the Zeus of the field, with the Nike Air Penny a clear rival and Scottie Pippen's Air Pippen (late '96) and Barkley's Air Max CB fighting it out for the next tier with the brand. The FILA Grant Hill 1 also rose in popularity along with its namesake, Grant Hill. But Reebok was floundering. They had about one-third of Nike's market share in the basketball space, and even though their lineup included stars like Shaquille O'Neal and Shawn Kemp, their shoes had yet to generate much buzz, let alone find a place in the pop culture pantheon like the Jordans and the Pennys.* Iverson, they believed, was the one man who could swing the company's reputation and fortune. Gaskins and Krinsky wanted to go after him. Hard. They just had to persuade a few of the more senior men at Reebok.

"When you've got a young guy that's a little smaller and plays off the dribble, that has an exciting game and can dunk in traffic—when you have all of those things, plus you're a good-looking kid and you've got a swagger and an urban profile—if you have three of those attributes, you're good," Krinsky said. "If you have all of them, it's like lightning in a bottle. Que and I were really, really pushing some of the older guys . . . and Reebok CEO Paul Fireman went, 'OK, you know what, let's do it!'"

With the green light, they went ahead designing the shoe and setting up meetings. Their one advantage, they believed, was that at Nike,

---

* The Shaqnosis was the one exception. It was unique and hard to take your eyes off of, you know, kind of like a hypnosis.

Iverson was going to be just another star with a shoe to promote. At Reebok, they were going to make him THE STAR.

"We took him around to different companies, and Reebok was really in need of a superstar," David Falk said. "I told them that if they wanted to have serious discussions with Allen, that he wanted his own shoe and aggressive promotion."

Gaskins and Krinsky were way ahead of Falk. In their first meeting they told Iverson their plan to make him the face of the company. In the second meeting, they showed him the prototype for "The Question" and announced that they'd have it ready for Iverson to wear on day one of his rookie year. They also made it clear that they had no interest in trying to polish or manipulate Iverson's image. Their pitch was basically, you be you, wear this dope shoe, and we'll promote the shit out of you. Also, here is a record-breaking amount of money.

It worked.

"All along, Reebok told me they didn't want to make me up. They didn't want it to turn out to be something I'm not. They wanted to let me be myself. They were just going to let me be, whatever that is," Iverson said. "I told Coach Thompson what Reebok was offering me and what Nike was offering me, and he told me it was a no brainer. He said, 'Well, you should sign with Reebok.'"

So, Iverson signed a 10-year deal worth $60 million, solidifying one of the most iconic apparel/athlete partnerships of the last fifty years. According to Gaskins, it was a page straight out of the playbook Falk ran for Jordan. Jordan had a guy named Howard White who was his main man at Nike to handle everything, and Gaskins was going to play that role at Reebok for Iverson. The minute the deal was signed, he started to make plans to move to Philadelphia. The deal also reinforced what Krinsky and Gaskins had believed all along: "There's a draft every year, but not an Allen Iverson every year."

True. True. True.

Legally, the signing of the document and the dotting of the Is and crossing of the Ts made the deal official on the business side for Reebok, but it was Iverson's crossover heard 'round the hoop world on Michael Jordan that announced the partnership to the public. The move and the moment took place in the spring of Iverson's rookie year, but the seeds had been planted one month earlier at the rookie game, when Jordan spoke to Iverson for the first time and shared these five heartwarming words with the budding star:

"What's up, you little bitch?"

"The first time I ever talked to him was that year, playing in the rookie game," Iverson told Complex. "I'll never forget it, because he said, 'What's up, you little bitch?' I looked at him like . . . 'All right, man.'"

A few weeks later, during a game in Philadelphia against Chicago, Iverson found himself one-on-one with MJ at the top of the key and decided to respond properly to MJ's "what's up" comment.

"It was time to put my moves to the test," he said later.

With a dribble between the legs, a hesitation, a mini-cross from right to left, a dribble, then another mini-cross to the left, he set Jordan up perfectly for a finger-snap quick deep crossover to the right, which left Jordan off-balance and facing the wrong way, as Iverson lifted up for an easy jumper that fell perfectly through the hoop and into the history books. It was an instant all-time highlight, leading *SportsCenter* for the week and becoming a video played on the anniversary of the crossover every year. While Iverson spoke about the move a few times afterward, he gave his most thorough account of the crossover on *The Fat Joe Show*.

"I didn't know nothing until ESPN and everybody else made a big deal of it," he said. "I was just playing. I was at war. I was playing against the greatest player to ever play the game. I always told my homeboys that if I play against him, with no disrespect, but I was gonna try my move on the best to ever play the game. I learned so much from him because I wanted to be like him, but I always looked at myself like a six-foot Shaquille O'Neal. Like, I wanted to dominate."

It was a highlight not only for the basketball ages, but for the sneaker wars as well. Basketball historian Brandon "Scoop B" Robinson, who practically grew up in his parents' sneaker store, says that "the reason the crossover was so iconic wasn't just because he did it on Michael, who everyone looked up to, but because he did it in the Reebok Questions, which for some people made them as iconic as the Jordan elevens. The tops of both sneakers looked very similar, with the patent leather tip. Nobody was buying Reebok sneakers before that. Now all these years later it's an iconic shoe. People are wearing the retros like they wear Jordans. And Iverson is still doing collaborations with modern stars like James Harden now. That's the impact Iverson had."

Robinson also tells a great story that illustrates how Jordan felt about the one sneaker that challenged his supremacy.

"Lil' Bow Wow was friendly with MJ's son and went to stay at his house with some friends and they were all wearing Iverson's shoes," Robinson says. "They left the shoes out and when the kids woke up, their Questions were gone. Jordan himself had replaced them with Jordans."

◘　　◘　　◘

"I'd say I had about 35 pictures on my wall of Iverson growing up," three-time Sixth Man of the Year Award winner and crossover extraordinaire Jamal Crawford says. "He's had more influence on my game than anyone. My handles. My pull-up jumper. It all came from him. He was an inspiration. He was like the little guy that could. The tattoos we all got came from Iverson. We could relate to him more. He had that mentality to take on the world."

First came the Questions; then came the ink, the shooting sleeves, the headband, the pre-game headphones, the hats, the jewelry, the baggy clothes, and more. Accessory by accessory, Iverson crafted a style that in the span of a few seasons became the image to emulate throughout the league.

"Iverson got the attention of a lot of people who maybe thought Jordan was too clean," Robinson says. "He got the attention of people from the inner cities who had never seen anything like Allen Iverson or who weren't vocal enough to express how much they really identified with that life. Iverson was part of their culture, but it wasn't like he did it with a branding mentality in mind. He did it just by being himself."

A perfect example of this is the story behind Iverson's iconic cornrows. The decision to go with that hairstyle wasn't made by a team of handlers or by Iverson poring over fashion magazines looking for a trendsetting way to do his 'do. Nope. He chose the cornrows for the single most relatable dude reason of all time: they were low maintenance.

"The cornrows came about because Iverson was tired of going to the barber shop all of the time," Robinson says. "When you get braids your hair just lasts longer. Iverson was always on TV and he wanted to make sure his hair was on point. You could either go to the barbershop or have a barber that you trust when you're on the road. But the cornrows made it easier."

Bobby Jones, a star player out of the University of Washington, was drafted by the 76ers in 2006 and as a rookie was assigned to Allen Iverson, which in the NBA's hierarchy meant he had to do whatever Iverson asked of him.

"I had to do anything he wanted whenever he wanted," Jones says. "It takes about a year before you stop feeling like a fan of your teammates. It's just how it is. You show up and you're like, 'Wow, you're Allen Iverson and you're my teammate now.' He always treated me with respect and he took me out for fun. I got to see firsthand how everybody just levitated [when they were] around him. They just adored him. His demeanor. The way he played. The way he attacked the tall guys.

And before him the only guy you saw with tattoos was Rodman. Then Iverson made them cool. Guys from the inner city connected to him. He was relatable and so down to earth. He wasn't going to change for anybody. He got the ultimate respect for that."

For basketball fans and players in the early '90s who grew up listening to Dr. Dre, Snoop Dogg, Tupac, Biggie, Jay-Z, and the rest of hip hop's golden age MCs, Iverson was the basketball embodiment of all of them. He brought the entire rap culture into the league and thus, into the sports culture at large. More importantly, he did it effortlessly and fearlessly. Just as urban kids and suburban kids blasted "Nuthin' But a 'G' Thang" in their basketball and football locker rooms because the beats and the lyrics empowered them, Iverson himself became a uniting force for all teenagers. He didn't take shit. And for millions of high school and college kids from every background, that was kind of the goal of growing up: to not have to take shit anymore, to be able to "do you" without parents or teachers able to stop you. Iverson's very existence showed that it was possible—with his clothes, his attitude, and most importantly, his play.

Iverson was the rebel you looked up to because physically he was you. He wasn't born 7', 275 like Shaquille O'Neal or even 6'6" 220 like Michael Jordan. He was 6' (maybe) and 165 pounds (on a full stomach). You saw dozens of guys bigger than him in your own high school league or at pick-up games in college. If you had no idea who he was, and he was waiting to get "next" on a court you were playing on, you'd just assume he was another average-sized guy trying to get a run in. Hence, the appeal; Iverson wasn't the strongest or the tallest, but he excelled in a professional sport that was almost the exclusive domain of the tall and the strong. And he inspired millions of athletes to try to do the same thing.

"Iverson broke the little guard barrier," Hall of Famer and nine-time NBA All-Star Gary Payton says. "How he was able to score and control the game. People were always saying that little guards weren't going to make it as scorers. When Allen showed that he could, then they set their talents to do it. And with the braids and the jerseys and the culture he embraced, he started a trend."

That trend ended up featuring a run of guys who made it to the NBA who credit Iverson directly for showing them that it was possible to be six-foot and under and be a star in the league.

"Allen Iverson was everything to me," three-time NBA Slam Dunk Contest Winner Nate Robinson says. "He was it. I wanted to dress like him. I wanted to play like him. I wanted his handles and his moves. I looked up to him in every way. He was who I wanted to be."

"He was a little guy who changed the way we played the game," 5'9", two-time NBA All-Star Isaiah Thomas says. "Pound for pound, he was the best to ever touch a basketball."

On this last statement, there is no doubt. Iverson finished his career with eleven all-star selections, the 2001 MVP Award, seven All-NBA selections, the Rookie of the Year Award in '96–'97, and he led the league in scoring four times and in steals three times. His number was retired in Philadelphia and he was inducted into the Pro Basketball Hall of Fame in 2016.

Upon his selection, LeBron James wrote the following in a congratulatory Instagram post, perfectly summing up how a generation of NBA stars felt about AI, while also speaking to his once-in-a-lifetime impact on the game:

"You're the reason why I got tattoos, wore a headband and an arm sleeve. Thanks for everything."

PITINO'S BOMBINOS

AARON HARRISON. KARL-ANTHONY TOWNS. DEVIN Booker. Andrew Harrison. Willie Cauley-Stein. Trey Lyles. Dakari Johnson. Tyler Ulis. Alex Poythress. Those are the record-tying nine Kentucky players who made it to the NBA from John Calipari's 2014–2015 Wildcats squad. That team went 38–1, with their sole loss occurring against Wisconsin in the Final Four of the NCAA Tournament.

Calipari had come close to getting nine future NBAers before.

On his 35–3 team in 2009–2010, a squad that also lost in the Final Four, he had eight, including two All-Stars: John Wall and DeMarcus Cousins, along with Patrick Patterson, Eric Bledsoe, Darius Miller, Daniel Orton, DeAndre Liggins, and Josh Harrellson.

A few years after that, he had seven NBA guys on his National Championship team: Anthony Davis, Doron Lamb, Michael Kidd-Gilchrist, Terrence Jones, Marquis Teague, Darius Miller, and Kyle Wiltjer.

At the time of this writing, there are enough Kentucky players in the NBA (25) to form two full teams and still have a few guys sprinkled around the G-League. Since his signing in 2009, Calipari has turned

Kentucky into the NBA's version of a AAA baseball team. The Wildcats
are the Pawtucket to the NBA's Red Sox.

You're probably thinking, 'Of course he's sent so many guys to the
NBA. That's Calipari's whole pitch! He recruits kids specifically to get
them to the NBA. He's the king of one and done. Seven guys. Eight
guys. Nine guys going to the NBA on one team! He's ruined college
basketball. Only in this crazy era.'

If that's what's on your mind, it's completely understandable. It's
also completely wrong. Twenty-five years ago, a different Kentucky
coach was running a fairly similar playbook. It wasn't "one and done."
It was more like "two and screw" or "three and flee," but still, the idea
was the same: amass ridiculous amounts of talent, take over college
basketball, and crank out Final Four appearances and NBA players like
F-150s rolling off an assembly line.

That coach was Rick Pitino.

o   o   o

Richard Andrew Pitino was born in New York City and raised in Bayville,
a strip of land in Oyster Bay that stands directly across the Long Island
Sound from Greenwich, Connecticut. He attended St. Dominic High
School, was captain of the basketball team, and was a good enough point
guard to sign with UMass Amherst to play in college. After leading the
team in assists his junior and senior years, he took a job as a graduate
assistant at the University of Hawaii (nice), before becoming a full-time
assistant in 1975. After leaving Hawaii due to an NCAA investigation
and sanctions (a common theme in Pitino's career), he took a job as
an assistant at Syracuse under Jim Boeheim. Two years later he got
his first head coaching job at Boston University (5 years), then took a
job as an assistant with the New York Knicks (2 years), then another

head coaching job at Providence (2 years and a shocking Final Four appearance) before miraculously being named head coach of the New York Knicks at 34.

In just two seasons, he helped lift a Patrick Ewing-led Knicks team that had won just 24 games the year before he arrived to a 52–30 record, the team's first division title in 20 years, and an Eastern Conference Semi-Finals appearance where they lost to Jordan's Bulls. In May of '89, Kentucky fired their head coach, Eddie Sutton, and Pitino talked openly in the press about going back to the college game.

"There's a lot I like about Kentucky," he said. "The big question is do I want to give up the Knicks . . . I would not be here, possibly leaving the New York Knicks situation—and a potential championship—if I did not believe that this program could be along the same lines as Duke and North Carolina."

I'll save you the suspense: Pitino did believe the program would be as good as Duke and North Carolina, and he left Madison Square Garden, which was a few blocks west of Lexington Avenue in Manhattan, for Lexington, Kentucky. By 1993, he had Kentucky in the Final Four, kicking off a six-year run in the mid-'90s that looked like this:

1993 – Final Four

1995 – Final Four

1996 – NCAA Champions

1997 – NCAA Finals

1998 – NCAA Champions (Tubby Smith Head Coach)

What does this have to do with Calipari and one-and-dones and the modern era of college basketball in particular and the NBA in general?

A ton.

Long before Daryl Morey and a legion of nerds took over front offices and re-engineered the game around the goal of jacking up as many high-percentage threes as humanly possible, Rick Pitino was giving his 1987 Providence College team the green light to let it fly as soon as they crossed half court. During the '87–'88 season, the Friars shot 260 more threes than the second-place three-point shooting team in the Big East.

"He really was the pioneer of the utilization of the 3-point shot," Stu Jackson, an NBA executive and former Pitino staff member, said on a Ringer podcast. "And I can tell you, I can remember like it was yesterday, Rick liked to have a lot of meetings with his staff, and I was on his staff at the time, and I remember the day he brought us into the sauna at Alumni Hall at Providence College, because he liked to meet in the sauna. I remember to this day, he sat down with a magnetic board and with a Sharpie and showed us the math. He said, listen, with this team, if we take X amount of 3-point shots and shoot 33 percent, it's better than taking X amount of [2-point] shots and shooting 40 percent. We were all sort of scratching our heads, but he was right."

Pitino's point guard on that team was Billy Donovan, who subsequently won several National Championships as the head coach of the University of Florida and is currently (in 2021) the head coach of the Chicago Bulls. He remembers that when the NCAA instituted the three-point shot for the 1987 season, many coaches rebelled against it and even refused to shoot it. Where other coaches saw a problem, Pitino saw a solution, or as author Ryan Holiday, a modern expert on Stoicism, would say, the obstacle is the way.

"I knew nothing about the 3-point shot, never played with the 3-point shot, never was around it, so I knew nothing about it," Donovan said. "But when Rick Pitino came in, he had NBA experience with the New York Knicks (assistant coach at the time). He may have been the only coach going into that season that really, really understood the magnitude of the 3-point shot. Nobody knew really how to take advantage of it. And this would never happen in today's day and age; the first six games of the Big East, not one team made a 3-point shot against us. We were taking 30 to 35 3-point shots a game, and you had a lot of very, very prominent coaches coming out who really opposed the rule, were down against it, saying 'We'll never take a 3-point shot, it's going to ruin the game.'"

Over time, teams would adapt, but not quickly enough. Pitino brought his love of the three to the Knicks and then again to Kentucky, where he coached with the ABC rule of offense: Always Be Chucking.*

Pitino was also a trendsetter when it came to his relentless pursuit of high school *Parade* All-Americans, regardless of position or depth chart. If you had a future in the NBA, and if you'd accept Pitino's offer and the environment, you had a spot on Kentucky's roster. Yes, maybe you'd play more at another school, but you likely won't be in the Final Four year after year and you won't be on national television as much or more than most small-market NBA teams. That was the choice facing five-star recruits in the early '90s when Pitino gave his closing pitch in living rooms across the United States.

It worked brilliantly.

After Final Four appearances in '93 and '95, Pitino put together his Mona Lisa of a roster heading into the '95–'96 season. Top to bottom, it was his magnum opus, filled with All-American seniors, NBA-ready juniors, and all-world freshmen. The team featured Tony Delk, Antoine Walker, Walter McCarty, Derek Anderson, Ron Mercer, Mark Pope, Jeff Sheppard, Wayne Turner, and Nazr Mohammed. The team had Mr. Basketball winners from six states! But no true point guard or dominant big man—neither of which mattered to Pitino because all of these guys

---

* I just made this up on the spot, but I really like it. Pitino never said this, but I imagine if he thought of it, he would have. I'm sure he likes *Glengarry Glen Ross*.

could play at the college level and the pro level and he was a straight shooter with them from the beginning.

"When you have 11 good players, you have to deal with the egos, because from the first man to the ninth man, they all think they're great players," Pitino said. "I tell them, when I was in the NBA, we never talked about how many points a player scores. We talked about rebounding ability, shot-blocking ability, can he guard his man? Everyone knows they're going to play, so they practice even harder."

It's hard to argue with the results. When all was said and done, these nine men collectively played 68 years in the NBA.

Sixty-eight!

Naturally, the 1995–1996 team opened the season ranked #1 and promptly dismantled #14 Maryland at the Tip-Off Classic. Then, in a surprise twist, they lost their second game of the year to thirty-six-year-old John Calipari's UMass team, led by Marcus Camby. The loss dropped Kentucky down to #5, but the Wildcats used it as fuel and proceeded to go on a twenty-seven-game winning streak that would last from December 2, 1995, to March 10, 1996, the last two months of which they were the #2 team in the country. The streak included crushing #16 Georgia Tech by twenty-three points (83–60), #25 Louisville by twenty-three (89–66), and #12 Mississippi State by eighteen (74–56). Most impressive was the way they closed out their SEC play, beating Georgia, Tennessee, Alabama, Florida, Auburn, and Vanderbilt by an obscene 156 total points. Every home game at the Rupp Arena was sold out or at 99 percent max capacity, with more than 24,000 people cheering on the blue and white.

When the SEC tournament started in early March, Kentucky planned to use it as a nice appetizer to March Madness; maybe get a small chopped salad and some tomato bisque before wolfing down the porterhouse that was the NCAA tournament. Things began as planned, with the Wildcats waxing the Florida Gators by 24 in the quarterfinals and then the Arkansas Razorbacks by 20 in the semis.

"Kentucky is the best team I've seen," Arkansas coach Nolan Richardson said after the game. "And I've been coaching thirty-one years. When you play Kentucky, your defense is under so much pressure because of their dribble penetration. That's what they do and they do it at all five positions."

Antoine Walker, Kentucky's Swiss Army knife of a sophomore, was even being compared to NBA All-Stars with his ability to pass and play down low. "Right now I keep saying that the more he plays like Magic Johnson, the better we become," Pitino said. "I just want him to stop emulating Dominique. He said he would emulate Dominique's dunk, but that he would emulate Magic Johnson everywhere else."

That's how good Walker was, and he was arguably the second-best player on the team next to scoring savant Tony Delk. With thoughts of a fifth straight SEC Tournament win and a #1 NCAA tournament seed dancing in their heads, the Wildcats took the floor as heavy favorites in the SEC tourney against the Mississippi State Bulldogs and . . . lost. Badly. They turned the ball over. They played terrible defense. Their shooting went ice cold. But Coach Pitino swore the loss was just what his team needed.

"I honestly believe, as great as you, the media, have made us out to be, that we could not make a serious run at a national championship without this loss," he said. "Things have come too easy. The loss will help us. It shows we're not invincible."

At the time, it was an easy comment to dismiss. Just days earlier he was talking about how there was no pressure heading into the tournament with a 27- or 28-game win streak and how not losing in four months was no big deal. Now, he was saying that they needed the loss. Classic coachspeak—everything that happens is exactly what we needed to happen, unless what we needed to happen didn't happen; then we didn't need it to happen.

In hindsight, however, Pitino was dead on.

Kentucky still earned a one-seed in the tournament and the road to the Final Four was a John Wick bloodbath of revenge.

The Wildcats machine-gunned San Jose State in round one by 38.

They took a samurai sword to Virginia Tech in round two and won by 24.

They emptied a full clip into Keith Van Horn's Utah squad to win by 31.

They got up close and personal to Tim Duncan's Wake Forest team, holding them to just 19 points in the first half before hacking off their championship hopes with a machete and winning by 20 points.

If you're scoring at home, the Wildcats destroyed their first four tournament opponents by 112 points. This set up a rematch with Calipari's UMass team in the Final Four. The Minutemen were the #1 overall seed in the tournament and had just dispatched Allen Iverson and Georgetown in their Elite Eight contest. Their motto was "Refuse to Lose." For the most part, the motto held true. Other than a fluky loss to George Washington, they did refuse to lose and entered their game against Kentucky 35–1. Unlike the Wildcats, however, they weren't winning with a team full of speedboats. It was more like they had one speedboat (Marcus Camby) and a bunch of dinghies.

Is this a little unfair to Donta Bright, Carmelo Travieso, Dana Dingle, Edgar Padilla, and the boys? Sure it is. They were all fine college players . . . who you'd never hear from again. Camby was the Hyperlux 42' Cigarette model that blew the other guys out of the water. He scored 20 points, grabbed 8 rebounds, and had 3 blocks a night as sure as he tied his shoelaces. He was selected Player of the Year by the Associated Press over Ray Allen, Allen Iverson, Tim Duncan, and Tony Delk.

The Final Four match-up between POY finalists Camby and Delk took place at the then-Continental Airlines Arena in East Rutherford, New Jersey, about 10 miles straight west of Pitino's previous home in Manhattan with the Knicks. Delk had a strong game, scoring 20 points, while Camby was outstanding, getting 25 rebounds, 8 points, and 6 blocks. The game was a slugfest and for a while, it looked like Kentucky might blow out the Minutemen just like they did everyone else. Midway through the second period they were up 54–41 and the rout seemed to be on . . . but then Travieso hit back-to-back threes and Camby scored a few buckets in a row and the game was all of a sudden 59–54 with six minutes left. More importantly, Kentucky was tightening up—and worse, Delk was on the sideline with a trainer trying to perform a Mr. Miyagi miracle on the knots and cramps that had suddenly developed in his leg.

This was exactly what Calipari had hoped for.

Stay close. Keep the pressure on. Let the Wildcats feel the weight of their immense talent and expectations. To capitalize, he switched to a 2–1–2 full court trap to prey on Kentucky's nerves and maybe force a few turnovers, but Pitino was ready. On the inbounds play with six minutes left, the Wildcats got the ball down court with 4 straight passes and ended up with an easy Jeff Sheppard lay-up. Pitino looked over at his counterpart on the Minuteman bench. Nice try, Cal.

Kentucky up 7.

But UMass kept coming.

A jumper by Bright, a turnover by Mercer, and then another tip-in by Bright made the game 63–60.

The 15-point lead Kentucky once had was down to 3, and Pitino called a time out.

"On the bench, we're saying, 'They hadn't been here before'," Calipari said. "They hadn't had close games before. We had."

Was Kentucky spent?

Were the Wildcats turning into the mild cats down the stretch?

Did they have any heart?

In order, no, no, and yes.

After an airball on a three by UMass that would have tied the game, Pope hit two clutch free throws for Kentucky to get them back up 5. Moments later, Antoine Walker hit a free throw, then stole the ball from Camby and threw a full-court pass to Sheppard, who threw down an epic dunk to put the Wildcats up 8 points with three minutes to go.

Thirty seconds later Kentucky was up 10.

Now the game's over, right? It's gotta be.

But UMass kept coming.

Kentucky turnover. Camby bucket.

Kentucky turnover. Camby free throws.

Kentucky turnover.

Now it's a 4-point game with 1:30 left.

On the next possession, Camby front-rimmed his shot and then Padilla got his shot blocked, which led to a Kentucky fast break and a foul.

Mercifully for Pitino, his team settled in and began to hit their foul shots. Then, with the Wildcats up 5 points with under a minute left, UMass lost Antoine Walker on an inbounds play under their basket and he broke free for a wide-open dunk to put Kentucky up 7 with 38 seconds left. After a stop and a bucket, Kentucky went up 9 with twenty seconds left.

The Wildcats exhaled.

The Minutemen finally (finally!) ran out of minutes.

Final score: Kentucky wins, 81–74

"We're a team that slugs it out," Calipari said afterward. "And we didn't slug it out well enough. We did our thing and they did their thing better."

Pitino, as always, knew this was exactly how it was going to go and knew exactly how his team would respond. "I always felt we'd play well in close games," Pitino said.

Even so, Walter McCarty had the quote of the night when asked how he felt about Kentucky's easy wins versus having to scratch and claw against UMass.

"I'd rather just keep blowing out people, to be truthful," he said.

Two nights later, the final against Syracuse was almost anti-climactic. Syracuse was just like UMass in that the team was largely built around one star, John Wallace, who had almost the exact same stats as Marcus Camby (22 points, 8 rebounds). He was also the only Syracuse player likely headed to the NBA, although he didn't have the career Camby had.

The Final belonged to Tony Delk, who hit a then Championship Game record 7 three-pointers. And to further validate Pitino's affection for the three, the entire Kentucky team hit 12 three-pointers, setting a record for that time as well. Ron Mercer added 20 points while Antoine Walker and Derek Anderson each added 11.

While Kentucky led 59–46 with eleven minutes to go, they once again gave up a big lead and found themselves in a 2-point game with two minutes left. This time, their nerves held. Down the stretch, a Walter McCarty put back, a Derek Anderson three, and a Pope jumper put the Wildcats up 71–64 and the game wouldn't be close again, with Kentucky winning, 76–67.

"I'm not out to prove I'm a great coach, good coach, bad coach," he said. "But the national titles, fair or not, define a coach. I wanted a championship on my resume so it would stop the dumb questions: When are you going to win it all?"

Wrote Brian Schmitz of the *Orlando Sentinel*, "Before Monday, Pitino may have been the only pro or college coach who ever authored more autobiographies (two) than titles (zero). With his swagger, *GQ* wardrobe and self-promoting style, you'd have sworn that this rising star was chasing John Wooden's legacy."

After '96, he had one title down, nine to go to catch Wooden.

Looking back on the '96 Final Four twenty-five years later, it's spooky how the coaches and teams were connected: Rick Pitino, Kentucky's head coach in 1996, beat John Calipari, Kentucky's head coach starting in 2009; and then faced Jim Boeheim, who gave Pitino his first big-time assistant coaching job. Then in 2012, Calipari, now coach of Kentucky, faced Pitino, then-coach of Louisville, in the Final Four (Kentucky won).

It was almost like Pitino was the star of his own *Back to the Future* series and Biff was screwing with his space-time continuum.

Nevertheless, the ripple effects of Pitino's style (the barrage of threes) and his recruiting tactics (grab as many McDonald's All-Americans as you can) are felt throughout college basketball to this day.

And of course, so are the negative consequences. Pitino himself has become a casualty of the system he revolutionized, having his national championship at Louisville vacated due to recruiting violations. Like the great Bambino himself, in order to build rosters of Pitino's Bombinos, Rick had to swing big, which meant he missed big, too.

ERIC WYNALDA
KICKSTARTS THE MLS

AMERICANS DON'T CARE ABOUT SOCCER.

Such was the conventional wisdom heading into the early 1990s.

Millions of kids played in the United States, but none of them ever had any interested in watching it as adults. It was bizarre, in a way. You could hardly find a field on an autumn Saturday that wasn't jam-packed with little kids running around with shin guards up to their knees and stuffing their faces with orange slices, but as those elementary schoolers grew up, interest inevitably waned. Those soccer players turned to baseball and football and basketball and anything else, really, when it came to sports spectating. Tennis. Hockey. WWE wrestling. All of them rated higher than soccer.

Nobody cared, but it wasn't for a lack of effort. New leagues pushing the world's most popular sport were popping up in the US all the time. We had the American Football Association (for soccer). Then the American Professional Soccer League, the Major Soccer League, the North American Soccer League, the United Soccer League, and the

Associated League of American Soccer Professionals (okay, I made that one up).

In 1993, as part of the United States' bid to host the World Cup, the US Soccer Federation formed Major League Soccer. After three years of planning, the league launched with ten teams in 1996. By 1998 they expanded to twelve teams, and despite early financial problems, the league has continued to expand almost every year since 2005 and plans to have thirty teams by the year 2023.

But it all began in 1996, and if not for Eric Wynalda, the league's first game might have been considered a disaster.

◻   ◻   ◻

Eric Wynalda gathered the ball on the left side of the pitch, his Dr. Seussian striped socks pulled up high over his shin guards. His uniform for the San Jose Clash was an ode to '90s GAP colors and giant preppie clothes. In addition to the hypnotic socks, Wynalda's shirt was split down the middle between pea green and white, with a blue v-neck collar and the name "Clash" written in bright orange. The shorts were made of a black satin. To top it off perfectly, both the shirts and the shorts were XXXL-sized, so the fabric billowed and blew in the wind like sails on a boat as the players ran down the field.

Wynalda received that fateful pass 87 minutes into Major League Soccer's inaugural game on April 6, 1996, between his Clash and D.C. United. The score was a very soccer-esque 0–0 at the time and the 31,683 fans on hand at Spartan Stadium were aching to explode.

"On that particular day there was an anticipation, a hunger that this was finally going to be our league," Phil Schoen, the broadcaster who called the inaugural match, said. "And this was just not our day, but the start of our new reality. It was like being a soccer fan and finally being able to burst out of the closet and wear your jersey with pride."

While the opening kick marked the official start of the new league, the feeling was that until a goal was scored, things weren't official official.

So here was Wynalda, one of the marquee players in the new league, suddenly out on the wing with a chance. The ball rolled out in front of him as he staggered his feet behind it.

One two.

One two.

Defender Jeff Agoos closed in just as Wynalda reached the goalie box and head faked briefly to his right before skipping the ball with the inside of his right foot over to his left. Agoos bit hard on the ball—and instead of shooting, Wynalda shifted his weight, deked him left, kicked the ball between Agoos's legs for a classic nutmeg, and slid right by him toward the middle of the field. A hair before two United defenders collapsed on him, he dug in his left heel, swung his right leg around and . . . blasted it into the upper-right corner of the net.

Gooooooooaaaaalll!!!!

Wynalda spread his arms out and sprinted in a quick circle as fans for both teams exploded, celebrating the league's first score. He ran off to the sideline, pulled his shirt off, and slid onto his knees, clenching his fists at his side as his teammates collapsed on him. Major League Soccer had its first official goal. The league really existed.

"I was trying to bait him," Wynalda said later about his move on Agoos. "I was trying to meg him and I knew that as tired as I was, that was the only way to beat him was to go through him. Once the ball went through his legs, there was just a half second where everything clicks in and goes into slow motion. You rely on your training, your ability to calm your nerves and just focus on what you're trying to do. The opportunity to play in the first MLS game was a big deal to me."

The goal was also important in a much larger context. The media was skeptical of the new league—almost antagonistic. It wasn't that anyone wanted it to fail, but there was this sense of another soccer league? We'll see how long this one lasts.

The knock on soccer in the United States forever has been that the games can be boring. That nothing happens. That nobody scores. The worst-case scenario from a public relations perspective would be a 0–0 tie in the inaugural game.

"You could argue that Eric Wynalda has scored prettier goals," Schoen said years later. "But considering the responsibility that he took, considering the creativity that he showed, and considering the significance of that goal, I'd be hard-pressed to say that he's scored a better one."

Sunil Gulati, the former President of US Soccer and former Deputy Commissioner of the MLS, put it this way:

"Thank God for Eric Wynalda."

9

WE GOT NEXT

LEAGUES HAD TRIED. LEAGUES HAD FAILED.
The Women's Pro Basketball League (WBL) lasted from 1978–1981. The American Basketball League and the Women's American Basketball Association lasted less than seven years combined. There had been so many leagues and associations that they practically ran out of words to put in front of "league" and "association." So when the National Basketball Association's Board of Governors "approved in concept" the idea of creating a women's basketball league on April 24, 1996, they settled on a simple solution for the league's name by just tossing "W" in front of the "NBA."

Like the famous scene in *The Social Network* where Sean Parker tells Mark Zuckerberg to drop the "the" from The Facebook "because it's cleaner," so too is the WNBA. It capitalizes on the brand and backing of the NBA while also giving it its own identity—one that then-NBA Commissioner David Stern felt was long past due.

"We are giving life to a concept that has been much discussed, much attempted, but that we feel is now ready to bloom," he said.

Sheryl Swoopes, Lisa Leslie, and Rebecca Lobo were invited to attend the inaugural press conference, and as the first three players signed to the league, they became known as the Original Three. Swoopes, an NCAA champion with the Texas Tech Lady Raiders in 1993, was the first player to sign. She'd eventually become a three-time WNBA MVP and a member of the Pro Basketball Hall of Fame. Lisa Leslie was a former college player of the year at the University of Southern California; she'd go on to win three WNBA MVP awards and two championships during her eleven-year career before joining the Basketball Hall of Fame. Rebecca Lobo was the college national player of the year in 1995 after leading an undefeated 35–0 UConn to a national championship. She's also a Pro Basketball Hall of Famer, has her number retired at Connecticut, and is a lead basketball commentator on ESPN to this day. All three women have multiple Olympic and international-play gold medals.

Now you know why these were the right women to start the league. Why was 1996 the right time?

The stars were aligned for a variety of business and basketball reasons, but Lobo believes there were two main catalysts that set the stage for the league's arrival. The first was Sheryl Swoopes's iconic 47-point game in the national championship against Ohio State in 1993, during which Swoopes broke nearly every offensive record that existed in women's college basketball: most points, most points in a half, most field goals made, highest free throw percentage, free throws attempted, most points scored in two Final Four games (78), and several more. It's a cliché to say that a person or a team rewrote the record book, but in this case, over the course of a few days, Swoopes actually took the record book, highlighted the whole thing, deleted it, and started typing all new numbers. Equally as important, her performance crossed over into the broader sports discussion and had many fans talking about women's college basketball for the first time.

The second inciting incident was Lobo's undefeated 1995 UConn basketball team that went wire-to-wire to win the national title.

"When Sheryl had that monster game it was the first time in a while there was a woman basketball player that general sports fans were aware of," Lobo says. "Not only her game, but her name—and people started paying attention to college basketball. That was in '93. Then in 1994, Charlotte Smith of North Carolina hit a three to win the national championship, and that kind of breathed life into our 1995 UConn team."

In terms of landmark women's basketball teams, Lobo's Connecticut squad was a pioneer, gaining attention from national media outlets and building a genuine general following among national basketball fans.

"During that season we were on *SportsCenter*, the *New York Times* was covering us, and it brought all kinds of attention to the women's basketball scene," Lobo says.

Following the '95–'96 college season, the US Women's National Team had their tryouts to prepare for the upcoming Olympic Games in Atlanta in 1996. It was during this time, when players were being selected, that talk of a women's league affiliated with the NBA began heating up. With NBA Entertainment as the marketing arm of USA basketball (both men's and women's), the timing never seemed better and the logic was sound: announce the league in '96, then use the Olympics at home in the US to promote the league and their stars heading into the inaugural season in '97.

"With the Olympics in the United States, there was certainly a lot happening in women's sports with us and soccer," Lobo says. "We felt we were a part of something big. We were on the cover of *TV Guide* and then we started doing the 'We Got Next' campaign and in my mind that was getting people ready for the WNBA."

The league launched with eight teams and promoted their stars, running the same playbook that the NBA used: sponsorships, sneaker deals, community engagement, appeal to families, and more. Swoopes and Leslie signed with Nike. Lobo signed with Reebok and Spaulding. There were joint appearances at the NBA All-Star Game, and as the teams got established there was a real camaraderie in the early days of women wanting to support other women.

"Women would come up to us and tell us how they loved basketball but they were from an older generation and there was no opportunity to play," Lobo says. "A lot of people came because they really wanted it to succeed. You could sense it."

Smash cut to twenty-five years later and the league has gone from women showing up to support women to its own fully formed fan base that includes some of the biggest names in the NBA, including LeBron James and the late Kobe Bryant. Bryant's late daughter, Gianna, was a budding basketball star and Kobe was often spotted with her at both NBA and WNBA games wearing an orange hoodie with the WNBA logo on it. The images of Kobe and Gianna on the sidelines went viral even before his passing, launching the popularity of the orange hoodie into the stratosphere. Following their tragic deaths, the hoodie became a symbol of solidarity with Gianna and Kobe and their love for women's basketball. In early October 2020, the WNBA announced that the orange hoodie was "the most popular item this season across official online retail partner Fanatics' network of e-commerce sites, including WNBAStore.com."

As we look back on how basketball history has unfolded, we can appreciate a tiny bit of sports poetry as the crown jewel of the NBA's 1996 draft class, Kobe Bryant, ended up giving the WNBA, founded the same year, a boost to take the league to new heights and to continue the momentum it had built in the public's eye toward the end of the last decade.

"I feel like there is a real groundswell now," Lobo says. "I felt that way in 2019. I felt that way through the 2020 season. It's not an afterthought. It's definitely a fun brand of basketball and we're having an explosion of popularity."

STONE COLD

EVER HEAR OF THE WWE SUPERSTAR OTTO VON Ruthless?

How about Chilli McFreeze?

Or Fang McFrost?

Or Ice Dagger?

No? None of these ring a bell?

You don't remember Ice Dagger headlining three WrestleManias or Fang McFrost being a six-time WWE Champion or Otto Von Ruthless becoming a two-time Intercontinental Champion or four-time Tag Team Champion?

There's a good reason for that.

Thankfully, the wrestler we all came to know and love as "Stone Cold" Steve Austin rejected that list of moronic monikers the moment they were presented to him at the start of his WWF career in early 1996. He believed, rightfully so, that if he entered the ring as Ice Dagger he'd be laughed out of town. When a listener asked him about those original names on his podcast years later, Austin didn't hold back.

"Man, when I was thinking about merchandise," he said with a hint of disgust in his voice. "Otto Von Ruthless. Fang McFrost. Ice Dagger. Ugh. Those are all so God danged bogus . . . Fang McFrost is just so corny, and that's the one I was about to pick. There was almost nothing behind Ice Dagger either."

According to The Miz, a WWE Champion, 8x Intercontinental Champion, Tag Team Champion, and current star of *Miz & Mrs.*, the names floated to Austin were B-list or C-list names.

"Those names were the kinds of names that sound like mid-card characters," The Miz says. "Those don't sound like Main Event type players. There are people who are characters and are entertaining and that's fine. But he was looking for a name that said, 'I'm a headline guy.'"

This wasn't the first time, or the second time, or even the third time that Austin had gone through a wrestling name change. His government name at the start of his wrestling career was Steve Williams, but that was the same as the wrestler "Dr. Death" Steve Williams, so a booker in Memphis, Tennessee, changed his last name to Austin to avoid confusion. From there, he wrestled under "Stunning" Steve Austin with the USWA and WCW, then "Superstar" Steve Austin with the ECW, and following that, he was billed as The Ringmaster for his debut match on the January 15, 1996, episode of *Monday Night Raw*.

It should be noted here, especially for you younger readers, that prior to '96, Austin was not wrestling as a bald badass with a goatee. He had stringy, flowing, platinum blond locks that fed into his earlier "Stunning" nickname. He was also skinnier with more of a big surfer dude, poser vibe than the power lifting, punishing menace he'd eventually become.

Upon Austin's arrival in the WWE, CEO Vince McMahon felt that it was necessary for him to change his look so WWE fans would forget about the Mr. Perfect-esque "Stunning" Steve and invest in the new character. Austin wasn't sure exactly what he could do to look different at the time, but he ended up getting a dose of inspiration from the one opponent he'd been losing to consistently throughout his early career: male pattern baldness.

"When I was in Atlanta wrestling for WCW, I was 25–26 years old and I started to lose my hair," Austin said. "I had that long blond hair but it was kind of thin and I was starting to get those widows peaks starting to creep up and I had that little crown in the middle—I knew my days with long hair were numbered."

Like everyone else who watched television in the mid-'90s, Austin was subjected to an ungodly amount of Hair Club for Men ads. You know the ones, with previously bald guys jumping into the pool and then shaking out their "new" hair, before Sy Sperling comes on the screen with a picture of his own previously bald head and then spouts his catchphrase: "I'm not just the President of Hair Club for Men, but I'm also a client."

Well, even the future Stone Cold wasn't strong enough to resist some good old-fashioned persuasive marketing, and he decided to walk in for an appointment.

It didn't go well.

"I went down there nervous as hell and to find out what I could do about hair replacement," he said. "I go into the examining room, a very attractive blonde lady picked up these wooden sticks, the kind they use as tongue depressors, and she starts looking at my hair, my scalp, and kind of brushing through it. She starts saying 'all right, well you know we can take this hair from the back and put it over here and we can use something from over here and put it on this side.' While she is telling me this I'm listening to everything she's saying and I'm thinking, 'Oh, hell no. I ain't getting no hair plugs. I ain't getting no bullshit on my head.'"

Cut back to Austin's conversation with McMahon about switching up his appearance, and he was running out of options. Then, he found inspiration from Quentin Tarantino.

"After watching the *Pulp Fiction* movie with Bruce Willis, that's the haircut that inspired me to get the buzz cut," he said. "Couple of months later I was traveling on the road with Dustin Rhodes [Goldust] and before I went to the show, I said fuck it. I went into the bathroom with a razor blade and shaved all my hair off . . . and it turns out that was one of the keys to my appearance. Then I grew the goatee and everything came full circle."

By the spring, Austin was beginning to have some success with the WWF, including a win in his first WrestleMania appearance, but he soured on the Ringmaster persona. He wasn't feeling it and it was falling flat with audiences, despite his considerable ring talents. After watching a television show called *The Iceman*, about hit man and serial killer Richard Kuklinski, Austin settled on the idea of wanting a cold-blooded character to work with. It was after he shared this idea with the WWE that they floated their list of "icy" names headlined by Fang McFrost.

He hated them all.

"One of the best things I've heard is that your character is just you turned up to 100," The Miz explains. "Those are the best characters. You take a piece of yourself and elevate it. Those names sound like they weren't going to do it for him."

Then, over a cup of tea, his ex-wife Jeanie Clarke serendipitously let forth the name that would define an entire generation of sports entertainment.

"The [WWE] was sending all these temperature-based names . . . they were all so hokey," she said. "None of them worked for Steve. One day he was just kind of pensive, a little bit worried-looking, and I just said, 'Drink your tea before it gets stone cold' and I went, 'There it is, Stone Cold.' He got a big smile on his face, and he liked it, so that's how it started, over that cup of tea."

The second most important part of the Stone Cold legacy boils down to one word and two numbers that would eventually be emblazoned on millions of t-shirts, posters, flags, hats, and more from 1996 on:

Austin 3:16

○   ○   ○

Steve Austin's giant black boot rained down blows on forty-one-year-old Jake "The Snake" Roberts's ribs like a jackhammer.

Boom.

Boom.

Boom.

Roberts twisted and sprawled and writhed in pain on the mat as the hits continued. To make each stomp count, Austin lifted Jake's left arm to get a cleaner shot at his rib cage. First he'd stomp Jake with this boot, then he'd clasp his hands together and clobber him with his balled up fists.

Stomp. Slam. Stomp. Slam.

Roberts had just taken a year off from the WWE and had only recently returned as a born-again Christian version of his old persona, complete with an Albino Burmese Python named "Revelations" to go along with his new bible and preaching. As Stone Cold mauled him, he looked old and hurt in large part because he *was* old and he *was* really hurt. He'd sustained a real-life injury in a match earlier in the night, so he and Austin had to improvise a way for the match to end quickly, and it centered around Austin going to town on Roberts's broken ribs.

The idea of pulling out of the final match was a non-starter. This was the WWE's iconic King of the Ring, single-elimination tournament and unless you were dead, you were fighting. And so the mostly one-sided battle went on for another 180 seconds of Austin pounding away at Roberts's ribs and shouting "get up!" as the former superstar moaned in pain (both pretend and likely real).

There's Stone Cold off the second rope into Roberts's ribs.

There goes Stone Cold off the top rope into Roberts's ribs.

Then there's Stone Cold winding up Muhammad Ali style and then landing a straight right to Roberts's ribs.

The announcer called it a "physical dissection of Jake Roberts," and he wasn't wrong. If this were a tee-ball game, parents on both sides would have asked for the mercy rule. But Austin was just getting started. After thundering away on Roberts's ribs, Stone Cold rips open Roberts's costume and starts tearing off the first-aid tape that was protecting his midsection. He'd tear some tape and crack Roberts. Then tear more tape and crack him again.

Stomp. Slam. Stomp. Slam.

Gorilla Monsoon, the WWF's president at the time, even interrupted the match to examine the damage Jake "The Snake" was sustaining, but when all the rib cracking and bone smashing was done, Stone Cold Steve Austin earned the coveted title of King of the Ring.

When the match ends, Austin heads over to take his rightful seat on the throne and claim his brilliant purple robe and gold crown.

Red, sweaty, and pissed off, Stone Cold, the new king, opens the post-fight interview with this:

"The first thing I want done is to get that piece of crap out of my ring!"

He's referring to Jake "The Snake," who needed assistance (again, probably both real and fake) to exit the wrestling mat and get back to the locker room.

"Don't just get him out of the ring, get him out of the WWF," Stone Cold hollers. "Because I've proved, son, you ain't got what it takes anymore!"

And then.

It happens.

"You sit there and you thump your bible and say your prayers and it didn't get you anywhere," Stone Cold yells. "Talk about your psalms.

Talk about your 'John 3:16' . . . Austin 3:16 says I JUST WHIPPED YOUR ASS!"

The crowd.

Goes.

Ballistic.

"When Stone Cold went to the WWE, he wanted to be the man," The Miz says. "It took him time to figure it out. But once you heard him say, 'Austin 3:16 says I just whipped your ass!' you could tell he found himself. He was the beer drinking, ass kicking, top caliber guy of his time."

And so, on that day, June 23, 1996, the unofficial start to the WWE's "Attitude Era" began. Within a few short years, Austin would take the WWE to heights it had never been before.

"He surpassed all of Hulk Hogan's records," Vince McMahon said. "In terms of merchandising and licensing, and pay-per-view and live events. Without question the most popular performer we've ever had."

And that's the bottom line, because Fang McFrost said so!

HOW JORDAN'S BULLS LOST TEN GAMES

REMEMBER THAT TIME YOU WERE PLANNING FOR two years to write a book on the 25th anniversary of the 1996 sports year, and a big chapter in the book was going to be on the historic '96 Chicago Bulls team that went 72–10 in the regular season and 15–3 in the post-season., but then, when you started writing it, a worldwide pandemic hit and ESPN fast-tracked a documentary called *The Last Dance* on Michael Jordan and the Chicago Bulls with never-before-seen footage from the '96—'98 seasons and it became the most popular, most talked about, most-viewed documentary of all time, and it covered almost the exact same stuff about the '96 Bulls team that you were going to cover in your chapter, including the big wins, the milestones, the winning streaks, and the personalities—so, you decided to take a completely unique approach to the Bulls' season and write something totally different and hope people enjoyed that, too?

Happens to everyone, right? Good, thanks for understanding. Before we continue, let's stipulate a few things:

If you're reading this, you most likely watched every episode of *The Last Dance* and you probably watched a few of them more than once.

You were most likely alive and experienced some or all of the Michael Jordan-era Bulls and have a more-than-passing familiarity with the '96 team and what they accomplished.

If you're on the younger side, between *The Last Dance* and YouTube and LeBron James winning his fourth title with the Lakers in the bubble in 2020 and igniting an endlessly pointless GOAT debate about LBJ vs. Jordan, then you still likely know a great deal about this famous Bulls team.

With that out of the way, we can concede that you're aware of the Bulls' amazing record that year, their 14-game win streak, their 18-game win streak, their five separate 6+-game win streaks, and then their near-perfect run through the playoffs. Because if you already know that Jordan was the league MVP, All-Star Game MVP, and the Finals MVP; and that Phil Jackson won Coach of the Year; and Toni Kukoc won Sixth Man of the Year; and that Scottie Pippen and Jordan were both First-Team All-NBA selections; and that Pippen, Jordan, and Dennis Rodman were each on the All-Defensive First-Team; then we're all on the same page about their greatness and we can properly dissect one aspect of that team nobody has focused on: the losses.

That's right.

Rather than write yet another piece that could be titled How the Hell Did the Bulls Win 72 Games!?!?, I thought we'd flip it: How the Hell Did the Bulls Lose 10 Games?!?!

Who were the teams? What were the circumstances? How did the Bulls feel? How did the opponents feel? As an added twist, we draw a shocking conclusion about what their real record should have been that year. Sound good?

Let's go.

LOSS #1:
NOVEMBER 14, 1995, AT THE ORLANDO MAGIC

The lasting image of the 1995 Eastern Conference Semi-Finals playoff series between the Orlando Magic and the Chicago Bulls was of the Magic hoisting ex-Bull Horace Grant on their shoulders in celebration after they clinched in Game 6. Jordan had returned from baseball a few months prior with one goal in mind: to win a title. The loss to Shaq and Penny was one thing, but the sight of Grant being hailed as a hero for helping to slay the Bulls made Jordan's insides rage; every synapse in his brain was like a splitting atom of fury.

"I think it was without question the biggest motivation coming that following season," Orlando Magic Coach Brian Hill said later. "Michael Jordan played the whole ['96] season with an unbelievable will to win. There were eight to 10 games where he basically willed his teammates into winning games. He was a man possessed."

Orlando Magic guard Nick Anderson, who was friends with Jordan, said that the loss ending his first comeback season drove him crazy. "He did not forget," he said.

You have to keep all of this in mind as we revisit the first match-up between the Bulls and Magic following that loss, which took place in mid-November of 1995. Heading into the game, the Bulls were 5–0 and the Magic were 5–1. It was as close to a proverbial "playoff atmosphere" as a pre-Thanksgiving game was ever going to get.

But there were two caveats.

The Bulls were playing without Dennis Rodman and the Magic were playing without Shaquille O'Neal. At first glance, this would heavily favor the Bulls, who had a fired-up Jordan and Pippen to take on Penny Hardaway without his fellow All-NBA teammate. Rage. Energy. Revenge. These were the three things on the mind of the Bulls from the opening tip, and they jumped to a 29–19 first quarter lead.

Then Hardaway, who was tasked with guarding Jordan all night, found his rhythm and stroked every club in his bag. Fast breaks. Whirling lay-ups. Turnaround jumpers. Inside moves. Three-pointers. It was a staggering show of efficiency: 12–18 from the floor, 4–7 from three, 8–9 free throw attempts, 36 points. All while keeping Jordan off-balance and holding him to 8–20 shooting for only 23 points.

Jordan could serve anything he wanted for his post-game dinner that night, but revenge was not on the menu, as the Magic won 94–88.

"Hardaway is playing with a lot of poise and confidence," Jordan said after the game. "It's a great feeling to have. I think this was a good test for us. Now we see what we're dealing with. I think we have a better sense of it now. We have to make some adjustments from here."

For Penny's part, he played it humbly, knowing the two teams would likely meet in the playoffs again.

"The best thing that happened to us was that Michael Jordan was off tonight," he said. "You can't really stop him when he's on. I just tried to take it right to him. That's all you can do."

Jordan would get his revenge six months later by sweeping the Magic in the playoffs.

LOSS #2:
NOVEMBER 26, 1995, AT THE SEATTLE SUPERSONICS

You know by now—because you lived it and then re-lived it while watching *The Last Dance*—that this was a preview of the '96 NBA Finals, but did you know that this 5-point loss to the Sonics came courtesy of an abysmal foul shooting performance by Scottie Pippen who shot 2–11 from the line?

"I felt good shooting them, but none of them went in," Pippen, a 70 percent career free-throw shooter, said. "I guess I'll have to practice them."

This isn't to take anything away from the Sonics. Not at all. They were awesome. Shawn Kemp continued his streak of being the best player on the floor during Seattle–Chicago matchups (the Bulls were never able to contain Kemp—even in the Finals). He had 25 points and 14 rebounds. And Gary Payton was brilliant, scoring 26 points, dishing 11 assists, and helping to hold Jordan to just 6 of 19 shooting and 22 points.

Even with Jordan getting bottled up, the Bulls led at halftime 64–51 and still had a 13-point lead in the fourth quarter thanks to Luc Longley's best game as a Bull, where he scored 21 points and grabbed 8 rebounds starting for the injured Rodman. Had the Bulls won, we may even be referring to this as "The Longley Game."

"The second half, we got alive, it seemed, energy-wise," George Karl said. "Then we just stayed alive."

Phil Jackson had the opposite assessment of his team, saying, "In the second half I thought our level of play didn't carry over from the first half. We got out of poise and out of character."

Also, Pippen was terrible at the foul line. The game was 77–74 late, and if he'd sunk even half of his free throws down the stretch, the final outcome may have been different. Then again, the Bulls couldn't match the Sonics' late intensity.

"For us to play like that in the first half and come back with some fire in the second half showed a lot about this team," Kemp said.

In the end, it was an exciting prelude to the collision in the Finals both teams thought was a real possibility. But really, Pippen blew it. The Bulls should have won. Let's mark this down for later.

LOSS #3:
DECEMBER 26, 1996, AT THE INDIANA PACERS

"Sure, I'm looking forward to seeing number 31, as long as he's looking forward to seeing number 23," Jordan said about Reggie Miller when interviewed before the Bulls' day-after-Christmas match-up against the Pacers. "We all have certain challenges and I think maybe I am a challenge for him to improve or compete against. I played against him a lot this summer and he's a competitor. And he's a talented player. A lot of the time his overall talent goes unnoticed and his scoring is magnified. But I think he's shown that he's one of the elite guards in the game. There's a competition that's always in the air when we play each other and I'm looking forward to that."

It was as magnanimous a statement as Michael Jordan ever made about a contemporary in the moment; so much so that you almost have to think he was buttering up Miller before their match-up. By this point in the season, the Bulls were 23–2 and the media were beginning to openly talk about whether this Bulls team had a shot at breaking the 1971–1972 Los Angeles Lakers' regular season record of 69 wins.

"It's too early to do that," Jordan said. "We're having success and learning at the same time. This is a good streak. I think it's building confidence among ourselves. You can see it." And the box score against the Pacers showed that confidence.

Jordan had 30. Pippen had 26. Rodman got his 11 rebounds. On a typical night, that's a Bulls double-digit win with MJ's only worry figuring out who's going to deal the $10,000-a-hand card games on the flight home. Instead, he left the arena with images of the Flying Dutchman, Rik Smits, on his mind. As usual, his foe Reggie Miller was solid, with 20 points, including 4–6 from three, but the story of the game was Smits, who shot 10–16 with 26 points in a game the Pacers led the entire way, from a 12-point lead in the first quarter, to a 59–40 lead at the half, and a final score of 103–97.

"It's a relief to have the streak over," Pippen said. "Even though we wanted to win this game. Now we can start another."

And that's exactly what they did. The Bulls wouldn't lose again until February 4, 1996.

LOSS #4:
FEBRUARY 4, 1996, AT THE DENVER NUGGETS

This is the first indefensible loss on our list.

The Bulls entered the game riding an 18-game winning streak.

The Nuggets had won 18 games *all year* and were eight games below .500, with an 18–26 record headed toward a 35–47 record on the season. Head Coach/GM Bernie Bickerstaff would be fired 13 games into the next year. The class of the Western Conference this was not, but the Nuggets had some talent, starting with their young center out of Georgetown, Dikembe Mutombo, and their point guard from LSU, Mahmoud Abdul-Rauf. They also had Dale Ellis and their number two overall draft pick out of Alabama in '95, Antonio McDyess. If the Bulls were a 45-day, dry-aged long-bone ribeye, the Nuggets were a sirloin on sale at Target.

Since the game was in Denver, you might be quick to blame the altitude for the Bulls' ineptitude, but you'd be wrong. This was just one of those nights where every skee-ball the Nuggets rolled off the side rail landed right into the 100 canister. McDyess was 7–10 from the floor. Dale Ellis was 7–13. LaPhonso Ellis was 6–8. Abdul-Rauf was 13–27 and sank four threes. The Nuggets raced out to a 34–20 lead to end the first quarter and then increased that to a 68–43 lead at halftime.

If you're trying to remember that time the '96 Bulls lost by 30 points during their legendary run, don't worry, it didn't happen. Jordan came out in the third quarter acting as if he were Harrison Ford and Bernie Bickerstaff had just tried to hijack *Air Force One*. He scored 22 points in the quarter on the way to a 39-point Bulls effort (but never yelled, "Get off my plane!"), cutting the Nuggets' 25-point lead all the way down to 84–82.

"That's one of those situations where I felt I had the opportunity and I tried to use my offensive capabilities to get the team sparking,"

Jordan said of his scoring barrage. "But they controlled everything down the stretch, which is an unusual situation for us."

Unusual and unlikely. The Nuggets stayed in the game on the back of an incredibly high percentage of their shots falling and a sudden ability to remain calm and execute in crunch time. "We never gave up and held our composure at the end," Abdul-Rauf, who had 32 points, said. "That's the best we can play."

It was just enough.

Jordan's onslaught netted him 39 points on the night, but the Nuggets still won 105–99.

"I expected us to lose sometime," The Worm said. "But I feel bad because we played bad. That team is not that good. I'm not going to give them any credit at all."

LOSS #5:
FEBRUARY 6, 1996, AT THE PHOENIX SUNS

If you're following the dates in this chapter closely, what you're seeing feels like a typo—but, in fact, the Bulls lost back-to-back games in early February to the Nuggets and Suns. It was their first official losing streak of the season, and to really add lemon juice to the paper cut, both the Nuggets and Suns were under .500.

Wait, weren't the Suns good? you just thought.

They were good for three of Charles Barkley's four years with the team, peaking with the '93 Finals appearance against the Bulls (which they'd lose). They followed that up with seasons of 56 and 59 wins in '94 and '95. But something was off in '96.

This Suns team was not the same one that the Bulls had faced in the Finals. They still had Barkley and Kevin Johnson, but Dan Majerle, Danny Ainge, and Tom Chambers were gone, replaced with Michael Finley, Wesley Person, and an aging A.C. Green. They were older, slower, not as dynamic, and didn't have nearly as much chemistry. Hence, their 20–24 record as they faced the 41–4 Bulls.

In many ways, Jordan and company should have seen it coming. Chicago was coming off of a tough loss in Denver after mounting a furious effort in the second half that took a lot out of them. Phoenix was at home, waiting for them, looking for a big win that might help them turn around their season. It was a trap. Tired Bulls versus a fired-up Barkley who was out to prove that neither he, nor his Suns, were dead yet.

"It looks like Barkley has been looking forward to this game since we beat them in Chicago," Steve Kerr said.

Chicago came out hot, mounting a 13-point lead in the first, before the Suns applied more and more pressure each quarter to wear down the Bulls, who only played seven guys. Jordan scored a hard 28 and Kukoc pitched in 18, but the Bulls never led after the half. And Kerr was dead on—Barkley had been looking forward to this game. He tallied 35 points and 16 boards while KJ added 20 points.

"The Bulls are the best team in the NBA, but they can be beat if you play well," Barkley said. "They're not going to cakewalk through the NBA like everybody thinks."

"It was a tough loss after falling to Denver the other night," Pippen said. "We didn't really come back with any energy or any type of enthusiasm."

Still, there would be no three-game losing streak.

LOSS #6:
FEBRUARY 23, 1996, AT THE MIAMI HEAT

Quick, name three people on the 1996 Miami Heat team. I'll spot you Alonzo Mourning and Tim Hardaway.

Anyone?

Still thinking?

Did you name Keith Askins? Or Bimbo Coles? Or Billy Owens? Or maybe you got Rex Chapman, so good for you. If not, don't feel bad. This team was Pat Riley's first in Miami and he blew through twenty-two players trying to find the right mix of guys to pair with Zo and Hardaway for his eventual run of strong teams that he'd field in the late '90s and early 2000s. In 1996 though, his team was 24–29 the night the Bulls came to town (now on a brand new seven-game win streak), and by all accounts they should have been victim #8.

Not if Rex Chapman had anything to say about it.

Yes, that Rex Chapman.

For you younger readers, before Chapman became known for his steady stream of feel-good Twitter shares, memes, GIFs, and puppy videos where he writes, "dogs, bruh," the man was a deadly shooter who scored over 1,000 points while at Kentucky and then scored almost 10,000 points in the NBA for the Hornets, Bullets, Heat, and Suns.

Let it also be known that on the night of February 23, he essentially beat the '96 Bulls all by himself, hitting an absolutely miraculous 9 of 10 three-pointers and scoring a total of 39 points. For once, there was nothing Chicago could do.

"Rex reminded me of Jerry West tonight," Pat Riley said. "He got us going, started making threes and we started to build our confidence."

Even Michael Jordan could only tip his cap to Chapman. "Rex hit some big shots for them," he said. "He played extremely well for them. They rallied around him."

"That was one of the best shooting performances I've ever seen," Mourning said. "He put on a clinic tonight. When Rex gets on like that, he's astonishing."

So, what's it like to beat Jordan, Pippen, Rodman, and arguably the greatest basketball team in the history of the sport almost by yourself?

"You're not even thinking," Chapman said. "You're just playing and it's like a good dream."

LOSS #7:
MARCH 10, 1996, AT THE NEW YORK KNICKS

In Jeff Van Gundy's first game as the Knicks head coach after Don
Nelson was fired, his squad lost to the Philadelphia 76ers—who were
then, in the words of iconic *Daily News* Columnist Mike Lupica, "one
explosive step from Jerry Stackhouse away from the Continental Basketball Association." In Van Gundy's second game, his Knicks, who had
lost seven of their last nine games, summoned the spirits of Earl "the
Pearl" Monroe and Walt "Clyde" Frazier to possess Madison Square
Garden with greatness, just for one night, as they demolished the Bulls
by a truly shocking 32 points, 104–72.

"All of a sudden, it was the old days for a little while," Charles
Oakley said, referring to the years under Pat Riley when the Knicks
were regular contenders.

The game was actually close for the first half and when the Knicks
began to pull away, the Bulls went on a 17–1 run in the third quarter to
close the gap. To everyone watching (and anyone who had paid attention to the Knicks for the past few months), the fourth quarter might
as well have already been played and the headlines already written: *Bulls
Win Yada Yada Yada.**

However . . .

Derek Harper got hot and scored 16 points in the last eight minutes of the third quarter, and by the time Charlie Ward drained two
three-pointers at the start of the fourth, the Knicks had outscored the
Bulls 37–8 to put the game out of reach with under ten minutes to go.

"I'm proud of my guys," Van Gundy said, in only the second game
he could call the Knicks *his guys*. "Most teams collapse after the Bulls
make a run like that."

---

*   Yes, in 1996 you can yada yada a Bulls win.

For one night in '96, the Knicks didn't collapse and Patrick Ewing was so giddy he got out over his skis a bit and told Van Gundy, "we're back" on the bench. Of course, they weren't back, but they did finish 13–1 under Van Gundy and sweep the Cleveland Cavaliers in the first round of the playoffs before losing in five to the Bulls in the second round.

LOSS #8:
MARCH 24, 1996, AT THE TORONTO RAPTORS

To properly put this Bulls loss into context, let me formally introduce you to the 1996 Toronto Raptors. This was a team headed for a 21–61 finish that was 17–49 when the Bulls showed up. They hadn't notched their tenth win of the season until almost February. The squad featured two bona fide NBA-level starters (rookie Damon Stoudamire and Tracy Murray) and seven other guys who at the time all would have gotten fewer minutes than Jud Buechler if they played on the Bulls (no disrespect to Jud).* The Bulls had already beaten the Raptors three times by a total of 21 points. The Raptors had about as much business beating the Bulls in 1996 as *Kazaam* did of taking home an Oscar.

And yet, Stoudamire scored a career-high 30 points with 6 three-pointers (breaking the then-record for three-pointers in a season by a rookie with 126), Tracy Murray added 23, and a bunch of guys you barely remembered playing in the NBA scored as well. Carlos Rogers had 15 points. Zan Tabak had 12. Alvin Robertson had 2.

Counter that with Michael Jordan scoring 36, including the Bulls' last 14 points, Toni Kukoc scoring 23, and Steve Kerr scoring 17 points, and you'd have thought the Bulls would have been able to pull this one out. Nope. The score was tied 108–108 when Oliver Miller, a career 63

---

* Meanwhile, future four-time All-Defensive Team player Doug Christie was on the bench for this team and was wildly misused and underutilized.

percent free-throw shooter, was fouled and sank one of two to give the Raptors a lead that would hold until the end, 109–108.

"Unbelievable," Murray said after the game. "This game meant more to me than the NCAA championship last year. I'm speechless. It was a huge win."

"We had enough offense," Jordan said, disappointed after the game. "Defensively, we let them get too many offensive rebounds and we fell asleep on defense. That was the whole difference in the game."

It should be mentioned here that Dennis Rodman was serving a 10-game suspension for head butting a referee and didn't play, and the Bulls other inside presence, Luc Longley, didn't even make the trip to Toronto due to tendinitis in both knees; you'd assume either one of them would have been worth at least 2 points to the Bulls, and they'd have won the game. Let's hold that thought for later.

LOSS #9:
APRIL 8, 1996, AT HOME
AGAINST THE CHARLOTTE HORNETS

Here are six facts about this early April match-up between the 66–8 Chicago Bulls and the 38–37 Charlotte Hornets:

Fact 1: Michael Jordan scored 40 points, had 11 rebounds and 5 assists.

Fact 2: The Hornets' roster was so thin that forty-three-year-old Robert Parish played the second most minutes in the game (32).

Fact 3: One week earlier, the Bulls had beaten the Hornets by 34 points in Charlotte.

Fact 4: The Bulls were up 50–40 at halftime.

Fact 5: Larry Johnson, the Hornets star, hurt his hand and barely played in the second half.

Fact 6: The Bulls were 37–0 at home up to this point.

Knowing these facts, a reasonable person would assume that the Bulls would win the game easily . . . even as it turns out, the Bulls themselves.

"I think we really lost our focus tonight," Pippen said. "I think we realized that this was possibly an easy win for us. In the second half, we just came out . . . and we are so used to winning at home, we lost our concentration. We underestimated this team. We felt the game was over in the first half and it wasn't."

Still, with eight seconds left and down by one, the Bulls had the ball and an excellent chance to win the game. After a Phil Jackson timeout, Toni Kukoc drove the lane hard to either create contact or make the game-winning basket, but neither happened. Instead the ball rolled off the rim and both Jordan and Pippen missed tap-ins for the win as time expired.

"Toni went to the hole aggressively and tried to get the foul," Jordan said. "We all went to the boards to clean it up. I think I had a shot, Pip got a tap, Dennis got a tap. It just didn't go in."

What are the odds that Kukoc, Jordan, Pippen, and Rodman would all have a shot to win a basketball game inside the paint and none of them would convert or get fouled? 100–1? 1,000–1? Regardless, the 20 points the Hornets got from Kenny Anderson and the 19 points they got off the bench from Dell Curry was enough.

Hornets win: 98–97.

"I told the guys that I was not disappointed with the loss on our floor," Phil Jackson said. "It let the team know going into the playoffs that we are not impervious on our home court. It's good to have reality set in."

LOSS #10:
APRIL 20, 1996, AT HOME
AGAINST THE INDIANA PACERS

This was the final Bulls home game of 1996 and a genuine record was on the line. If Chicago won, they would finish the season tied for the best home record of all time (40–1). Lose, and they'd have to settle for second best, something Michael Jordan enjoyed about as much as being told a golf course gave away his tee time.

The Pacers had already beaten the Bulls earlier in the year (a plus) but they'd be playing without Reggie Miller, who had a busted eye socket (a minus). Nevertheless, Indiana was a proud team and had no interest in being the Bulls' last home victim of the season and having to answer questions like, "What was it like being on the floor when the Bulls tied the all-time record for home wins?"

Competitors like Dale Davis, Derrick McKey, and Antonio Davis would rather get their post-game rubdown with thumbtacks than be a part of NBA history that way. To spoil the celebration, Larry Brown emptied out his bench, played all ten of his guys double-digit minutes, and did his best to wear down the Bulls, believing that the toll of chasing the record plus nonstop fresh legs would force Chicago to buckle.

Phil Jackson also played his bench heavily, logging twenty-two minutes for Kerr, twenty-one for Randy Brown, and nineteen for Jud Buechler; but his goal was to give his big three rest. Neither Jordan, Pippen, nor Rodman played more than thirty-one minutes, far below their season average. Jordan still had 24 points and Rodman still grabbed his typical 15 rebounds, but unfortunately for Chicago, the added minutes for the role players didn't lead to added production as Kerr and Brown shot a combined 4–18 from the floor.

"I wanted it really bad," Jordan said, referring to the record. "I wanted to be 40–1. I wanted to tie the record. That would have been another notch in our belt. And you just want to continue to win at home. You don't want to give any teams motivation coming into the playoffs that they can win on your home court."

Alas, MJ and the Bulls would have to settle for a 39–2 home record and a 72–10 record overall, becoming the first team in NBA history to break 70 wins and obviously the first to win 72.

But one question remains:

Should their record have actually been better?

WHAT THE 1996 CHICAGO BULLS' RECORD SHOULD HAVE BEEN

Let's agree that luck goes both ways—the Bulls won some games they shouldn't have and lost some games they shouldn't have over the course of an 82-game season.

Keeping that in mind, there are four Bulls losses that "should have" gone the other way:

1. Their inexplicable loss to Denver (a complete and total brain fart).
2. The game against the Sonics when Pippen missed nine free throws (even making half of them likely wins the game, but the Sonics were awesome, so who knows).
3. The 1-point loss to the 18-win Toronto Raptors.
4. The home loss to the Hornets with Grandmama sitting the second half.

If we split the difference on these, and just pick two that truly should have gone the other way, the Bulls' record really could have been and should have been . . .

. . . drumroll, please . . .

74–8.

They'd be one game better than the 2015–2016 Golden State War-riors that went 73–9.

Too bad, Bulls.

Like Robert De Niro would tell Sylvester Stallone in 1997's *Copland*, "You blew ittt!"

INTO THE
SHAQ-VERSE

1996 EASTERN CONFERENCE FINALS, GAME 4:
Chicago Bulls vs. Orlando Magic

With 8:29 left in the fourth quarter, Penny Hardaway has the ball out on the wing on his home court. He's got half a shot clock and a full suite of options. The nearest defender, Toni Kukoc, is still eight feet away (and a hundred horsepower short of keeping up with him), so the 6'7" Hardaway can dribble, drive, pull up, and shoot . . . whatever he wants.

In the tenth of a second that Hardaway surveys the floor, he spots a rare and beautiful sight: Shaquille O'Neal one-on-one on the block. All night, the Bulls treated Shaq like a one-man game of Red Rover, sending another man over the instant he got the ball. Luc Longley, the Bulls' center who was tasked with guarding Shaq, had been giving up his body all night long, dumping fouls on the big man with little to no effect. To this point, Shaq was 10–12 from the floor, shooting an efficient 88 percent.

Hardaway recognized the opportunity and fired it in to O'Neal, who threw his billboard-sized back into Longley. As the towering Australian absorbed the blow, O'Neal took a dribble, ducked his right shoulder, swung his left foot over Longley's, and then spun toward the baseline.

Longley is in trouble.

Kukoc bails on Hardaway to set up a double team and arrives just in time to sandwich O'Neal, who barely flinches at the second defender. With Longley on his back and Kukoc leaping at his side, O'Neal gives a two-handed pump fake, then another, then a one-handed ball fake back to Hardaway that Kukoc bites on, before spinning around Longley one more time and going up for an easy lay-in.

Swish.

It was a display of unstoppable, unbelievable, unmatched low-post dominance at its finest and Orlando fans rightly believed it would carry the team and the city to a basketball dynasty before the close of the decade.

If only.

The baby floater, which went through the net with approximately 8:19 left in the fourth quarter to pull Orlando within three (80–83), was Shaquille O'Neal's last basket as a member of the Magic.

He would never again score wearing the silver and black and blue.

That night the Bulls completed a 4–0 sweep of the Magic behind Michael Jordan's 45 points. Less than two weeks later, the Bulls famously defeated the Seattle SuperSonics in the Finals in six games, touching off Jordan's second three-peat.

But what of the Magic?

At the end of the '96 season, they were a team that embodied the famous Zig Ziglar quote, "designed for accomplishment, engineered for success, and endowed with the seeds of greatness." They'd already made it to the NBA Finals in 1995 and the Eastern Conference Finals in 1996. They had two All-NBA players under twenty-five years old: Penny Hardaway (24) and Shaquille O'Neal (23). They had two strong complementary starters in Dennis Scott and Nick Anderson, both under thirty, both perfectly suited to play off the ball and off of O'Neal, and the team had veteran leadership and toughness from the recently signed Horace Grant, who himself was only thirty years old.

The future should have been bright.

It should have been full of trophies.

It should have ended with banners hanging from the rafters right next to Shaq and Penny's retired jerseys.

If only.

Pre-internet, pre-Adrian Wojnarowski, and pre-24/7/365 NBA coverage, if you had asked the average fan in 1996 about O'Neal's future most people would have reasonably thought that he would re-sign with the Magic as a free agent following the season. It was a star-studded free agency year, with Jordan, Gary Payton, Reggie Miller, and Dennis Rodman all hitting the market along with Shaq, but the conventional wisdom was that all five guys would stay put (four out of five did).

What was the conventional wisdom regarding Shaq in '96?

It was simple, really. Orlando had the two most important assets you needed to retain a young star: talent and money. Between potential hall of famer Penny Hardaway as a longtime teammate, the lack of a luxury-tax penalty, and no rules in place for a maximum salary offer, the Magic were in position to give Shaq the best chance at winning a championship and pay him more than any other team in the NBA. There was nothing stopping them from looking at the contracts of the league's highest-paid players (7 years, $105 million—Alonzo Mourning and Juwan Howard) and simply saying, "We'll give you $1 million more." Considering 'Zo and Juwan were at best brown belts to Shaq's black belt in NBA prowess, this would have been the smart, sensible thing to do. It would have assuaged Shaq's ego, given him the title of "highest paid player in the league," and extended the Penny/Shaq title window by three or four years.

If only.

Instead, what happened was tantamount to sports franchise malpractice. In the words of Joel Corry, who was a consultant for Shaq's agent, Leonard Armato, in 1996, the Magic's handling of Shaq was "the most botched negotiation on the part of an NBA team that I can recall in my 16-year career in the athlete representation business. There is no way Orlando should've lost O'Neal."

Corry wrote a scathing first-hand account for CBS in 2016, listing all the ways the Magic blew it. In part:

> There are some aspects of Shaq's free agency that I remember like they happened yesterday, and that initial offer is one of them—$54 million over four years with none of the yearly salaries specified . . . . They lowballed him. Almost offensively so.
>
> It's a low offer, but not the first time two sides have been far apart in initial negotiations. The more baffling part of the call, and I'll never forget this, was that the Magic, I guess in an attempt to create some kind of leverage, actually criticized O'Neal's rebounding and defense. Are you kidding me?
>
> That was the tone Orlando set for this negotiation. The Magic didn't seem to appreciate that Shaq was a franchise-altering talent, even though he had already completely altered theirs.

The entire process was baffling to everyone on Shaq's team, including Shaq.

"When the Magic offered a paltry $54 million, he [Shaq] didn't just view it as an opening salvo in contract negotiations," wrote Jeff Pearlman in his excellent book on the 1996–2004 Lakers dynasty, *Three-Ring Circus*. "No, to O'Neal and Armato and Tracey and the entire Shaq crew, it was an effort to put a superstar in his place. Even worse, the team backed its hesitancy at offering O'Neal enormous dollars by explaining how, in another year, Hardaway would be a free agent, and the Magic *needed* him to stay in the fold. According to O'Neal, Gabriel literally told him, 'We can't give you more than Penny. We don't want to upset Penny.'"

"When he said that," Shaq told Pearlman in the book, "I was out. Inside I was fuming. I said to myself, I'm not messing with these guys. They're worried about Penny's feelings being hurt?"

Ironically, when it came to paying Shaq, Penny was actually on his teammate's side. During a radio interview on *Tiki & Tierney* in 2019, the subject of Shaq's negotiation came up and Hardaway said, "I thought, 'Give this man whatever he wants.' But I don't really think Shaq wanted the contract. I think he wanted to leave anyway. I think he really saw LA as an opportunity for movies, music, and to be with Kobe."

Penny was right; Orlando should have given Shaq whatever he wanted, and Shaq also wanted to leave. His agent, Armato, had been talking up a move to Los Angeles from the day Shaq was drafted, and the draw of the entertainment industry that Penny mentioned was true. Shaq had recently released his second movie, *Kazaam*. He'd already put out two music albums, *Shaq Diesel* and *Shaq Fu: Da Return*, and when it came down to which city could better support his Superman-sized ambitions, Orlando offered the roller coaster ride while Los Angeles offered the reality.

At one point, Orlando upped their financial package considerably when they realized there was a distinct possibility that Shaq was bolting, but once Jerry West finished his three-dimensional chess moves with the Lakers roster to free up money, he was able to offer Shaq more: $120 million over seven years. That, plus the allure of LA, plus the opportunity to be the next legendary Lakers center—grabbing a torch that had been passed from George Mikan to Wilt Chamberlain to Kareem Abdul-Jabbar—put the purple and gold over the top.

It was an offer Shaq couldn't refuse and on July 18, 1996, the Los Angeles Lakers won what *LA Times* writer Mark Heisler dubbed "the highest stakes bidding war in American sports history." Shaquille O'Neal officially became a Laker—and unofficially destroyed the Magic's title chances for a decade.

"We had a special situation our first couple years," Hardaway said in his interview. "He left to go to the Lakers, but if we would have stayed together and stayed on that trajectory we were headed to, it would have been big time. You have to win championships. I felt like we would have. I think he and I would have been able to be in the top-five duos."

If only.

"When Shaq left, I knew the magnitude of that instantly," Hardaway continued. "I knew it was over. We were done."

Many years later, when Shaquille O'Neal was being inducted into the Orlando Hall of Fame, he expressed remorse about having left the Magic.

"Knowing what I know now," he said during the induction ceremony, "I would've stayed and fulfilled my seven years and looked at it differently after my seventh year. This is where I started. This is where I should've stayed. I just wish I would've had more patience . . . Even when I got there [to LA], I still got bashed and it still took four years to win. But I was very impatient. I was very young, and I thought that if I go there with those guys out there, that I could win right away. And that wasn't the case."

True, but it wasn't like the move to Southern California didn't work out for Shaq.

He won three titles.

He cemented his legacy as one of the greatest centers to ever play the game.

He did it with one of the NBA's signature franchises in one of America's signature cities, raising his hoops status and his Hollywood star power to heights he may never have reached if he stayed in central Florida. All in all, it worked out pretty well for the diesel, but his talk of wishing he'd stayed in Orlando brings with it some interesting ramifications that greatly affect the legacies (some good, some bad) of fellow NBA stars and even fellow NBA icons.

We know what happened when he left the Magic.

The real question is: What would have happened to everyone else had he stayed?

◦   ◦   ◦

THE SIX LEGACIES MOST AFFECTED BY SHAQUILLE O'NEAL SIGNING WITH THE LAKERS

Penny Hardaway

In order to fully understand how big of a star Penny Hardaway had become in the mid-'90s, we need to talk about Lil' Penny, his two-foot tall, trash-talking, supermodel-dating, catchphrase-dropping alter ego voiced by Chris Rock. For two years, Nike ran a series of commercials featuring Lil' Penny and Penny as a modern-day *Odd Couple*, with Penny as the laid back, unassuming star and Lil' Penny as the loud, irresponsible, cash-in-on-Big-Penny's fame sidekick.

If you were over eight years old in the '90s you can close your eyes and picture the entire first commercial: Penny is in Orlando's locker room getting ready for a game against the Timberwolves and Lil' Penny is sitting in his locker, singing loudly and obnoxiously while listening to a Lil' Walkman. The voice Chris Rock summons for the character is part high Pookie from *New Jack City* and part opening segment from *Bigger and Blacker*. It's brash and energetic and has a touch of little-brotherness that is perfect.

Mid-song, Lil' Penny stops singing and starts peppering Big Penny with questions and strategy. "What are those shoes called?" "Who are you playing?" "I want you to work them inside and outside." As

Lil' Penny jabbers on, the most subtle and underappreciated move in this commercial takes place, when Big Penny leans over to take off Lil' Penny's headphones so they can talk. It is the perfect big brother gesture. We can see from Big Penny's eye rolls and body language that he just wants to tie his shoes and get to the court, but he knows Lil' Penny is just gonna keep talking and keep shouting if his headphones are on, so he indulges him while also making himself more miserable. It's such a great touch. As Big Penny gets up to leave, Lil' Penny drops the to-this-day quotable lines from the commercial:

Lil' Penny: Penny! Penny! Penny! I want you to say hello to my man Kevin Garnett.
    Big Penny (confused): Kevin Garnett?
    Lil' Penny: Yeah, yeah, yeah, Garnett, we went to high school together. Tell 'im Lil' Penny from the science club says hello. Can you DO that for a brother?

Fade out.
Genius.
The Lil' Penny commercials ran for two years and went from featuring just the real-life Penny Hardaway and Lil' Penny to a "co-starring" role by Tyra Banks to the climax of the Lil' Penny series—a Super Bowl spot that included Michael Jordan, Ken Griffey Jr., David Robinson, Tiger Woods, Barry Sanders, Stevie Wonder, Michael Johnson, and even Jonathan Lipnicki, the kid from *Jerry Maguire*.

When it came time for NBC to put together their opening-night package for the 1996 Eastern Conference Finals, did they ask a big-name actor to record the hype video narration and introduction to the series? Did they ask Samuel L. Jackson, Tom Cruise, Denzel Washington, or Spike Lee?

No, they didn't.

They asked Nike to put together a two-minute Lil' Penny spot, and that is what ran right before tip-off of Game 1. That's how big of a star Penny was. In terms of sheer popularity, he was a Top Ten guy. Maybe Top 5. Jordan, Barkley, and Shaq were bigger. Grant Hill was probably tied, and in that next tier were Shawn Kemp, Gary Payton, David Robinson, and let's say Pippen and Reggie Miller. No matter how you slice it, Penny was right there. He was an eventual three-time All-NBA player and a four-time All-Star, so the stardom was earned; but some percentage of it was certainly because of his pairing with Shaq, and another was due to the Magic's visibility and deep runs in the playoffs.

Once Shaq took off for LA, Penny was correct in saying the team "was done." After winning 60 games during the '95–'96 season, the Magic's record dropped faster than the elevator in *Speed* after Dennis Hopper blew the brakes. They won 45 games in '97, 41 games in '98, and then Penny was gone after '99. Over the course of his final Magic years, he battled through injuries, including a crushing ACL injury that he never fully recovered from in '97. Following the 1999 season, he was moved to Phoenix in a sign-and-trade, but injuries kept him in and out of the lineup. After four-and-a-half years with the Suns, he spent three seasons with the Knicks and about three seconds with the Miami Heat before retiring.

Would Penny have sustained the same injuries if Shaq had stayed in Orlando? Who knows? Maybe he would have played fewer minutes . . . or less stressful minutes . . . or maybe they'd have recruited different trainers or more talent or any number of things that may have kept Penny healthy. We can only speculate on that part; but what we know for sure is that *with* Shaq, Penny was always on prime time (before the NBA League Pass), was always in the playoffs, and would likely have cashed in at least one title as the team improved and the Bulls aged. He'd also have been part of a legendary, title-winning tandem with Shaq—and with titles comes Hall of Fame consideration and all kinds of goodies. *Without* Shaq, none of that happened. The Magic were .500 and done by May his last two years.

No Finals appearances.

No 'chips.

If there's one person whose basketball legacy took the biggest direct hit from Shaq's move to the Lakers, it's Penny.

Kobe Bryant

If nobody had more to lose by Shaq's departure than Penny, then nobody had more to gain by his arrival than Kobe. In an alternate universe where Shaq re-signs with Orlando, Kobe's career championship total is likely cut in half, with the new over/under number at 2.5 career titles. This isn't a knock on Kobe at all, it's just that two very significant factors are now in play if Shaq stays with the Magic.

One, there's almost no way that Kobe wins a title in just his fourth season, at the age of 21, without Shaq. The Lakers roster at that time was built around Shaq (including Kobe), and it's doubtful that even if Jerry West whiffed on Shaq, that he could have assembled a team around Kobe strong enough to compete. Shaq was a singular force in the NBA from 1996–2004. There was no other available big man the Lakers could have signed and paired with Kobe that would have guaranteed a championship result so early in his career.

Two, Shaq's presence is what lured Phil Jackson out of retirement to take over for the ineffective Del Harris. He said so in his own book, *Eleven Rings*, when he wrote, " . . . I remember sitting in my hotel room during my cross-country trek and watching the . . . Western Conference semifinals. It had been painful to watch. The Spurs' big men, Tim Duncan and David Robinson, were forcing Shaq to take off balance fadeaway jump shots instead of his power move to the middle and then beating Shaq downcourt to break through the Lakers' defense. Watching those games, I'd found myself visualizing ways to counter the Spurs' strategy and transform the Lakers into the team they were destined to be."

And that's why Kobe's career championship totals are cut in half. No Shaq likely equals no Phil, which likely equals a longer road to a championship. Even Jordan didn't win a title until year seven. Of course, maybe Kobe would have eventually followed Jordan's path to a string of five or six titles later in his career, but without Phil Jackson joining the Lakers the first time around, there's a good chance he doesn't join the Lakers the second time around, which lowers the odds again.

From everything we know of Kobe's work ethic, drive, and otherworldly determination, he clearly would have found a way to win one, two, three, or even more titles, but they may not have been with the Lakers—and they would most likely have come in the back half of his career. But with so much of his basketball legacy riding on a) the five championships and b) never having to leave Los Angeles to chase a title, it's reasonable to assume that Kobe's legacy would take a big hit if Shaq stayed in Orlando.

Phil Jackson

If Phil Jackson never filled out a W-4 form for the Los Angeles Lakers, his legacy would have been secure: six championships with the Chicago Bulls, two three-peats, a 72-win season. He was fine. Hall of Famer. One of the all-time greatest coaches. Done and done.

However, if he'd stopped at six, then Jackson likely would have been stuck in tier two of the all-time great coaches list, rather than residing in tier one. Tier one is reserved for the best of the best, the guys with trophies named after them: John Wooden, Vince Lombardi, Red Auerbach, Bill Belichick (no namesake trophies, but still). Specifically, the conversation between who was better, Jackson or Auerbach, wouldn't be taking place because Red's nine championships, including eight in a row, trump Jackson's six.

If Shaq stays in Orlando, there's a very good possibility that Jackson never goes to the Lakers. After all, the Shaq–Kobe combo is tailor-made for his triangle offense and without Shaq, the attraction wouldn't be there. Jackson had received interest from both the New Jersey Nets and the New York Knicks during his mini-retirement, but nothing moved him to act, likely because neither team had a one-two combo like Shaq and Kobe.

Now here's an interesting theory . . . If Shaq had stayed in Orlando, you know who would have been a one-two combo like Shaq and Kobe? Shaq and Penny. And do you know which coach the Magic players pushed out at the end of the '97–'98 season? Brian Hill. So, let's imagine a scenario where Jackson leaves the Bulls after the *Last Dance* season and the Magic have a struggling Chuck Daly (who replaced Hill) as head coach. Suddenly, Jackson is available. The Magic, who have just two years left on the deal Shaq signed, decide to go all-in to appease the big fella and call Jackson, who agrees to coach the Magic (in this bizarro world) for the same reason he agreed to coach the Lakers in our real world: the Shaq–Penny combo.

If that happens, maybe Jackson cashes in another two or three titles with Orlando and gets his name up there with Auerbach anyway.

But one thing's for sure. Without Shaq on the Lakers, there's likely no Phil Jackson in LA either.

Michael Jordan

You're thinking: *Whaaaat? Why the hell is Jordan on this list? He has the most secure legacy ever. He's the G.O.A.T.!!!*

Yes, I believe he is, too. But let's just say that Shaq chooses to re-sign with the Magic . . . and let's also say that he and Penny are livid after they get swept in the Eastern Conference Finals in '96, so they decide to spend the off-season together training like Rocky and Apollo—and they come back with a vengeance in '97. At this point, the Bulls were still the top dog, so Orlando may or may not beat them in the hypothetical Eastern Conference Finals in '97. But the series at least goes seven, right?

For the sake of this discussion, let's use the Bulls' early struggles against the Pistons as a guide, which means that after losing back-to-back heartbreaking series to the Bulls in '96 and '97, they finally break through in '98 against an aging, clearly out-of-gas Bulls team. That Orlando team then likely goes on to win their first Finals.

The ripple effects of that single win are enormous—for one, Jordan now only has five NBA Finals to his name. The back-to-back three-peats are gone. The six-for-six is gone. The legacy of going out a champion is gone (ignoring the Wizard years) and the final shot on Bryon Russell never happens.

Is Jordan still the G.O.A.T.? I think so . . . But without those moments and that last three-peat, he's a little less G.O.A.T.-ey . . . Which opens the door for . . .

LeBron James

Imagine a world where LeBron James wasn't chasing Jordan's six titles and six Finals MVPs, but his five titles and five Finals MVPs. Imagine a world where Jordan only went to half of the NBA Finals that LeBron did and where LeBron either finishes with four championships (one less than Jordan in this scenario) or the same five championships? Now in that world, a hand of five championships, five Finals MVPs, with ten Finals appearances from LeBron likely beats a five, five, and five set of cards that Jordan would be carrying, right?

Right?

In this alternate universe, the tired Jordan vs. LeBron G.O.A.T. debate barely happens because in this alternate universe, LeBron would be the clear G.O.A.T.

Relax, LeBron stans . . . We don't live in an alternate universe.

Chris Webber

There might be no NBA star whose career could have used a championship to lift his legacy from "good" to "great" more than Chris Webber. From his timeout flub with Michigan in the NCAA tournament to his glory years with the Sacramento Kings, Webber was usually good, occasionally great, but always coming up short. In the three years that the Lakers won their championships with Shaq and Kobe, Webber's Kings won 55, 61, and 59 games, and were deep enough and talented enough to win a championship, though they never did.

The Kings' most heartbreaking moment came in the 2002 Western Conference Finals, when they lost to the Lakers in overtime of Game 7. It was a gut-wrenching, franchise-crushing loss that came to define the team never being able to get over the hump—AKA the Lakers—to get to an NBA Finals.

But think about this . . .

If Shaq had re-signed with the Magic in '96, maybe that Kings team in 2002 represents the West in the NBA Finals. And since the Lakers swept the New Jersey Nets that year, it's reasonable to assume that a Kings team that took the Lakers to overtime in Game 7 would have at least beat the Nets in five or six games, if not also swept them. In that case, Webber would have been the best player on a championship team, and his entire NBA legacy would be thought of in a whole new light.

The irony here is that on draft day in 1993, the Magic actually drafted Webber as the number-one overall pick before trading him to Golden State for Penny Hardaway.

Too many what-if scenarios in that one to consider.

KINGPIN

AND THE NOMINEE FOR BEST MAINSTREAM movie where bowling is prominently featured is . . .

Kingpin.

Relax, all you *Big Lebowski* lunatics. We're talking about 1996 here. And when *Kingpin* was released on July 26 of that year, it was by far the funniest and best (and only) bowling movie ever made. It held this title for two solid years until March 6, 1998, when *The Big Lebowski* debuted in theaters and Jeff Bridges's "Dude" and John Goodman's Walter supplanted Bill Murray's Ernie McCracken and Woody Harrelson's Roy Munson as cinema's bowling duo du jour.

The casual shoving aside of "Big Ern" for The Dude and the dismissal of *Kingpin* is a cinematic travesty. To the untrained eye, *Lebowski* features better acting, a cleverer script, heavier undertones, and is an overall more serious piece of work.

To the trained eye (like ours), the movies are strikingly similar on nearly every level. They were both directed by brothers (Joel and Ethan Coen for *Lebowski* and Peter and Bobby Farrelly for *Kingpin*); they were both headlined with Oscar nominees (Bridges and Julianne Moore for *Lebowski* and Murray and Harrelson for *Kingpin*); they were both follow-ups to wildly successful films from the directors (*Fargo* from the Coens and *Dumb and Dumber* from the Farrellys); and they both completely bombed at the box office, before gaining a second life and a cult following once their DVDs came out, back when people bought DVDs.

See that? They're basically the same movie. The only major difference is that two of the most prominent film critics of all time, Roger Ebert and Gene Siskel, both liked *Kingpin* while Siskel said this about *Lebowski*: "I just think the humor is uninspired. Jeff Bridges plays a too self-consciously created character named Jeff Lebowski, a laid-back '80s dude in surfer shorts . . . . Isn't kidnapping for ransom a tired plot these days? *Kingpin* was a much funnier film set in the world of bowling. Jeff Bridges's character wasn't worth my time. There's no heart to him like, say, the Frances McDormand character in *Fargo*. *The Big Lebowski*, a big disappointment."

Siskel loved *Kingpin* so much that he even put it on his Top Ten Movie list for 1996. It was probably this exchange that hammered things home:

> Claudia: It must be hard to spank your monkey.
> Ishmael: You have a monkey?

Or maybe it was this one:

> Roy: Thomas can raise a barn, but can he pick up a 7–10 split?
> Ishmael: God blessed my brother to be a good carpenter. It's okay.
> Roy: Yeah, well he blessed you, too, and I'll give you a hint what it is. It's round, has three holes, and you put your fingers into it.
> Ishmael: You leave Rebecca out of this.

Whether it was Murray's performance as Ernie McCracken, a man who "clearly has done for bowling what Muhammad Ali did for boxing," or Harrelson's believability while acting with a hook for a hand, if *Kingpin* was good enough for Gene Siskel's Top 10 Movie list of 1996, it's good enough for ours.

And there's also this cool tidbit:

Kingpin was such a box-office disaster that the Farrelly Brothers figured the next film they were making was going to be their last in Hollywood—so they tried to make it as memorably raunchy and over-the-top as possible, putting in every bit and gag they could think of to win over audiences.

That movie was *There's Something About Mary.*

14

KOBE'S DRAFT CLASS

BEFORE ADDING KENNY SMITH AND CHARLES Barkley to *Inside the NBA*, before the Emmy nominations and Shaquille O'Neal, and even before he switched to wearing a bowtie, Ernie Johnson hosted the 1996 NBA Draft live on TNT. The event took place in East Rutherford, New Jersey, at the then-Continental Airlines Arena, formerly known as the Brendan Byrne Arena and subsequently known as the Izod Center (and as of this writing, without a basketball team, it is simply the Meadowlands Arena).

Johnson's main co-hosts for the night were the omni-present and ageless (because he's looked 60 for 60 years) Hubie Brown, and Kentucky Head Coach Rick Pitino, who won a national championship in that very building not four months earlier. TNT also ran a second booth at the arena with Craig Sager in a sadly boring tan and taupe suit and Peter Vecsey, NBC's NBA insider on loan for the night to TNT.

David Stern stepped on the stage smiling, read his prepared statement (as he got booed), and then kicked off the draft with, "Let's get started. The first pick in the 1996 NBA Draft will be made by the Philadelphia 76ers, who have five minutes to make their selection."

The first round that night went as follows:

1) 76ers, 2) Raptors, 3) Grizzlies, 4) Bucks, 5) Timberwolves, 6) Celtics, 7) Clippers, 8) Nets, 9) Mavericks, 10) Pacers, 11) Warriors, 12) Cavaliers, 13) Hornets, 14) Kings, 15) Suns, 16) Hornets, 17) Blazers, 18) Knicks, 19) Knicks, 20) Cavs, 21) Knicks, 22) Grizzlies, 23) Nuggets, 24) Lakers, 25) Jazz, 26) Pistons, 27) Magic, 28) Hawks, 29) Bulls.

To properly relive this draft, we have to do a bit of *Men in Black*-level mind erasing and forget everything we now know. We also have to remember that many of the teams at the top of the draft were in rebuilding mode and already had young players at certain positions from earlier drafts, which is why they may have passed on someone we now know to have become a superstar. Also, NBA front offices often do dumb things. The point of this little series of caveats is to warn us against the knee-jerk reaction of, "How the hell was Kobe not taken first overall?" or "Wait . . . someone named Todd Fuller was taken four spots ahead of Steve Nash?"

Just like CD towers, physical answering machines, and Blockbuster Video, certain things can only be explained properly within the right context—and NBA Drafts are one of them. The weeks leading up to this draft weren't consumed with talk of whether the 76ers should take the local high school kid from Lower Marion, Kobe Bryant, as the number-one overall draft pick, even though Bryant said years later that he was "really upset that the Sixers didn't take me number one in '96."

Bryant thought it was a possibility. The Sixers thought it was too risky. Only one year earlier, Kevin Garnett became the first prep-to-pro player to go straight to the NBA in twenty years. At the time, he looked promising, but nobody knew how good he'd be. With so few test cases, there just wasn't an appetite at that point to use the #1 overall pick on a kid who could still be grounded by his parents.

That's not to say that the Sixers weren't intrigued by Bryant.

In Jonathan Abrams's book, *Boys Among Men*, he reveals that Sixers scout Tony DiLeo had a vision of the team's future that included both Iverson and Bryant, and he even went so far as to discuss trading Jerry Stackhouse for a second lottery pick to make it happen; but that's all it led to, discussions.

The only question concerning the Sixers heading into the draft was whether they would trade the pick down to Vancouver (if Vancouver could put together a package of picks and the right player fell). The rumor persisted right up until draft night, when Sixers owner Pat Croce finally confirmed that his front office wasn't stupid.* The other hot-take topic for sports talk radio was whether the Sixers should go with Georgetown star Iverson or Georgia Tech star Stephon Marbury, with the number-one overall pick.

Iverson averaged 25 points, 3.4 steals, and 4.7 assists on 17 shots per game.

Marbury averaged 18.9 points, 1.9 steals, and 4.5 assists on 14 shots per game.

They were both point guards. They were both scoring prodigies. They were both capable of putting butts in the seats.

Just prior to David Stern walking to the podium to announce the selection, TNT had Peter Vecsey chime in to end any speculation: "I talked to Brad Greenberg, the 76ers' General Manager . . . he loves Iverson for a number of reasons. He thinks he's the quickest guy in the draft, the fastest, the most competitive, the most mentally tough, the most persistent, and he feels he's very capable of running the team and making everybody happy. Other than that, Brad Greenberg isn't sure of the pick."

Vecsey's got jokes.

---

* That's not exactly what he said, but trading out of the #1 spot is largely an ill-advised move for an NBA team unless you're a contender, which Philly was not.

And the Sixers got Iverson.

After hugging and kissing his family at the roundtable backstage, the future Answer threw on a white Sixers hat, brim cocked slightly to the left, with the tag still attached and dangling down the right side of his head. His baggy, beige suit looked like it belonged to an uncle or relative who was twice his size. The shoulders and sleeves hung huge on his slight frame, and despite the fact that he could have passed for a little brother attending his big brother's wedding, the confidence and coolness in his walk were unmistakable. He had the ever-so-slight hitch in his step, the LL Cool J licking of the lips, and to top it off, the gold bracelet and ring on his right hand, catching the glare of the lights perfectly for his famous handshake with the commissioner.

The TNT graphic read:

Strengths: Excellent Speed, Great Court Vision

Weaknesses: Sometimes erratic play; shoots first, passes second

As if foreshadowing a decade-and-a-half of highlights, Craig Segar's first question to Iverson was, "Hubie Brown says there's nobody in the league quicker than you. Is there anybody that can stop you one-on-one?"

"I don't know, I hope not," Iverson says, with a grin. "I don't think so."

The short answer is "no."

o   o   o

The Toronto Raptors entered the NBA in 1994 as an expansion team with Detroit Pistons Hall of Fame point guard Isiah Thomas as a part-owner and Executive Vice President calling the shots. Thomas's credentials as an all-time point guard are unassailable (two-time NBA

Champion, Finals MVP, twelve-time All-Star, five-time All-NBA), but his record as an executive is totally assailable. If he were applying for a regular job, his LinkedIn resume has a few landmines: he bankrupted the Continental Basketball Association, was fired by Larry Bird as coach of the Indiana Pacers, and took a flame thrower to the Knicks roster and salary cap before getting replaced there as well.

Prior to all of that, he had a nice little run of draft selections for Toronto that actually panned out, starting with his pick of point guard Damon Stoudamire, AKA Mighty Mouse, out of Arizona in 1995. Stoudamire averaged 19 points, 9 assists, and 4 rebounds a game and won Rookie of the Year in his first season. His success meant the Raptors weren't in need of a point guard, which took Marbury and Nash off the table; that left guys like Marcus Camby, Shareef Abdur-Rahim, and Ray Allen.

The smart money was on Camby, considering he was so confident that he'd be a "top two" pick that he only worked out for the top two teams, Philadelphia and Toronto. During his Toronto workout, he played Stoudamire one-on-one (but he wasn't allowed to back the 5'10" point guard down) and Mighty Mouse beat him 5–4. The loss, however, was a win. Camby realized he'd love to play with Stoudamire and the Raptors discovered that they could have a near-seven footer who was athletic enough to hang with one of the smallest, speediest guards in the NBA. They were so enamored that a couple weeks before the draft, Thomas stated in a televised interview that Marcus Camby was the guy he wanted—and that's who they got.[*]

As the slender Camby made his way to David Stern and held a #21 jersey that was about the same length as the commissioner, Pitino gave his assessment of Camby, fresh off playing him in the Final Four.

---

[*] Thomas's draft picks with Toronto were Stoudamire, Camby, and Tracy McGrady. Not bad, but I'm not sure Knicks fans feel it makes up for Renaldo Balkman and Mardy Collins as first-round picks.

"This young man has what all NBA teams look for," Pitino said. "He's a great shot blocker. He's extremely quick. He has a great low post game and if you try to double down on him, he finds all the open men. [He] has fabulous potential and with Stoudamire, the Raptors have a great future."

The only weakness TNT identified for Camby was that he needed to "add more weight."

"I had a gut feeling it was going to be Toronto," Camby said after the draft. "Isiah gave his word, so I was thinking about what he said. I slept fine last night. I feel fine right now. I was projected to go number two and that's where I went. It is just a big dream come true. I'm just happy it is a reality right now."

He was also happy that he didn't fall to the next team in line, the Vancouver Grizzlies. During the pre-draft meetings Camby voiced his concern that he wouldn't be thrilled about playing in Vancouver with his family so far away in New England. Truthfully, very few players were thrilled about the prospect of playing in Vancouver.

Even though the city is only 120 miles north of Seattle, for most NBA players from the East Coast, Vancouver's home court might as well have been in Russia's Vostok research station on Antarctica. From New York City, the flight itself was two hours longer than flying to London and the fact remained that no kid playing in the Big East, ACC, SEC, or Big Twelve dreams of playing ball in British Columbia.

And then there was the actual team, which easily (and cleanly) could have swapped out its "Grizzlies" name for the "Bad News Bears." They only won 15 games during the 1995–1996 season and trotted out a cast of NBA players as anonymous as a Twitter profile with an egg avatar.

If I asked you to name any of the top six players for the Grizzlies for the '95 season, and you were spotted Bryant "Big Country" Reeves and a few random guys like Chris King, Blue Edwards, and Kenny Gattison, could you name anyone else?*

When you add up the location, the losing, and a cast of anonymous teammates, it was hardly an ideal scenario for a rookie to wind up in Vancouver. Stu Jackson, the team's General Manager for its first five seasons, had to take all this into consideration when drafting players (no reason to waste a lottery pick on a guy who'd never be happy playing for your team in your city). Case in point, according to Jackie MacMullan of *Sports Illustrated*, Stephon Marbury made it abundantly clear that he had no intention of ever playing in Vancouver.

So, you take out Marbury, Camby, Iverson, and other East Coast guys like Ray Allen, John Wallace, and Kerry Kittles and you've got . . . Shareef Abdur-Rahim, or potentially, Steve Nash from Santa Clara University, who grew up 70 miles south of Vancouver across the Strait of Georgia.

Nash would have loved to go #3 overall.

The Grizz weren't having it.

There was simply no version of the draft where Jackson was taking the "little white dude from a little off-brand school"—as *Slam Magazine* writer Ryan Jones labeled Nash—with a top-three pick. A pick that high was typically reserved for a player you were in love with, not a player you'd keep on the bench in *NBA Jam*. That honor fell to Abdur-Rahim out of Cal, the first freshman to ever win the Pac-10 Player of the Year Award. He averaged 20.5 points, 8.2 rebounds, 1.8 assists, and 3.9 blocks per game in his lone college season and was, in the words of his high school coach Doug Lipscombe, "a super nice kid, unselfish, a good leader and a very hard worker. He's mature, family-oriented and very religious. If athletes are to be role models, he'll be a great one."

---

* Don't lie and say you knew Greg Anthony and Benoit Benjamin were on that team. C'mon, we're all friends here.

One thing Abdur-Rahim wasn't great at, at least for a while, was deciding whether or not he wanted to enter the NBA as a twenty-year-old. He declared for the draft, then rescinded the declaration, then declared again, which led to some draft experts leaving him off their mock drafts entirely. It also led to Ernie Johnson dropping a dad joke in his analysis, saying, "the complexion of the draft kind of changed a bit with Shareef Abdur-Rahim. First he said he was going to come out, then he said he was going back to school . . . now I'm coming back out. We could make his name Shareef Abdur-I'm Not So Sure Rahim . . . "

Badump-tisss!

Abdur-Rahim said that he vacillated because he wanted to make sure he was doing the right thing. He'd been wanting to go the NBA for so long, he didn't want his enthusiasm to cloud his judgment and lead him to leave too early.

"This is something that's been going on longer than anybody knows," he said about wanting to play in the Association. "It's something I've been striving for my whole life. The NBA's been a dream ever since I started watching it."

Once he officially declared, the Grizzlies knew he had the tools and the talent to be their guy in the third spot. Also, he didn't hate Vancouver, which helped them make him the earliest freshman ever taken in the draft.

"When you compare Abdur-Rahim to Camby and Marbury, he probably starts out a little slower because physically, he's a little bit weaker," Jackson said. "But his upside . . . he may have the most upside of anyone in the draft."

o   o   o

The weight of the Marbury name hung on Stephon's shoulders like a vest made of concrete. All three Marbury men ahead of Stephon had NBA aspirations. All three came up short. His oldest brother Eric earned a full ride to the University of Georgia and played with Dominique Wilkins in the early '80s. Although he was drafted in the 6th round by the San Diego Clippers, he got cut before the season started. The next Marbury man up was Donald, who took the junior college route to an eventual scholarship to Texas A&M, where he led the Southwest Conference in scoring but didn't sniff the NBA. Marbury man #3, Norman, AKA Jou Jou, was the chosen one who was all-city at Lincoln High and who earned a scholarship to Tennessee. The scholarship was eventually pulled over his SAT scores, and after attending three different junior colleges he played for a few teams overseas before ending his professional career.

That left Stephon Marbury, AKA Starbury.

He scored 30 points per game in high school.

He followed fellow New York City legend and NBA All-Star Kenny Anderson to Georgia Tech.

He won ACC Rookie of the Year, earned First-Team All-ACC, and was an AP Third-Team All American.

Surrounded by his brothers, his two sisters, and his parents, he was selected as the fourth overall pick in the 1996 NBA Draft by the Milwaukee Bucks, and as Ernie Johnson described, "pandemonium raged backstage." Stephon's selection was the culmination of a near two-decade quest by the Marbury men to reach basketball's promised land; and when it was finally realized, the emotion was uncontrollable. Hugs. Tears. Kisses. Even a full family group hug/huddle was in the cards.

The roughly 4,000 Milwaukee fans in attendance at the Continental Airlines Arena ate it up. While Marbury and his bed-sheet-sized suit shook David Stern's hand, the Bucks faithful hollered in approval and cheered all through his interview with Craig Segar.

"I can't even explain the way I feel right now," Marbury said, fighting back his emotions during his interview immediately after his selection. "It's been twenty years. Twenty long years I've waited for this day. And it's here. It's here now. It feels so good. I can put a smile on my mother's face."

The feeling was so real and so raw and so genuine you couldn't help but root for the kid. And Bucks fans were enamored with the prospect of pairing a dynamic passer and scorer like Marbury with the weapons the team had in place, namely Vin Baker and Glenn Robinson.

"I can't wait to see Marbury bring the ball up the court with Vinnie [Baker] and Glenn [Robinson] on the wings," Bucks reserve forward Marty Conlon said right after the pick. "He can create and make things happen for them. Anybody who is a fan of the Bucks has to be excited."

Bucks General Manager Mike Dunleavy was not excited.

Before Marbury could dry the tears from his eyes, Dunleavy traded him down one spot to the Minnesota Timberwolves for Ray Allen and a draft pick. The Bucks fans on site were not pleased. Wrote Gery Woelfel, who covered the draft for *The Journal Times* out of Wisconsin, "The [Bucks] fans went bonkers. They screamed their lungs out. They jumped up and down, clearly showing their disapproval. Others yelled 'no trade!' or 'keep Marbury!'"

But it was too late.

The deal was done.

And Marbury was elated. If you had to rank Marbury's goals before the draft, his first was to be a top-five pick, and his second was to somehow end up in Minnesota to play with his good friend, and fellow 1995 McDonald's All-American, Kevin Garnett.

"When I found out I was going to Minnesota, a chill went down my back, because I really want to be there," Marbury said.

"Everybody knew that. I'm on Cloud Nine. I can't believe I got to go where I want."

The trade came on the heels of the Timberwolves front office reaching out to nearly every team ahead of them to make sure they got their man. In the days leading up to the draft, they called Philadelphia, Toronto, and Vancouver to try to make a deal. In their minds, Marbury was the number-one pick in the draft and Wolves General Manager Kevin McHale wasn't going to let the fact that they had the fifth pick ruin their plans.

"We had him rated higher than Iverson," McHale said. "That was our number one priority, to get him. There were a lot of guys in our league, you ask around, who had him rated higher than Iverson."

T-Wolves Coach Flip Saunders was all-in as well, dropping the mic about his team's bright future with this quote about having a pre-prime KG and Starbury:

"We have the two best 20-year-old players in the world."

◘   ◘   ◘

The grand irony of Minnesota trading Ray Allen to the Bucks so that the Wolves could pair Stephon Marbury with Kevin Garnett for a title run, is that twelve years later, the Celtics traded for Kevin Garnett to pair with Ray Allen to make a title run of their own.

It worked for the Celts.

Not so much for the T-Wolves.

None of this was known, of course, in late June of 1996, when the Bucks and T-Wolves both declared victory with the trade.

"Ray is a very good all-around player," Bucks coach Chris Ford said. "He brings a shooting touch to three-point range. I think he shot 46 percent from three-point range."

There was also a cool bit of history with the selection:

Chris Ford, who drafted Allen for his three-point shooting, happens to have hit the NBA's first ever three-point shot. Go ahead and win a few bar bets with that one.

Focusing on just the three is a little unfair to Allen's full set of skills. We picture him now stroking from downtown, calmly knocking down threes in the Finals or the playoffs for the Celtics or the Heat, but that's just a case of recency bias. Allen wasn't a one dimensional, Craig Hodges-type, spot-up deep threat. He was a smooth shooting, driving, pull-up jumper hitting savant who could score from almost anywhere on the floor.

"We looked at Ray Allen as a big-sized two guard," Dunleavy said. "He's 6'6", a great shooter from outside, a great free throw shooter and a great athlete."

He was also sneaky-fast and had an underrated vertical leap, leading a few people to even call him a poor man's Jordan (though even Allen said that was an "unfair assessment"). Yes, Iverson stole the headlines in the Big East, but keep in mind that it was Allen, not Iverson (confusing, I know) who won the 1996 Big East Player of the Year.

"I want to come to Milwaukee and be my own person and develop my own image," he said after learning of the trade. "We'll see what happens. I definitely want to go in and push my teammates so we can be a better team. I felt Milwaukee was the best situation for me, where I would feel my best. The sky is the limit at this point for us. I want to make a lot of good things happen."

o   o   o

The Boston Celtics have had several NBA Draft hot streaks that would make the MIT Blackjack Team jealous. In 1956 and 1957 they drafted Hall of Famers K.C. Jones, Sam Jones, and Tommy Heinsohn. In '69 and '70 they drafted Hall of Famers Jo Jo White and Dave Cowens.

From 1977 to 1980, they selected Cedric Maxwell and two more Hall of Famers—Larry Bird and Kevin McHale.

They have had some legendary cold streaks as well, none icier and more arctic-chilled than 1993, 1994, and 1995. For those who don't remember, during those three years the winningest franchise in NBA history selected Acie Earl, Eric Montross, and Eric Williams in the first round like Tom Emanski's back-to-back-to-back AAU National Champions (only without the championships).

It was into this barren wasteland of draft picks that the Celtics and their beleaguered coach/director of basketball operations, ML Carr, entered the 1996 draft. They originally had the ninth spot but traded Eric Montross, AKA the Montrossity, to the Mavericks to move up to the sixth pick. Keep in mind that this was during the nadir of the Celtics franchise's existence. If the Celtics were Sylvester Stallone, and the heyday of titles was *Rocky, Rambo, Tango & Cash*, and *Demolition Man*, the mid-'90s were the Celtics' version of *Eye See You, Avenging Angelo*, and *Shade*. Oh, you've never heard of those last three? Exactly.

After the glorious '60s, outstanding '70s, and dominant '80s, the team in green dropped off a cliff(hanger), going from 56 wins in '91 to 51 in '92 to 48 in '93, to 32 wins, 35 wins, 33 wins, and then a lowly 15 wins in the '96–'97 season.

On draft night, the Celtics and ML Carr needed a franchise boost, and to their mind, there was only one man who could deliver it to them: Antoine Walker. Well, Walker or Ray Allen, who Larry Bird felt was the best player in the draft.

"I liked Ray Allen a lot, too. At the end of last season I said that Allen would be number one or number two if he came out," Bird said. "Ray Allen and Walker, to me, were the elite of the whole draft. The Celtics' number one choice was down to Allen or him."

With Allen off the board one pick earlier, that left ML Carr to take the man he coveted so much that right before the pick, he did a call and response at the microphone in a ballroom full of corporate sponsors.

"Who shall we pick?" Carr shouted.

"Antoine Walker!" the crowd shouted back.

And so it was that Walker, eventually nicknamed Employee #8 after one of his Adidas sneaker commercials, became a Celtic.* He also became an instant draft legend by rocking a pair of sunglasses with his olive suit backstage. Rick Pitino, Walker's coach in college who just won a National Championship with him, raved about his skills to EJ and Hubie Brown, going so far as to say that while Walker's family is crying tears of joy, the fans of Kentucky were crying tears of sadness because he's gone.

Easy, Rick.

But ML Carr was thrilled and even acknowledged that while he had been gaga over the last three Celtics picks and taken some knocks for it, he was really, truly, genuinely pumped up to have Walker.

"I know everyone likes to talk about the excessive optimism I have," Carr said following the Walker selection. "But let me tell you something, this organization is on the way back!"

Bird agreed, or at least, he hoped Carr was right.

"God, I hope so," he replied when asked if he felt the tide was turning in Beantown. "It's time to buckle down and give the fans what they really deserve—a winner."

◘   ◘   ◘

To borrow an album title from Green Day (the perfect mid-'90s band), picks seven through twelve of the 1996 NBA Draft were "Dookie" for

---

* Why was Walker #8? Because the Celtics have retired so many players that all the numbers Walker wanted were taken, so he randomly just said, "I'll take 8."

NBA executives. They contain a collection of men that run the gamut from "solid pro" to "absolute bust" (sorry, Todd), and no matter how defensible the selection was at the time, within twenty-four months it was clear that, to be blunt, these six franchises blew it. This isn't 2021 revisionist history. This is 1997–1998 near-immediate regret.

It's one thing as a general manager to look in the mirror and know that taking Iverson, Camby, Abdur-Rahim, Marbury, Allen, or Walker was the right basketball call at the time. They all made the '96–'97 All-Rookie Team (1st or 2nd) and there were two bona fide Hall of Famers (Iverson and Allen), several all-stars (Abdur-Rahim, Marbury, and Walker), and Camby was a four-time All-Defensive Team player. It's quite another thing to know that you took one of these half-dozen guys:

Lorenzen Wright – Los Angeles Clippers

Kerry Kittles – New Jersey Nets

Samaki Walker – Dallas Mavericks

Erick Dampier – Indiana Pacers

Todd Fuller – Golden State Warriors

Vitaly Potapenko – Cleveland Cavaliers

Over Kobe Bryant. Or Steve Nash. Or Jermaine O'Neal. Or even Peja Stojakovic. That's a clean 35 All-Star Selections from picks 13 to 17 versus none from picks 7 to 12.

Ooooof.

Even in the moment, there was a lack of sexiness to picks 7 through 12. In person, Kittles was the fastest coast-to-coast player in basketball and showed flashes of excellence, but few projected him as an all-star caliber talent. Wright, Walker, Dampier, and Potapenko became serviceable, and in some cases, solid NBA players. But as they came off the draft board, Hubie Brown and other analysts used phrases like "will help shore up the defense" and "this helps them get bigger" and other vague, roster-rounding-out terms, rather than things like "game changer" and "potential superstar" and "special talent" which he, and other draft gurus, reserved for the man picked after all of these guys: Kobe Bryant.

It's worth noting here that just because Bryant wasn't discussed as a #1 overall pick, it's not as if *nobody knew* how good Bryant could be. In fact, a lot of people suspected he could be the prize of the draft: they just didn't have the guts to put their jobs on the line for a high school kid, or they got talked out of it, or bullied out of it, or both.

John Calipari, the New Jersey Nets' new head coach, *really* wanted him. He worked him out three times, each time becoming more and more convinced that Bryant was going to be special. So why didn't he take him with the eighth pick? There are three versions: one of them involves Calipari, a first-time NBA head coach, pleading with ownership to take him, but getting turned down. He described the scenario like this:

"I had the eighth pick in the draft, and everyone thought I was nuts," Calipari said. "A seventeen-year-old kid, a high school kid who's just now getting to the NBA? It shows you don't know what you're doing."

Version two was described in Jeff Pearlman's book, *Three-Ring Circus*, and it involves Kerry Kittles's agent strong-arming Calipari and telling him that if he didn't take Kittles (instead of Bryant), he'd never let any other clients sign with the Nets.

Version three involves Kobe Bryant's agent, Arn Tellem, talking to Calipari and telling him that if he drafted Bryant, the teenager would never suit up for the Nets.

"It was a calculated gamble," Tellem told the *Charlotte Observer*. "I remember meeting with John Calipari and John Nash, pressing them not to take him if he fell. I left not knowing if they would pass. I thought they would pass, but didn't know."

In the end, it really doesn't matter which version is right, or even if it's a combination of all three. Calipari and the Nets didn't select Kobe Bryant and neither did the next four teams in line—or any of the top twelve teams in the draft. It was only at Jerry West's urging, after a trade involving Lakers Center Vlade Divac, that Kobe went off the board and found his way to the Lakers.

West coveted Bryant like card collectors covet the Honus Wagner T206, and he planned to do whatever it took to land him. He worked with Tellem to limit Bryant's workouts. He massaged Vlade Divac's hesitation about going to Charlotte (Vlade once threatened to retire if traded).

As Bryant fell in the draft, West realized that his plan was coming to fruition when the Hornets selected him. And then the whole thing almost fell through because, well, someone on the Hornets said, "Holy shit, we just got Kobe Bryant."

"There was such excitement about the pick that Charlotte didn't want to go through with the deal," Mitch Kupchak, Los Angeles' assistant general manager in 1996, said. "There was a time there, whether it was Vlade [Divac threatening to retire] or just pressure on the franchise, where the deal was actually in jeopardy."

But it got done.

And instead of Bryant joining Anthony Mason, Glen Rice, Dell Curry, and Muggsy Bogues in Charlotte, he teamed up with Shaq in Los Angeles . . . and you know the rest.

□   □   □

Imagine a world where the 1996 NBA Draft simply started with the Sacramento Kings and the 14th pick—but in this world, none of the other 13 players exist, so the Kings 14th pick becomes the number-one overall pick. In this game, we roll with the picks as they were made as if they were at the top of the draft and see how they stack up—meaning that with the number-one overall pick, the Kings take Peja Stojakovic, an eventual three-time NBA All-Star, an '04 All-NBA player, and a 2011 NBA Champion. Up next, the Phoenix Suns at number two take a chance on a skinny Canadian point guard from Santa Clara, Steve Nash, who was actually a future Hall of Famer and an eight-time all-star, a seven-time All-NBA selection, and two-time MVP. We'll skip over the Tony Delk pick at three in this scenario and go to pick number four, the Portland Trail Blazers, who choose to roll the dice with Jermaine O'Neal, a high school kid on the road to a career that would net him six all-star appearances and three All-NBA teams.

If those were the top four picks in the hypothetical world mentioned above, that would be one hell of a draft. A Hall of Famer, three perennial all-stars, and three All-NBA guys in the top four. Very few drafts can claim to be so top heavy. That's how impressive the 1996 draft was. In the usual no-man's land of the early and mid-teen picks, NBA teams threw bullseyes. And this isn't even to mention that two-time All-Star Zydrunas Ilgauskas and five-time NBA Champion Derek Fisher were yet to come.

Talk to the hand, 1984 Draft Class.

▫   ▫   ▫

With twenty-five years having passed since that epic day in East Rutherford, New Jersey, the legacy of the draft has been solidified. Like a movie that opens with a montage of a leader getting the gang back together for one last ride to glory, we've got:

"The Icon" Allen Iverson.

"The Legend" Kobe Bryant.

"The Revolutionary" Steve Nash.

And "The Statesman" Ray Allen.

Looking back on his class, Allen says, "You've got to remember where our mindset was. We're walking into a league with Jordan, Barkley, Patrick Ewing, Reggie Miller, Hakeem Olajuwon, Scottie Pippen. There were some horses in this league that we were stepping into that we had been watching forever. We didn't think we were the next coming or next generation, but we were excited to be there."

Allen explains that the toughest part about being drafted is balancing your excitement with any inclination to sit back and say, "I made it." Guys who do that don't go far. He goes on to say that one thing that '96 draft class shared was the mentality to keep pushing yourself and to self-motivate like you're on a mission.

"When you look at myself, Nash, Kobe, Iverson, Marbury, Camby, Shareef, Jermaine, Peja, Fisher, Walker, all these guys, they were all good to great in college and scored a lot of points," Allen says. "But they weren't in it to be famous or liked by everybody. It was evident in someone like Steve Nash, a white kid from Canada out of Santa Clara, he was on a mission. Kobe came in from high school and he was on a mission. Marbury wanted to prove what the legacy of New York City ballers could do, and he was on a mission. I came from meager beginnings and I was on a mission."

That was the big differentiator between past "great draft classes." Rather than two or three or even five guys with the mindset to chase greatness, the '96 class had a dozen.

"That's the reason the '96 draft class is thought of as one of the best," Allen says. "It's the mentality we had. We were all on a mission to be better than we were. For all of us, there was a constant search to win. Every year the championship was a carrot we were chasing. I didn't win until my twelfth season. It comes down to watching basketball in June or playing basketball in June. This class had a lot of guys play in June. We knew what it took."

MADISON SQUARE
GRETZKY

AFTER TWENTY-FIVE YEARS OF THE LAVA-HOT
AstroTurf on the field at Busch Memorial Stadium, the St. Louis Cardinals replaced it with nearly three acres of all-natural Bermuda sod between the 1995 and 1996 seasons. The days of 100-degree scorchers in the stadium would remain, but players would no longer have to endure the 120+ degree temps bouncing off the searing plastic grass. The place that Casey Stengel once said "holds the heat well" was remodeled and beautified for the start of the 1996 season, which was set to feature two stars in the twilights of their careers on the field (Dennis Eckersley and Ozzie Smith) and one in the stands (The Great One himself, Wayne Gretzky).

No, the Cardinals didn't spiff up their stadium because they thought they'd have hockey royalty on hand regularly, but it didn't hurt to know they'd be getting some extra attention and media whenever he did choose to attend a game.

Gretzky, who played nine years with the Edmonton Oilers and seven-and-a-half with the Los Angeles Kings, was traded to the St. Louis

Blues on February 27, 1996, after publicly declaring that the Kings roster wasn't built for success—and giving an ultimatum that if ownership wasn't going to bring in new talent, they might as well trade him. This went over with Kings fans about as well as a collective case of pink eye.

"The Kings wanted to rebuild the hockey club," Gretzky said. "It was probably the right move but no one told me that's what they were doing. So I forced their hand and ended up being portrayed as the bad guy."

Originally, the Kings were going to trade Gretzky to the New York Rangers, where he'd be paired once again with the Pippen to his Jordan, Mark Messier. But the general manager and coach of the St. Louis Blues, Mike Keenan, laid out a Godfather offer to the Kings that included three prospects and two draft choices for the then thirteen-time all-star—and the Los Angeles ownership happily accepted the haul.

It was a ballsy move by Keenan. Gretzky was going to become a free agent on July 1 of that year, and to give up that many prospects and picks without an agreement for a new contract left him uncomfortably exposed (though it was worth the gamble considering who he was dealing with). He also had a few things going in his favor in terms of getting Gretzky to re-sign. First, he'd get to play on the same line with fellow future hall of famer and friend Brett Hull, and second, Gretzky's wife, Janet, was born in Bridgeton, Missouri, a short twenty-five minutes from St. Louis.

With Gretzky's good buddy on the team, a roster that gave The Great One a shot at another Stanley Cup, and Janet's family from the area, Keenan figured all he had to do was offer Gretzky a fair deal and he'd have him locked up and ready to retire as a member of the Blues.

Even Gretzky was on board with the plan, and by the time the regular season was ending, his agent and the Blues' ownership had already knocked out the larger points of a three-year deal that would make everybody happy.

"Heck, I'd already put down $9,000 for four season tickets to the Cardinals," Gretzky said.

Then came the famous Game 2 loss to Detroit in the second round of the 1996 Stanley Cup Playoffs, when the Red Wings smoked the Blues, 8–2.

Bernie Miklasz, a columnist for the *St. Louis Post-Dispatch* at the time, wrote, "The Blues got humiliated. They were an embarrassment to their fans and the city of St. Louis. Strip the blue note from the sweaters. Stop this mismatch. Put an end to this series, this season. Do it as quickly as possible . . . Please put the Blues out of their misery."

It was a scathing takedown of the hometown team by a hometown writer. The Red Wings had won 62 regular season games that year and were the prohibitive favorite to win the Cup, but that was no excuse for the complete no-show in both effort and heart by the Blues on the road. To make matters worse, Keenan and Jack Quinn, the team's president—the men who effectively mortgaged their team's future for Gretzky—made the unusual choice to not only throw The Great One under the bus, but to roll over him, put it in reverse, back up over the body, and then do it again.

"I don't know what's wrong with Wayne," Keenan said after the game. "He keeps telling us he's not hurt, so if he's not hurt, there's something bothering him and I'm not sure what it is."

Okay, that's not the best way to call out the greatest player in the history of the sport, but it's not unforgiveable. You could chalk it up to a coach letting off steam after a blowout and you can walk it back in the locker room if you have to. Probably apologize to Gretzky and move on.

But Keenan kept going.

"Wayne let his man go twice, and that's pretty well the end of the hockey game," Keenan said. "It's over in five minutes. I don't know what's wrong. I haven't got a clue. If he's hurt, he's not telling our trainers and he's not telling me."

Ooof.

Gretzky was asked about Keenan's comments almost immediately after he said them, and he owned them. "He's right. I let the team down. Both losses were my responsibility," Gretzky said.

Keenan did apologize for his tirade and Gretzky got over it. Coaches do what they think is best to motivate their teams and star players. Sometimes the tactic works. Sometimes it doesn't. Gretzky could handle that. The problem was that Keenan's words were merely shots across Gretzky's bow. Quinn was the one who fired the Mark 11 torpedoes directly into Gretzky's broadside.

Later that night, after the loss, Quinn called Gretzky's agent and took the contract offer they'd been working on together off the table. As Gretzky told *Sports Illustrated* at the time, "The money had already been agreed to. We were just discussing the length of the deferred payments and the interest. You want to play for people who believe in you. If that's all the faith they had in me—to take a deal off the table after one bad game—right then I decided I would never sign with the Blues, which I'd had every intention of doing."

So never mind that the Blues won Game 3 in overtime and that Gretzky had an assist. And never mind that they won Game 4 to tie the series in a 1–0 nail biter where Gretzky had the lone goal.

And forget about the fact that the Blues won Game 5 to go up 3–2 in the series behind another goal and another assist from Gretzky, and that the series ultimately went seven games and came down to a double overtime, stomach-punch loss.

The damage was done.

There was no way in hell Gretzky was staying in St. Louis.

Bad for the Blues.

Good for the Rangers.

"We wanted him during the season and we never stopped wanting him," Madison Square Garden president Dave Checketts said. "But there came a point when I really thought he was going someplace else."

Gretzky had about eight teams on his original wish list once he officially put St. Louis behind him, and over the course of just a few weeks that number was whittled down to two: Vancouver and New York. Realistically, it was a one-horse race. Few people believed that once Gretzky removed St. Louis from the mix that he wanted to skate off into the sunset playing for what would basically be a Mid-American Conference media market. Vancouver was a nice city with a decent team, but with around 600,000 people, it was nowhere near the bright lights of Los Angeles, which he'd become accustomed to, or the draw of New York City's eight million people.

"Going into Vancouver would have been going into media darkness," Checketts said. "I always thought if it came down to the two of us, that would be our edge."

That, and the fact that he'd get to reteam with Messier, with whom he'd already won four Stanley Cups while a member of the Edmonton Oilers in the late 1980s. There was just the little matter of money that needed to be sorted out. Messier won a Stanley Cup with New York in 1994 and was the team's captain and highest paid player. The Rangers front office didn't want to pay Gretzky more than Messier from both a financial and optics standpoint, even though it didn't bother Messier one bit. "I have absolutely no problem with him coming in here and making more money than me," he said.

There was some talk about a three-year deal versus a two-year deal and different yearly base salaries and deferments, but on July 21, 1996, Gretzky took less money to join his old Edmonton pal on the ice at Madison Square Garden for what they hoped was one last hoist of the Cup.

As Mike Lupica wrote in his column following the announcement, "New York gets one of the best guys in the world of sports, a champion and a gentleman."

They also got a first-class, sky-high Q-rating, capital S.T.A.R.

For New York City in the early and mid-'90s, this was actually a bigger deal than you'd expect. On the day of the Gretzky signing, the Big Apple was in the midst of a big drought of transcendent stars. The Yankees hadn't won a World Series since 1978 and while they had some former big names from the '80s on their roster, like Don Mattingly and Wade Boggs and even Darryl Strawberry, these were mostly baseball-centric stars. You knew who Boggs and Mattingly were, but your mom didn't, and neither man in 1995 was pitching Nike or Gatorade or McDonald's in national ad campaigns. Bernie Williams and Paul O'Neill would soon become Yankees icons, but their appeal remained mostly within the confines of the five boroughs.

The Mets, now ten years removed from their '86 World Series win against the Red Sox (when they were headlined by true crossover star Doc Gooden and Mr. *Seinfeld*-cameo himself, Keith Hernandez), were a 70-win team whose best player was . . . any guesses?...any at all?... no, Mike Piazza wasn't there yet . . . okay, you can give up . . . it was Bernard Gilkey.

The Knicks had Patrick Ewing (NBA all-star and future hall of famer, but not a national media darling), Allan Houston (NBA all-star and good guy), and Larry Johnson (formerly Grandmama), all of whom were a big deal in basketball circles, but didn't have Madison Avenue lining up to make them the face of national brands at this point in their careers.

The Giants were starless and terrible, and if you can name the starting quarterback of the '96 G-Men off the top of your head and you aren't a die-hard fan then there's a good chance you're a member of Dave Brown's family. Who's Dave Brown? He was the quarterback of the Giants in '96. They had a few players who would soon be stars, most notably Michael Strahan, but at the time they were mostly known to football fans.

And let's not forget the Jets.

Actually, yes, let's forget the Jets; Wayne Chrebet was not exactly a threat to supplant Wayne Gretzky in household name recognition. And they were about to embark on a glory-less 1–15 season.

This is why The Great One choosing the Rangers held more significance than it may have in future years when guys like Derek Jeter and Eli Manning were the toast of the town. In '96, New York City was in desperate need of a transcendent star and they got their man.

"Wayne attracts attention wherever he goes," Messier said in a *Sports Illustrated* piece just before the season started. "He's fun to be around. As a teammate you feed off that energy. The guys will feed off it. I call it catching the wave. That's what gets a team through a season, feeding off each other's energy. Wayne's always going for records, there's a full house every game. It's like a carnival atmosphere around him."

The carnival atmosphere at Madison Square Garden turned out to be an elixir for Gretzky, who led the Rangers with 97 points in the regular season (4th in the NHL) and 72 assists. The team itself finished 38–34–10 and made it to the Eastern Conference Finals where they lost to the Philadelphia Flyers. Sadly, there would be no perfect ending to the Messier–Gretzky reunion, which would only last one year. Following the 1997 season, Messier signed with the Vancouver Canucks and left Gretzky to finish out the final two years of his career in NYC without his old friend.

On April 16, 1999, wearing a Rangers jersey and sitting in front of a Rangers backdrop, Gretzky retired from the NHL. In his speech listing all the teams he played for, he said, "New York . . . was a wonderful experience and something I'll never forget," which is exactly how you'd politely sum up a relationship with someone you still like after it didn't work out. In fact, he sounded a little bit like Wayne Regret-zky (ba-dump tis!).

VENUS MEETS STEFFI

THE CRAMMED AND CONGESTED INTERSECTION of Rosecrans and Sepulveda in Manhattan Beach, California, is crowded with big-box stores, the Manhattan Village mall, office buildings, banks, and parking lots. Tucked away in the northwest corner, sidled up to the always-busy Manhattan Village Field, sits a hidden tennis treasure, the Manhattan Country Club. It's the kind of place where Irwin M. Fletcher might order two portions of beluga caviar, lobster thermidor, and two bottles of Dom Perignon on the Underhills's tab. It has a pristine lap pool and over a dozen outdoor hard courts, one of which served as the main stage for the star athletes competing in the 1996 Acura Classic.

On a near-perfect, mid-August, 78-degree day in Los Angeles, where the smog was light and you could see the ocean from the Pacific Coast Highway, 5,514 fans sat at center court to watch the number-one ranked female tennis player in the world play a third-round match.

But this wasn't just any third-round match.

It was the future of the sport versus its present.

A sixteen-year-old versus a twenty-seven-year-old.

Prodigy versus legend.

It was a girl with 14 professional matches against a woman with 20 Grand Slam victories, including her Golden Slam in 1998 (when she won all four Grand Slam tournaments consecutively in the same calendar year).

It was Venus Williams versus Steffi Graf, and for a very brief moment, it looked like the sport's future was getting impatient. Williams won the first point; then the second; then the third; and the fourth and fifth and sixth.

This was nothing new at all for Williams. Be it Steffi Graf or a teenager we'd never heard of, Venus was used to having her way on the court. At one point she was 63–0 on the United States Tennis Association Junior Tour. Her actual professional tennis debut had taken place on October 31, 1994, at the Bank of the West Classic in Oakland when she was fourteen. In the second round, she miraculously took the world's then-number-two player, Arantxa Sanchez Vicario, to the limit, going up a set and service break before coming back down to earth. From that point on, the buzz about Venus and her sister Serena, two tennis wunderkinds from Compton, steadily built.

Their father, Richard, who also served as their head coach, had learned tennis as a boy from a man he has only identified as Old Whiskey, whom he paid in pints of booze. According to a piece in the *New Yorker*, Richard Williams composed a 78-page manifesto for turning two yet-to-be-conceived daughters into tennis stars.

Wrote Reeves Wiedeman, "Once they were born, he put up signs in the family's front yard to emphasize lessons about life ('Venus, You Must Take Control of Your Future') and tennis ('Serena, You Must Learn to Use More Top Spin on the Ball'). Boyfriends were not allowed, and, to discourage any impulse toward early motherhood, Richard would rip the heads off of any dolls Venus brought home."

It was under this tutelage and this scrutiny and this level of seriousness about the sport that the Williams girls thrived, beginning with Venus, the elder sister. Over time, through a gauntlet of repetition and fire and their own friendly rivalry, the two African-American girls forged a path that would guide them to the top of a mostly white crop of players—and that would one day lead to a mind-boggling combined 30 individual Grand Slam titles (Serena 23, Venus 7) and 14 doubles titles. But we're not there yet. We're in Manhattan Beach, California, in 1996 and Venus, officially ranked #192 in the world and just old enough to drive, is in her 15th professional match somehow mopping the floor with the best female tennis player alive.

"There were some amazing points," Graf said. "I saw her play only once before and she looked slow, but she was a different player today."

After the six straight points, Graf shook off the blows, put her head down, and got to work. First, she broke Williams's serve and held to go up 2–1. Then Williams broke her serve to go up 3–2. Then Graf broke at 4–3 and served out to take the first set, 6–4.

In the second set, Graf jumped out to a 5–2 lead on the teenager, but Williams refused to give in. She battled back to make the match 5–4, including two clutch aces that had Graf, if only for a moment, on her heels. She then regained her footing and won four consecutive points to win 6–4, 6–4.

The crowd stood up and cheered.

For Venus.

The eighty-one minutes of the match stood as a wakeup call to the entire women's tour. The Williams Sisters were coming.

"She's a different player from before," Graf said. "She really goes for her shots, she has great range, and she has great ability. She showed me some great tennis. Before, she played slower and made more mistakes. She didn't do that tonight. I had to really focus, not on her game but on my game."

Venus was truly and refreshingly unfazed. She said that despite losing, the match wasn't very difficult and that there wasn't any part of Graf's game that, in her words, "made me go, 'whoa,'" like she couldn't handle it.

"I just played my game and had a lot of fun," Venus said, already learning to talk in athlete-speak. "Steffi Graf is a great champion, and I learned a lot from this match. I should have gotten more first serves in, and there were a couple shots down the line I should have gone for. It didn't bother me to play her. Each tournament, I play better and I'm pleased with my progress."

One year later, that progress would lead Venus Williams to become the first woman to make the US Open Finals in her first entry into the tournament (unseeded, no less). Williams and Graf would meet four more times before the elder player retired, all in 1999, with Graf winning two matches and Venus winning two matches.

Ultimately, Serena would be the Williams sister to break Graf's all-time women's Grand Slam singles match record, tying her with her 22nd Grand Slam win at Wimbledon in 2012 and then getting her 23rd Grand Slam win to take sole possession of the record, again at Wimbledon, in 2016, beating none other than her sister, Venus, in the Final. But it was on that picturesque day in August of 1996 that the two tennis generations first met.

Fittingly, after her 23rd Grand Slam, the most famous number 23 ever (and an official 1996 icon), Michael Jordan, sent Serena a congratulatory letter and a pair of custom-made Jordans.

ALI IGNITES ATLANTA

NOBODY KNEW.

Not the 85,600 people in attendance at the Centennial Olympic Stadium in Atlanta. Not the estimated 3.5 billion people watching around the world on television. Not President Bill Clinton, who officially opened the 1996 Olympic Games, nor former president and Georgia native Jimmy Carter.

As legendary composer John Williams directed the Atlanta Symphony Orchestra to play the first official song of the '96 Olympics, "Summon the Heroes," not one of the thousands of athletes waiting to be summoned to the stadium for the parade of nations was aware of what was going to take place.

Not track star Michael Johnson. Not swimming speed demon Gary Hall Jr. Decathlete Dan O'Brien had no idea. Olympic icon Carl Lewis wasn't clued in, and future WWE star Kurt Angle, who would win wrestling gold, didn't know either. Lisa Leslie and Dawn Staley and Rebecca Lobo didn't know. None of the Dream Team III members were in on it either. Not Shaq or Penny or Barkley or Hakeem or The Glove. Even The Admiral was unaware.

Even basketball star Teresa Edwards, who was reciting the Athlete's Oath on behalf of all the Olympians, didn't know.

"I'm standing at the bottom of the stage. I am about to go on the stage and I'm going to recite the Athlete's Oath. I'm as nervous as ever," Edwards said. "I don't know who's going to come out. I had no idea."

Nobody knew.

This was the 100th anniversary of the Olympic Games and the Olympic flame had been held by over 10,000 torchbearers in its lifetime to get to the stadium in Atlanta, and still nobody knew who was designated to light the Olympic cauldron to kick off the Games.

Up until about seven months before the Atlanta Games, the organizing committee had decided that it was going to be Evander Holyfield. He checked all the boxes. He'd grown up in Atlanta and won the Boys Club boxing tournament in the city at seven years old. He'd competed in the Junior Olympics, was a Southeast Regional Champion as a teenager, and won a bronze medal at the 1984 Olympics in Los Angeles. In 1990, he defeated Buster Douglas to become the undefeated, undisputed heavyweight champion of the world. Holyfield was the exact kind of hometown hero that the committee believed should light the Olympic flame for the host city.

Former NBC Executive (and sports television revolutionary) Dick Ebersol disagreed with the committee's assessment.

This was the ONE HUNDREDTH Olympics.

This was bigger than one city.

This was bigger than one country.

This torch ceremony needed an international icon.

And he knew just the one. All he had to do was convince Billy Payne and the rest of the Atlanta organizers to get on board with the only man he felt had the gravitas for the moment. Ebersol recalled the exact conversation he had with Payne for the *Sports Business Journal*.

"I don't think there's any question about it," Ebersol said. "It should be Muhammad Ali. Muhammad Ali may be, outside of perhaps the

Pope, the most beloved figure in the world. In the third world, he's a hero. In the Muslim world, he's a hero and a fellow traveler. To anybody young—just about—in the United States, he's a man of great moral principle who was willing to go to prison."

At first, there was pushback. Ebersol wasn't the only person to have presented this idea. Olympic Historian Dr. Bill Mallon had contacted Payne, as well.

"I'd actually written to the Atlanta Organizing Committee saying 'you need to pick Ali,'" Mallon said. "And I don't think I was the only one that did it."

Payne and a few others on the committee were still in the mindset that Ali was considered a draft dodger or too controversial. Ebersol wouldn't hear it. The first thing he did was get in touch with the Ali family to make sure that The Greatest was going to be able to handle the torch. Ali suffered from Parkinson's disease and it wasn't a given that he'd be able to control the flame. Once his wife, Lonnie, told Ebersol he was capable, he was a man on a mission.

Over the next few months Ebersol built his case, including the assembly of a file that could have been titled "Why Muhammad Ali is Awesome and Don't Ruin This Moment for the World" that he presented to Payne.

Finally, just two months before the Olympics, Payne agreed . . . but there was a problem. The organizers built a tower with the Olympic cauldron at the top of it, and Payne wasn't sure Ali would be able to make it up to the top on his own.

No problem, Ebersol said, and then he explained his makeshift plan to have Ali light a rocket somewhere else in the stadium that would carry the flame up to the cauldron. It would be a scintillating, spectacular finish worthy of the moment.

Picture it! The rocket's red glare shines on Ali is it soars to the cauldron. It'll be spectacular!

The committee was in.

Now all they had to do was keep it a secret from, well, everyone.

◦   ◦   ◦

Al Oerter, a four-time discus gold medalist for the United States, is the last man to hold the Olympic torch outside of Centennial Olympic Stadium before handing it to the man who had gone from top billing to the night's main undercard, Evander Holyfield. One month removed from defending his WBA Heavyweight belt against Mike Tyson, Holyfield grabs the torch with his battered hands and jogs through a labyrinth of hidden hallways and alleyways in the bowels of the stadium.

Holyfield had discovered a short time earlier that he was only carrying the torch, and not lighting the official Olympic flame.

"At twelve o'clock, midnight, they told me that I was going to be carrying the torch," Holyfield recalled. "Then they told me I wasn't going to light it. Then I said, 'Who in the world has done more than me in Georgia?' And they said, 'well, we can't tell you.'"

With the knowledge that a mystery icon would have the honor of lighting the torch in his hometown, Holyfield, Georgia's favorite son, emerges onto a stage in the middle of the field to a deafening cheer. Soaking it in, Holyfield runs a lap around the track with Greek athlete Voula Patoulidou, to connect the first Olympic Games to the current one, and then hands the flame to Olympic swimming icon Janet Evans, who does a lap around the track. She passes the 197 countries gathered in the infield as hundreds of camera bulbs flash and Beethoven's Ninth Symphony thunders through the warm Atlanta air.

At the end of her lap, Evans ascends a broad, black ramp that is lined with thousands of bulbs on each side. The torch looks like a two-foot-long silver flashlight, with a six-inch spot in the middle for athletes to hold on to. Evans runs and smiles and the music gets louder and louder as the crowd cheers. She reaches the top platform after nearly a full-minute jog upward, and as the fans clap and scream we see . . .

Blackness . . .

Nothing but Evans and a spotlight and an empty stage . . .

And then . . .

Seemingly out of nowhere . . .

Muhammad Ali appears holding a torch.

Whoooooooaaaahhhhhhhhh.

"When Ali appeared, it was the greatest collective gasp any of us had ever heard," Ebersol said.

Even the television announcers that night, Bob Costas and Dick Enberg, were unaware that Ali would be involved, which was just the way Ebersol planned. He wanted Costas to describe the moment with raw, unprepared emotion. Ali, whose left hand and arm shook from his Parkinson's, held the torch high in his right arm for all to see—and Costas described the scene as only he could.

"Muhammad Ali, of course, an Olympian as young Cassius Clay, gold medal boxer, 1960, the games of Rome," he voiced. "Look at him. Still a great, great presence...Still exuding nobility and stature . . . And the response he evokes is part affection, part excitement, but especially respect."

Ali then held the end of his torch against the prepared rocket and, after a few false starts, it finally lit and rose to the cauldron. There were shouts. There were cheers. There were tears. It was a rare, completely unexpected and breathtaking moment for the Olympics and for the world. Over time it has simply become known as the greatest opening ceremonies moment of all time.

Evander Holyfield remarked, "Later when I found out that it was Ali [instead of me], I think they made the right decision."

Yes, they did.

MICHAEL JOHNSON'S GOLDEN FEET

GOLD EARRING. GOLD CHAIN. GOLD SHOES. GOLD. Gold. Gold. American Sprinter Michael Johnson wore gold, dreamt of gold, and would have had a diet that consisted of gold food if he could. He'd dedicated his life to gold and the one time he turned his back on it, it cost him. Big time.

It was a balmy night in Salamanca, Spain, about two weeks before the start of the '92 Olympics. Johnson had just participated in a warm-up meet in preparation for running the 200 meters at the Games, and he and his agent decided to head out for some dinner. They originally planned to dine at the safe and familiar Burger King, but at the last second, they headed to a place called El Candil. They'd eaten there the previous night and enjoyed a wide variety of grilled and smoked meats. Only this time, something went wrong. Both men came down with ferocious cases of food poisoning. Johnson spent days recovering, losing hard earned fast-twitch muscle and sapping his strength heading into Barcelona, an event he'd spent two years preparing for.

Ever since Johnson graduated Baylor University in 1990 as a five-time NCAA Champion in the 200-meter dash, the Olympics were his goal. In college, he was only allowed to race the 200, but after graduation, he took up the 400 and became the first athlete in the sport's history to be ranked #1 in the world in both events. He even toyed with running both events in 1992.

"There's always been a stereotype," Johnson said. "If you ran the 200, you also ran the 100. If you ran the 400, that was all you did."

Johnson was different; in the 24 months after getting his diploma he was dominant in both events, putting him in ideal position for the Olympics. While game planning their strategy, Johnson and his coach, Clyde Hart, decided that he'd focus only on the 200 for Barcelona, since he had a stronger chance of winning. Then, Johnson made the disastrous decision that night to abandon the gold-crowned home of the Whopper for some local fare. The damage from the stomach bug was too much to overcome and he flopped at the Olympics. After being projected to finish first, he didn't make it out of the semi-finals and finished with the eleventh-best time.

It was a literal gut-wrenching turn of events for Johnson, and all he could do was set his sights four years into the future . . . to Atlanta. But this time, there would be no hedging. No choosing the 200 or the 400. No bullshit. This time Johnson was going to call his shot and enter both races as a heavy favorite.

Gold in the 200.

Gold in the 400.

Try and stop him, fools.

"I had run world championships, been ranked number one in the world, but if I don't win gold, nothing else matters," he said. "My coach and I talked about running the two hundred meters and four hundred meters, becoming the first man to win gold medals in each one of those events. Once I announced that I was going to attempt to make that history, it just sort of caught everyone's imagination."

The simplest way to describe Johnson's fame and popularity heading into the '96 Games for a 2021 audience is to say that Johnson was Usain Bolt before Usain Bolt—if Bolt had the added press (and accompanying pressure) of competing in Jamaica. Johnson, a star American in an Olympics hosted by America, was the face of the Games, and when you factor in the gauntlet he laid down for himself, he was one of the most recognizable athletes in the world. Even though most people only paid attention to track and field every four years, there was still the general understanding that speed demons were built in one of two models: there were 100-meter and 200-meter types, like Carl Lewis, or the 400-meter models, like Johnson. Nobody in the history of running really fast had ever been the fastest in the world in both. This was something that sports fans, Olympic fans, and even casual fans viscerally understood; Michael Johnson was out to make history. Which begged the question:

Could he do it?

And if he did it, would he be considered the fastest man alive?

According to Johnson, *yes.*

"If people want to call me the fastest man in the world, I'm not going to argue with them," he said at the time. "That's a great title to have. I feel good that I'm the first person who's not a one hundred meter runner to hold that title. Traditionally, the hundred meter guys have always been the fastest guys, but since I came along, I've changed a lot of the rules of sprinting so this is just another one."

In Johnson's mind, if he took home double gold medals in the 200 and 400 the fastest-man title undoubtedly would be his. And since there was no doubt, he might as well look good doing it.

That's where the iconic gold Nikes come into play.

Like most runners at Johnson's level, he wore hi-tech shoes made specifically for his events. He worked directly with Nike to come up with a design called the "MJ Special." It had a minimal foam heel (because the heel almost never hits the ground in a sprint), a specific wrap on each shoe for the left turns, six permanent spikes made of aerospace composite one-third the weight of steel, a stiff nylon front plate, a one-piece upper design, and an aerodynamic lace cover to reduce drag. They were as close to physically attaching running spikes to the human foot that any design had ever come. Each shoe weighed a slight 3.5 ounces, lighter than a deck of cards and a full two ounces less than any shoe Johnson had ever worn. In his words, they were the lightest and most stable track spikes ever made. They were designed to help Johnson run like the Flash, but that was also the thing they were missing: flash.

"The shoe was one-hundred percent Michael," Tobie Hatfield, Nike's designer on the shoe told the *Bleacher Report.* "He wanted to feel the track. He really wanted to make sure that every single gram was out of the shoe that didn't need to be there. Then it was a matter of, 'What is it going to look like?'"

The first prototype had a mirror-like gold color that was reflective, but Johnson's coach didn't like it, saying it looked cool close up but to people in the stands it was just going to look like a silver shoe. That's when a light bulb went off in Johnson's head.

"As soon as he said the words 'silver shoe,' I immediately thought, 'I want my shoe to be gold,'" Johnson said.

He'd already declared to the world his intention to do the impossible, and he already had the biggest track-and-field target possible on his back—why not push in all his chips with gold shoes? They were at once a declaration and a dare to his fellow competitors.

Hell yes, I'm gunning for two gold medals.

You gonna do anything about it?

They were also a stroke of branding genius (Johnson had a degree in marketing), and he displayed them in every Olympic photo shoot—including the pre-Olympic cover of *Time Magazine,* when they were on his feet, and the post-Olympic cover of *Time Magazine,* when they hung around his neck with his medals. On the track, they were a dizzying sight, mere flecks of gold churning at a super hero-like RPM at the bottom of Johnson's unmistakable upright running stance.

Their first test run in a gold medal final took place on the night of July 29, 1996, in front of a packed house at Centennial Stadium for the 400-meter race. Johnson was in the midst of a 53-race winning streak in the event and as the runners were introduced, he prowled back and forth in lane four, with his hands on his hips, his head down, and a stare that said, *you're all running for second place.* When his name was called, he raised his right hand, briefly looked up and gave a slight wave to the American-flag filled crowd.

He was dialed in.

When the gun went off to start the race, because of Johnson's lane, it appeared he was merely holding his position on the track after a fast start. But as he hit the backstretch and his legs spun with his arms pumping tight against his chest, it became clear he was accelerating at a rate none of the other racers could keep up with. He passed lanes five, six, seven, and three on the turn and as he rounded the corner like a slingshot, he looked like a fighter jet coasting past a bunch of prop planes. He never led by less than 8 meters the entire final straightaway, winning gold in an Olympic record, 43.49. As he raised his hands in victory, a smirk crept across his face, but there was no fist pumping or screaming or any kind of emotional release. It had the feel of a business-like victory, as if he'd just wrapped up giving a nice sales presentation at the office. The reason for the subdued nature of the win was obvious: Johnson had set out to win two medals in Atlanta, not one, and his mission was only half over.

Three nights later, on August 1, once again in front of a capacity crowd, Johnson lined up in lane three for the final of the men's 200-meter sprint. This time, there was no pacing from Johnson near the starter's blocks. No. This time he lightly shifted his weight from foot to foot with what can only be described as a death stare on his face. It was part Clubber Lang, part lion about to run down a gazelle, and all badass.

A moment later, he was in the blocks and . . .

Bang!

Johnson's start was velocity personified. He went zero-to-sixty like a Lamborghini. Four seconds into the race and he was already up on the two men next to him. Seven seconds in and halfway around the turn he was tied with the men who began ahead of him due to the staggered starts. At the eleven-second mark, blasting off the turn, Johnson was flat out blazing. Thirteen seconds in he was five meters in front of everyone, moving at a speed only a handful of humans have ever experienced. His arms swung wide. His golden feet streaked the surface of the track. His lead grew wider and wider and then . . .

He crossed the finish line in an unheard of 19.32 seconds, shattering the world record by .34 seconds, which might has well have been an eternity in the 200. He'd done it. He'd made history. He'd achieved the impossible. While 80,000-plus fans hollered his name he finally let himself enjoy the moment. He swung his arms up and down, hopped, screamed, shouted, waved widely to the crowd, shouting "Yeah! Yeah! Yeah!" as he grabbed the top of his track suit and flexed the "USA" for all to see.

"Not in 100 years have we seen a better performance," Bruce McAvaney, the famous Australian sports announcer, said. "You might say I'm carried away by the moment, but I'm not. No one has ever run a better race. You have seen something extraordinary."

After all the hugs and handshakes and smiles, about four minutes after the race, Johnson collapsed to the ground, his head buried on his forearms, as he caught his breath and absorbed the magnitude of the moment. When he got up, he pointed both hands to the sky and strutted down the track, enjoying the title he said he'd be happy to have: Fastest Man Alive.

A few weeks later, on *The Charlie Rose Show*, Johnson was asked what he was thinking about in that moment of victory on the track, after all the years of lifting weights for two hours in the morning and training two hours in the afternoon; after all the other titles that weren't Olympic titles; after all the expectations he put on himself and that he accepted from Nike and his sponsors and USA Track and Field.

What was he thinking about?

Who was he thinking about?

"Me," he said. "I was thinking of Barcelona. I thought about how in 1992 when I didn't win an individual Olympic Gold medal and now I finally did it.

Now I don't have to go through the rest of my career being afraid that I'd finish my career and people will say that 'he was the greatest two hundred and four hundred meter runner ever, but he never won an Olympic Gold medal.'"

Nope. Back in '96, the only thing people said was, "There goes the man with the golden feet, the fastest man in the world."

DREAM TEAM III

YUP, DREAM TEAM III.

You're thinking . . . wait . . . Dream Team I was in the 1992 Olympics, so wouldn't Dream Team II be in the 1996 Olympics? Technically, yes, but there is a forgotten all-star roster of NBA players who participated in the 1994 FIBA World Championships that was, officially at least, referred to as Dream Team II. That team was coached by Don Nelson, had an 8–0 record, won the gold medal, and was going to be the team for the '96 Olympics. But an excessive amount of taunting, shit-talking, and openly embarrassing international opponents led the powers that be to scrap much of the team prior to the Atlanta Games to avoid any sportsmanship issues on the Olympic stage.

The Dream Team II roster included Derrick Coleman, Joe Dumars, Kevin Johnson, Larry Johnson, Shawn Kemp, Dan Majerle, Reggie Miller, Alonzo Mourning, Shaquille O'Neal, Mark Price, Steve Smith, and Dominique Wilkins.

Yeah, that's one helluva squad, but only Shaq and Reggie carried over to the '96 Olympic team, which is often referred to as Dream Team II but is really Dream Team III.

Got it?

Now, let me save you some time. Otherwise, you'll start reading, then you'll put this book down or close the reading app on your phone, open Google, and start searching for "Dream Team I roster" and "Dream Team III roster." You'll end up down a '90s Olympic basketball rabbit hole, which is essentially what this section of the book is anyway; so here you go: Dream Team I, 1992 Olympics, Barcelona, Spain

PG – Magic Johnson

PG – John Stockton

SG – Michael Jordan

SG – Clyde Drexler

SF – Larry Bird

SF – Scottie Pippen

SF – Chris Mullen

PF – Charles Barkley

PF – Karl Malone

PF – Christian Laettner

C – Patrick Ewing

C – David Robinson

Dream Team III, 1996 Olympics, Atlanta, Georgia, United States of America

PG – Penny Hardaway

PG – Gary Payton

PG – John Stockton

SG – Reggie Miller

SG – Mitch Richmond

SF – Grant Hill

SF – Scottie Pippen

PF – Charles Barkley

PF – Karl Malone

C – David Robinson

C – Hakeem Olajuwon

C – Shaquille O'Neal

Five men played on both teams: John Stockton, Scottie Pippen, Charles Barkley, Karl Malone, and David Robinson.

Of the players who didn't carry over from '92 to '96, Larry Bird and Magic Johnson were retired and Christian Laettner wasn't good enough. Drexler and Mullen were past their primes; and Olajuwon, O'Neal, and Robinson were simply better than Ewing. That left a pretty big meatball hanging out there—the biggest meatball of all, in fact: Michael Jordan.

Of course, Jordan *could have* joined the team if he wanted to, but in a rare move of magnanimity from the famously cutthroat competitor, he decided that it was time for other NBA stars to enjoy the Olympic experience. It's often forgotten that the Dream Team in '92 was Jordan's second Olympic Gold medal. In the 1984 Games in Los Angeles, he led Team USA in scoring with 17.1 points per game and won his first gold. When the time came to go for a third, he graciously bowed out.

Let the young guys have some fun.

It wasn't until the 1996 NBA Finals, just a few months before the Olympics were going to start, that a reporter asked Jordan about not playing and what he thought of the new team and the selection process. He seemed particularly irritated that the men in charge left off Shawn Kemp, who was giving his Bulls all they could handle in the Finals.

"I really don't know what the criteria was for picking the Olympic team," Jordan said. "When you look at the caliber of players on the team or in the league, you can put together two or three different teams. To leave Kemp off, I really don't understand. That's one of the reasons I chose not to perform . . . to give people like him a chance to play. Why they didn't pick him, I don't know."

The new guys who did make the team had one thing in common: they were noticeably younger than their 1992 counterparts (when they played).

In 1992, Larry Bird was thirty-five years old. He was replaced with twenty-three-year-old Grant Hill. Magic Johnson was 32 in '92. He was replaced with Penny Hardaway, who was 25. Patrick Ewing was 29 when he played in Barcelona. The committee swapped him out for Shaquille O'Neal, who was only 24 heading into Atlanta.

Overall, Dream Team III was filled with younger, up-and-coming stars who had yet to rack up MVPs or titles, which was a departure from the end-of-their-primes, loaded-with-rings-and-trophies Dream Team I. If you remove the guys who played on each team, at the time of the '92 Games, the Dream Team boasted 14 NBA Championships and 11 MVP awards to . . . 0 NBA titles and 0 MVPs (yet) for the newcomers to Dream Team III.

Unlike the "Dream Team" name that the media gave the first group of legends, the new guys on the "Dream Team III" squad weren't quite legends just yet; more like potential legends. Looking back, it's easy to downplay two of the "next Jordans" on the team, Penny Hardaway and Grant Hill, both of whom had their careers significantly altered due to injuries. But prior to getting hurt, Hardaway and Hill were on the path to icon status. Hill was a version of LeBron before LeBron. Hardaway was a version of Magic after Magic. They had the all-star nods, the All-NBA selections, the shoes, the commercials, and the skills to be the next faces of the NBA. So, when you see a comparison of the teams, it's not a given that swapping Penny for Magic was a significant downgrade or that losing Bird for Hill was some kind of huge drop-off in talent. It was a somewhat negligible dip (considering the points they were at in their careers) at best, and a slight dip at worst.

Lenny Wilkens was the head coach of Dream Team III, but also had been an assistant under Chuck Daly back in '92 for the original team. When he compared the rosters, he said, "Back then, there were more players with the legend moniker attached to them. These players aren't in that category yet. But certainly they are talented and they have great versatility and desire."

The moment the Dream Team III roster was announced they were just as big a favorite to win Olympic Gold as their first iteration. International basketball had not yet reached the level it would by the mid-2000s, and not a single country posed a legitimate threat to stop the Americans. In fact, the toughest game DTIII played on their road to gold actually took place three weeks before the Olympics, on June 6, 1996, at the Palace at Auburn Hills in Detroit against the USA Select Team, which was made up of under-22 college stars.

The game was supposed to be a friendly exhibition where the pros on Team USA let the college kids share the court while they worked out the kinks in their lineups and developed chemistry. The college kids, led by Tim Duncan, Chauncey Billups, Paul Pierce, and a bunch of guys you don't remember like Geno Carlisle, Louis Bullock, Shea Seals, Austin

Croshere, and others were supposed to be content with the opportunity to bask in greatness; you know, show up, take a few photos with their idols, get a good run in and then smile while getting blown out by 50.

Or not.

In front of 21,454 fans and millions on live television, the select team treated Team USA like a bunch of JV posers. The college kids hit eight of their first ten shots to jump out to a lead that stretched to 34–20 after Chauncey Billups hit a lay-up midway through the first half.

"We caught them off guard and I'm sure they took us too lightly," Croshere said. "We didn't care if they dunked on us. It was bound to happen anyway."

The Billups basket seemed to wake up the NBA stars, spurring them to go on a 20–5 scoring blitz that ended with the old guys having the lead, 40–39, with about six minutes left in the first half. Now things were back as they should be and Team USA would coast to a win against the twenty-two-year-old kids, right?

Wrong.

Guard Shea Seals, from Tulsa, was feeling it. Croshere was feeling it. Duncan was feeling it. Instead of cowering to the Olympians, they crushed them, going on a 20–2 run to end the half, which included six three-pointers on 63 percent overall shooting. Seals sank the last of the six threes right at the buzzer to put the Select Team up 59–42 at the half.

"I wasn't enjoying it, but I wouldn't say I was concerned," John Stockton said.

"I was concerned," Olajuwon said.

Dream Team III came out of the locker room after the half determined to knock the snot (and the swag) out of the cocky college kids. They methodically ate into the 17-point deficit and through big-boy defense, intimidation, and focus, finally took the lead 78–76 with almost seven minutes to go. They led the rest of the way and finished off the youngsters, 96–90, behind 17 points from Pippen and 16 from Olajuwon.

"We thought we had them," Northwestern guard Carlisle said. "We got out there and started to make some baskets. It was like we were in a dream."

Karl Malone strongly disagreed.

"Today we weren't the Dream Team," he said. "In fact, for a while, we were the nightmare team. We got our wake-up call, and now it's time to start making a statement."

The statement would come in the Olympic tournament where they tore through teams like Godzilla through a row of townhouses. In Game 1 they beat Argentina 96–68. In Game 2 they beat Angola 87–54. They beat Lithuania by 22, China by 63, Croatia by 31, Brazil in the quarterfinals by 23, Australia in the semi-finals by 28, and then they smoked Yugoslavia in the gold medal game, 95–69.

Their average margin of victory was 31.6 points per game, which was not quite as high as the 43.8 point-per-game margin of victory of Dream Team I, but still impressive. Charles Barkley led the team in scoring and rebounding (12.4 points and 6.6 rebounds per game) while playing only 18 minutes a contest. Payton and Hardaway both averaged almost five assists per game. It was, by any measure, a success.

"It's great to be able to represent your country on a world stage," Wilkens said.

Surprisingly, the most memorable moment of the tournament wasn't winning the gold medal for Team USA. Instead, it was the halftime ceremony.

What kind of halftime ceremony would overshadow an actual Olympic Gold? This kind:

At halftime of the championship game, with Team USA ahead of Yugoslavia 43–38 at the Georgia Dome, the members of Dream Team III took the court early to make a special presentation to none other than Muhammad Ali. In the 1960 Rome Olympics, Ali, then Cassius Clay and only eighteen years old, won the boxing gold medal.

Sometime after 1960, Ali lost the gold medal, and with Ali present in Atlanta, the International Olympic Committee made the decision to present him with a new medal at halftime of the men's basketball final. Ali stood at center court and got a standing ovation while he waved and kissed the medal, before being enveloped by the basketball players who idolized him. Even with Parkinson's ravaging his movements, Ali managed a smile as Reggie, Hakeem, Malone, Barkley (jabbering away), Pippen, and Penny circled him and hugged him while the Superman theme blared over the loudspeakers and fans chanted, "Ali! Ali! Ali!" The players gathered for a quick photo (with Shaq essentially photo bombing everybody in the way back) and then went out and won the game easily by 26 points.

"I grew up watching the champ," Reggie Miller said. "He was a role model. To have him out there with us in the center of the court, to have a chance to reach out and touch him—it meant a lot to the people on this team. It was very special."

Almost as special as winning the gold.

KERRI STRUG & THE MAGNIFICENT SEVEN

NORM MACDONALD IS WEARING A BLUE SPORTS jacket, a patterned tie, and white dress shirt behind the Weekend Update desk on *Saturday Night Live*. He aims his dry, nasally delivery right at the camera. It's the September 28, 1996, season premiere of *SNL* and of all the stud athletes in their prime in 1996, only one is making an appearance on this episode: Kerri Strug. Strug is playing herself, next to Chris Kattan, who is playing her brother, Kippy Strug, a made-up male version of the famous gymnast with the same high-pitched voice and mannerisms. The skit works and the jokes land . . . all because of the historic and gutsy vault performance that Strug had in the Olympics a few weeks earlier.

That was the last time most of America had seen her, when she was holding up a bouquet, posing with a gold medal around her neck in Atlanta as a member of the "Magnificent Seven," the first women's gymnastics team from the United States to ever take first place in an Olympics. She was wearing only the top of her warm-ups because prior to the photo, she was getting her entire left leg bandaged in an Olympic hospital tent and she didn't have time to put on her pants when her coach, Bela Karolyi, carried her to the podium to join her teammates for the medal ceremony and photo.

She had jacked up her ankle in competition that day. Twice. The first time she did it by under-rotating the landing of her vault and tearing the medial and lateral ligaments in her ankle. At the time, she heard the unmistakable sound of the tear and felt the searing pain of the injury, but she didn't know how badly she was hurt. She also didn't have time to dwell on it. Team USA was in a dead heat with the Russians and in the moment, it appeared that they needed her to land her second vault to clinch the win.

"Do we need this?" she asked Karolyi.

He told her "yes" and then cheered her on, screaming the now famous lines, "You can do it, Kerri!" over and over again.[*]

Believing that her team needed her to land a second vault to win the gold, Strug blocked out the pain, went to the top of the runway, raised her hands, took a deep breath, exhaled ever so slightly, and took off sprinting for the beam. Routine, repetition, muscle memory, adrenaline, and thousands upon thousands of hours of practice took over as she raced, planted, leapt, spun, and then hit her vault.

You remember the landing.

She stuck it on one foot and then stood up with her left leg bent off the ground, putting all the pressure on her right. The 30,000 fans at the old Georgia Dome went ballistic as Strug raised her hands and saluted the judges while fighting back tears of pain before finally collapsing to the mat.

"It felt like a bomb," she later said about the pain in her foot when she landed.

---

[*] She didn't actually need it. In the heat of the moment, some people who were paid to know how to add scores quickly forgot to add. The US had clinched the gold, but none of the athletes or coaches were aware of this. Somehow.

As she was helped off the mat, she had no idea that by the time she had her ankle treated, she would become a household name and one of the breakout stars of the Olympics. She'd appear in a famous "This is *SportsCenter*" commercial, where Karl Ravech, Keith Olbermann, Rich Eisen, and even Sparty, the Michigan State Mascot, carried her around the office in a spoof of Karolyi carrying her off the mat at the Olympics. There were Wheaties boxes, meetings with President Clinton, a *People* magazine cover, a *Time* magazine cover, an autobiography—appropriately titled *Landing on My Feet*—and yes, the unforgettable appearance on *SNL*.

But it wasn't just a magnificent performance by one person. While Strug received most of the spotlight due to her crunch-time vault performance, Shannon Miller, Dominique Moceanu, Dominique Dawes, Amy Chow, Amanda Borden, and Jaycie Phelps rounded out the squad that would go down in history as The Magnificent Seven.

Miller is the second-most decorated American gymnast in Olympic history and won the only individual women's gold in '96 on the balance beam. Amy Chow won a silver medal in the uneven bars. In 2008, all seven women were inducted into the United States Olympic Hall of Fame in the team category.

To this day, they are the standard by which every US Women's Gymnastics Team is measured.

AGASSI REINVENTED

THE PREMISE OF NIKE'S FLAGSHIP ANDRE Agassi-as-rebel commercial is simple: the bad boy of '90s tennis (Agassi) and the bad boys of '90s rock and roll (the Red Hot Chili Peppers) team up to show us just how badass they can be.

At tennis.

The spot is a 30-second whirlwind of absurdity. We open on a fast zoom into Anthony Kiedis and Flea sitting in a tennis umpire's chair and Kiedis asks, "Wanna play rock and roll tennis?"

Then we get electric guitar licks, drums, Agassi sitting in a lounge chair spinning a tennis racket, Flea banging his bare chest like King Kong, and a graphic that says "AGASSI'S ROCK & ROLL TENNIS CAMP"—after which Agassi says to the camera, "Let's dance." Kiedis and Flea respond by screaming in the umpire chair like they're about to fall into a zero G drop on a roller coaster.

And that's only in the first six seconds of the ad. Over the course of the next twenty-four seconds, Flea and Kiedis make a combined 459 weird faces and yell like they're on a bad mushroom trip while Agassi smashes forehands on stage at what looks like a rock concert that Flea and Kiedis are performing in while being in the umpire chair at the same time, I think. Put a *Mad Max* fight scene in a blender with tennis balls and a Fender guitar and you're close to the feel of this spot, which ends with Agassi asking, "Any questions?"

Yeah, Andre, I've got a few questions.

Why are Flea and Kiedis snuggling up in a lifeguard seat that's a stand-in for an umpire's chair? Shouldn't they be playing against you? They're the rock and roll stars and they're not even playing rock and roll tennis? What? Also, are you going to be lighting up the Chili Peppers with forehands to the face or something? They seem terrified of you. So yes, I've had a few questions about this commercial for twenty-five years and I appreciate you letting me ask them.

Why bring up this commercial (other than to let me vent)?

Because it perfectly illustrates the brand that the late '80s/early '90s Agassi projected. From Agassi's famous "image is everything" tag line for his Canon camera spots, to his feathered hair and mullet, to his sunshine yellow and highlighter orange and hot pink tennis outfits, to the iconic Nike Air Tech Challenge Threes with the neon colorways (practically the only tennis shoe acknowledged by sneaker heads and my dad), every single thing about Agassi in the '90s was about flash and fame and lifestyle and, to use his own word, *image*. He was one of the sports world's few super spokespeople, a celebrity for several years in the mid-'90s on par with Jordan, Griffey, Shaq, Deion, and all the other big time, high Q-rating stars.

In a Justice League-advance moment for sports legends, Agassi was a member of the investment group behind the ill-fated Official All-Star Café chain of restaurants, a sort of Hard Rock meets Planet Hollywood type of restaurant with a sports theme. The investment group included Griffey, Shaq, Joe Montana, Wayne Gretzky, and Monica Seles (the theme failed, closing down in 2001).

On the endorsement front, he had deals with Head tennis racquets, Penn tennis balls, and Nike shoes and equipment. During his career he was sponsored by Mountain Dew, Canon cameras, American Express, Deutsche Bank, Schick (worldwide spokesman), TwinLab, DuPont, Ebel, Mazda, and then Kia. There was even the *Andre Agassi Tennis* game for Sega and Super NES, because were you even a sports star in the '90s if you didn't have your own video game?

Agassi arrived on the tennis scene at the exact moment he was needed—right when American stars John McEnroe and Jimmy Connors were ending their careers and preparing to leave the tour. By the time Agassi won his first Grand Slam in 1992 at Wimbledon, it had been eight years since McEnroe's last Grand Slam win (the US Open in 1984) and ten years since Jimmy Connors's win in the 1982 US Open. While there were plenty of dominant American men's tennis stars to pick up the slack in terms of performance, most notably Pete Sampras, Michael Chang, and Jim Courier, none of those athletes even sniffed the off-the-court celebrity that McEnroe had in his heyday—a stardom that Agassi would soon surpass.

◘　　　◘　　　◘

Like Lebowski's rug, Agassi's hair tied his whole look together. It was part lion's mane, part cockatiel. It whooshed and flipped and flared and was as much a part of his legend as Davy Crockett's coonskin cap. At times, it seemed to have a life of its own. The lengths varied, the colors changed, and even the feathering seemed to ebb and flow. To Agassi, it was the source of his strength, like Sampson. To tennis fans, it was the ultimate symbol of the rebel with a racket. To Brooke Shields, his new girlfriend in 1993, it was . . . not exactly real-looking, but she didn't say anything until he brought it up after their third date together. They were back at Shields's brownstone in Manhattan, about to get romantic, and suddenly Agassi stops the action to begin a sequence of look-altering (and life-altering) talks about his hair that he revealed in his acclaimed biography, *Open*.

"This isn't easy to admit, Brooke," he says. "But, look, I've been losing my hair for quite some time and I wear a hair piece to cover it up."

"I had a feeling," she smiles, before assuring him that she's falling in love with him, not his hair.

Cut to January of 1995 and Agassi is about to prepare for the Australian Open. He's just come off a spectacular finish to the '94 season, where after hiring new coach Brad Gilbert, he becomes the first men's player in thirty years to win the US Open unseeded for his second Grand Slam. He's never played in the Australian Open before, but with his new training regimen he feels like Superman and wants to give it a go. A few weeks before the tournament, Shields has one suggestion.

"I think you should get rid of that hairpiece," she says. "And that ponytail. Shave your hair short, short, short and be done with it."

"But I'd feel naked," he says.

"You'll feel liberated," she says.

At first, he basically responds with helllllll noooooo.

But a few days later, he's in.

"Let's cut it off," he says. "Let's cut it all off."

As the shearing is taking place, he's having doubts and starts to freak out.

What have I done??? I am my hair! My hair is me!

When it's over, he feels like a new man. Or at least a different man. And he thanks Shields.

"You were right," he says. "My hairpiece was a shackle, and my natural hair, grown to absurd lengths, dyed three different colors, was a weight as well, holding me down."

For the very short term, Agassi was right. Sporting a goatee, a bandana, a hoop earring, and an outfit that was part Pirates of the Caribbean and part Miami beach bum, he ripped through the brackets of the Aussie Open and then faced down his nemesis, Pete Sampras, in the final to win his second Grand Slam in a row and third overall. Gone were the neon colors and dyed blond flowing locks. In their place were a seemingly XXL horizontal striped polo shirt, paisley-esque shorts, and the most important accessory of all: the Norman Brookes Challenge Cup that he was able to hoist after winning the Slam.

The win was widely considered the best match of his career, and with back-to-back Slams under his belt, there was no reason to believe that Agassi wasn't about to go on a hairless tear and collect more hardware. And for a time, he did, reaching the ranking of the world's number-one player for the first time in his career in April of 1995. He was even somewhat invincible over the summer, winning 26 times in a row. On the year, he won 73 matches and lost 9. It was a remarkable streak, but somehow didn't include any more Grand Slams.

You can collect all the Cincinnati Open wins and Canadian Open wins you want, but what matters to the history-book writers is one category of triumph: Slams. Agassi had no way of knowing that following his Australian Open win, he'd go a full four years without winning a Grand Slam again. Sadly, a litany of problems (a surprising crystal meth issue), injuries (his wrist again), and personal issues (relationships) would soon have him hitting career and real-life rock bottom in 1997, when he failed an ATP drug test, only played in 24 matches, and nosedived down to a ranking of 141.

However, he did have one lone bright spot between the end of 1995 and his stunning comeback of 1999: the 1996 Olympic Games in Atlanta.

◻   ◻   ◻

Mentally, Agassi was in a dark-ish place in the summer of 1996. He was about to get married, but he wasn't all that excited. His stellar tennis play had dropped off. He felt listless. He needed something—anything, really—to fire him up.

Enter: the Atlanta Games.

"As the summer [of '96] approaches, there is only one elaborate pageant that interests me. And it's not my wedding," he writes in *Open*. "It's the Atlanta Olympics. I don't know why. Maybe it feels like something new. Maybe it feels like something that has nothing to do with me. I'll be playing for my country, playing for a team with 300 million members. I'll be closing a circle. My father was an Olympian, now me . . . As the Games begin, sportswriters kill me for skipping the opening ceremonies . . . But I'm not in Atlanta for opening ceremonies, I'm here for gold, and I need to hoard what little concentration and energy I can muster."

Yeah, there was a lot going on in the mind of Andre Agassi in August of 1996 as he flew to Georgia. Outside of his own head, however, he was the #1 seed in the tournament (Goran Ivanisevic was #2; Sampras and Becker didn't participate) and as an American competing on his home soil, there was the added pressure to win. It certainly didn't help him that he'd flamed out early at both Wimbledon and the French Open earlier in the year. Still, he was disappointed that more of the world's top players didn't show up to compete.

"It's disappointing," he told reporters. "I think [the Olympics] deserve more respect and attention. But it didn't change my desire to be here."

Agassi won his first two Olympic matches without dropping a set, winning 7–6, 7–6 against Jonas Lars Bjorkman from Sweden in the first game and winning 6–4, 6–4 against Karol Kucera from Slovakia. In round three he got beat in the first set against Andrea Gaudenzi before recovering and winning 2–6, 6–4, 6–2.

In the quarterfinals, Wayne Ferreira, a South African who would never win a Major but randomly retire with a positive win record against Roger Federer, gave Agassi a tug-of-war type match that sucked the life out of him. Agassi won the first set, 7–5, lost the second 6–4, then won the third set 7–5. The Semi-Final against Leander Paes started off the same, with a marathon first set in the steamy Atlanta heat, which Agassi won 7–6, before dropping the hammer in the second set, 6–3.

Now, all that stood between Agassi and Olympic Gold was the 6'2", spindly and speedy Sergi Bruguera from Spain. Bruguera was an excellent clay court player with a two-handed backhand that came off his racket like it was blasted out of a pitching machine. He won back-to-back titles in the French Open in 1993 and 1994 and rose to the highest ranking of his career, #3 in the world, in the summer of 1994. Bruguera also had a habit of stomping the greatest players of his generation, beating Pete Sampras in three of their five matches and handing Roger Federer the worst loss of his entire career, defeating him 6–1, 6–1, at the 2000 Barcelona Open.

Having tumbled out of the top 50 in the world rankings, Bruguera's scoring a win against Agassi would be the cornerstone of a comeback he'd been dreaming of. And doing it on Agassi's "home court," in America, would be that much sweeter. As the men took the court at the Stone Mountain Tennis center, the giant-slayer Bruguera was envisioning what Agassi would look like as a notch on his belt.

Agassi, on the other side of the net, didn't care what Bruguera was envisioning. He had the feeling. The ball launched off his racket. His feet felt like he was floating over the court. On days like this, it didn't matter who he was playing. It could have been Bruguera and Federer and Sampras all together.

He wasn't losing.

Wearing white sneakers, a billowing white shirt, and a white hat, Agassi treated Bruguera like a dad toying with his kid on a racquetball court. He hung around center court and smashed winners all day while the Spaniard sprinted back and forth, dumping shots out of bounds and into the net, unable to keep up with Agassi's power and accuracy.

The gold medal match was best of five, rather than best of three like the earlier rounds, but Agassi still only needed three, winning 6–2, 6–3,

6–1. On a double break point in the third set, Agassi jammed Bruguera on the return and as had happened all day, the volley came back long, putting him one game away from victory.

On the third gold medal point, Agassi blasted a serve to Bruguera's left and he could only manage a tapper of a backhand back over the net, which Agassi destroyed to his weak side. Bruguera slumped. It was like he was playing another species of tennis player. All he could do was smile.

Agassi smiled and raised his hands and pumped his fists—he'd won his gold medal.

"When he's on, he's the best player in the world at this surface," Bruguera said. "He played too well for me today."

Tom Gullikson, the US Olympic coach, said, "He didn't play a sloppy point all day. It was the sharpest I've seen him all year."

For Agassi, the win was much more than a medal. It was a reckoning. His father, Mike Agassi, was an Olympic boxer as a kid in Iran and never won a medal—so in a way, it was a full-circle moment for the Agassi men.

"It was a memorable embrace we'll have forever," Agassi said of the hug with his dad afterward. "I let him get closer to the gold than he ever got."

As for the way he mowed down Bruguera, the new gold medalist didn't mince words.

"The way I was playing today, I didn't care who was on the other side of the net," he said. "I was going to win."

The gold medal would end up being the great differentiator for Agassi when his career finally wrapped up around 2006. He'd won 8 Grand Slam titles, including the career Grand Slam (winning the Australian Open, French Open, Wimbledon, and the US Open). There have been only seven other men's career Grand Slam winners, and of them, only Rafael Nadal also has an Olympic Gold.

"To me, this is the greatest thing I've accomplished in this sport," Agassi said at the time. "I'd keep this over all of them."

TIN CUP & THE FAN

LET ME PITCH A MOVIE TO YOU.

Ready?

Robert De Niro is going to play an unhinged San Francisco Giants fan who starts off the film teetering on the edge of normalcy before taking a swan dive into a sea of insanity.

Wesley Snipes is going to play Bobby Rayburn, a Barry Bonds type who signs a record-breaking deal to play with the Giants (and who is also DeNiro's favorite player).

Benicio Del Toro plays the Giants' current superstar, who immediately resents Rayburn and refuses to relinquish his lucky number eleven.

Rounding out the cast we've got John Leguizamo as Snipes's agent/manager and Ellen Barkin as a local sports media personality. And as a kicker, I'm throwing in Tony Scott (*Top Gun, True Romance, Crimson Tide, Man on Fire*) as the director.

How "in" are you for this movie? 100 percent in? 1,000 percent in?

Now I'm going to hit you with the finisher:

The movie's final scene involves DeNiro, standing on the pitching mound at Candlestick Park, about to pitch KNIVES to Wesley Snipes in the batter's box.

Now how "in" are you? A zillion percent?

By now you have either a) guessed that this was a real movie, b) are one of the small group of viewers who have seen it on HBO, cable, or Amazon Prime, or c) you were one of the truly lucky human beings who experienced this film in the theater on August 16, 1996. By lucky, of course, I mean rare. The movie only made $17 million and is nowhere near the top of any all-time greatest sports movie lists—or even must-watch baseball movie lists. It's noteworthy for our purposes not because of the quality of the film (though I personally like it), but because the film exists at all.

Do you know what the chances of a major studio making a baseball movie are now? Let alone a baseball movie not based on a true story or an established star? Let's just say it's about one percent . . . and we're being generous.

In 1996, throwing DeNiro and Snipes into a thriller about baseball made total sense because baseball was still a top-of-the-food-chain choice for entertainment. Not anymore. Unless you're Ryan Coogler, if you rolled onto the Universal Studios lot with a big budget for a fictional baseball movie you'd get thrown out before you even got your parking validated.

And you know what's even more awesome/different about '96?

The Fan *wasn't even the only star-driven sports movie to come out on the weekend of August 16, 1996.*

Robert DeNiro, Wesley Snipes, and John Leguizamo actually had to share that weekend with Kevin Costner, Rene Russo, and Cheech Marin, who all starred in *Tin Cup*, which premiered on screens the same day.

Yeah, a baseball movie and a golf movie headlined by A-List stars hit theaters together. *Tin Cup*, however, is a bona fide excellent sports movie. Also, if you're reading this book chronologically, then you'll recall that *Happy Gilmore* had come out in February of '96, which means that two thirds of the holy trinity of golf films (obviously *Caddyshack* is the first) came out in 1996.

Unlike the literal theatre of the absurd that was the finale in *The Fan*, the finale of *Tin Cup* was "loosely based" on a hole played by the film's golf advisor, Gary McCord. It's been twenty-five years, so if you haven't seen this movie, this is your spoiler alert . . . but in the film's memorable third act, Roy "Tin Cup" McAvoy is on the fairway on the 18th hole of the US Open. There is a large pond in front of the green and all he has to do is lay-up on his second shot, chip it over the water and onto the green on his third shot, and then sink a birdie to win the tournament. Despite battling his demons the whole movie, "Tin Cup" is incapable of laying up. His caddie, Cheech Marin, begs him to play it safe. His girlfriend/psychologist, Rene Russo, flips the script and tells him to "go for it."

What follows is one of the most memorable sequences in sports movie history. It's based on a hole Gary McCord played at the 1986 FedEx Cup St. Jude Classic, when he faced a 209-yard shot over the water on the sixteenth hole of the Colonial Country Club. McCord hit his four-iron five times into the water and with one ball left in his bag, he hit a three-iron over the water and then sank his putt for a score of 16 on the hole. After the hole, reporters wanted to interview him but his only response was, "just say I cut my wrists and bled to death, so I can't talk."

Screenwriter/director Ron Sheldon and his co-writer, John Norville, got the idea to have McCoy be the kind of player who couldn't stand playing it safe when he watched actual PGA golfer, Chip Beck, lay up on the approach at the par 5, fifteenth hole at the Masters in Augusta in 1993.

"When Chip Beck laid up, we immediately called each other and said, 'That's the key to our guy: He won't lay up,'" Sheldon told ESPN.

Costner learned how to play golf for the film by taking lessons from McCord, and Sheldon and Costner both say that he hit a majority of the golf shots in the film. A veritable who's who of mid-'90s golf pros made cameos in the movie, including Phil Mickelson, Craig Stadler, Johnny Miller, Lee Janzen, Corey Pavin, Fred Couples, and Peter Jacobsen. To heighten the reality, the producers worked with the USGA on the courses and the tournament scenes, and enlisted Jim Nantz, Ken Venturi, McCord, and other actual golf announcers to provide play-by-play and commentary for the tournament.

The movie raked in over $75 million and has enjoyed a long life on cable. While *Caddyshack* will always be the most legendary golf movie, and *Happy Gilmore* is the most outrageous (and even rivals *Caddyshack* for most quotable), *Tin Cup* is the best actual golf movie.

The Fan, on the other hand, well . . .

Let's just say it's not overtaking *Major League*, *Field of Dreams*, *Bull Durham*, or *The Sandlot* anytime soon.

TIGER'S FIRST ROAR

WHEN YOUR DAD AND GRANDFATHER WATCHED golf, the golfers all had names like Ian Woosnam, Paul Azinger, and Mark O'Meara. They all looked 45-ish but were really thirty. You tried to pay attention maybe for the last few holes on a Sunday afternoon if it was a Major tournament, but the pace and the patter and the putting were all sooooo dull.

Your dad told you stories about "Arnie's Army" and his rivalry with Jack (always "Jack," never Jack Nicklaus). But Jack hadn't won jack since 1986, and Arnold Palmer's last major win was in 1964, for God's sake.

You'd hear about "great ball striking," and what Lee Trevino could do, and how hard Nick Faldo worked . . . but really, who cared? Not you, because all the golfers seemed to be faceless forty-something dudes who were considered athletes but often sported bellies and couldn't do fifty push-ups if their lives depended on it.

They looked slow.

They played slower.

They were dorks.

Aside from the beer-drinking, chain-smoking, mullet-loving excitement of John Daly's second out-of-nowhere win in '95 (finally a golfer who was interesting), the PGA Tour had about as much personality as a bowl of Grape Nuts. Here is a list of Major Championship Winners in 1995 after Daly: Corey Pavin, Steve Elkington, and Ben Crenshaw. And here are your winners in 1996: Tom Lehman, Steve Jones, Mark Brooks, and Nick Faldo.

Lehman, Jones, and Brooks is a great name for a small-business CPA firm in Omaha, Nebraska, but had no shot of drawing huge ratings in a major American sport.

Golf in the early '90s was a broken planetarium; they had no stars.

They didn't have a single guy that a teen, a college kid, a twenty-something, or a Gen-Xer could relate to or even try to give a shit about. There was nobody to attract new fans and certainly no dominant force to create any kind of buzz. From 1980 on, only two golfers even won back-to-back Majors (Watson and Faldo). And yes, we're ignoring the smaller tournaments because if you can't get big names to win big tournaments, casual fans are never going to watch small names win small tournaments.

Golf needed a savior.

Golf needed someone who was thrilling to watch, who appealed to young people, who showed emotion, who came up clutch, who shouted and pumped his fist and stuck it to all the old-timers.

Golf needed someone like Tiger Woods.

o   o   o

By now you've seen the grainy footage of a two-year-old Tiger Woods scurrying on to the stage of *The Mike Douglas Show* from October of 1978. Woods is wearing a red hat, a white golf shirt with a red collar, and khaki shorts. His feet move cartoon-quick as he exits backstage with his red golf bag (nearly his size) slung behind his back. The studio music plays and the audience claps, and Woods reaches an indoor putting green. Standing on the artificial turf are Bob Hope, Jimmy Stewart, Mike Douglas, and Tiger's dad, Earl. Once they do away with the pleasantries (how old are you, young man?), two-year-old Tiger channels twenty-two-year-old Tiger and pounds a few drives into the deepest part of the stage. A few moments later they suggest a putting contest with Bob Hope, who quips, "you got any money?" It's a funny line in the moment, but the real joke is that within a few short years, Bob Hope and nearly every adult not on the PGA Tour would likely lose to young Tiger in not only putting, but a full round of golf.

At three years old, Tiger broke 50 playing nine holes at the Navy's golf course next to the Joint Forces Training Base in Los Alamitos (shot a 48).

At five years old, standing 4 feet tall and weighing only 48 pounds, he regularly shot in the low 100s from the championship tees.

That same year, 1981, he was featured on the *Today Show* with Bryant Gumbel, when his first coach, Rudy Duran, said, "I think he's one of the best players I've ever played with. He's the equivalent of a touring pro. He's just too small. He's like taking a touring pro and shrinking him down to four feet tall. He has great instinct for timing. His swing is repetitive. He learns so fast that he amazes me."

When Gumbel asked the five-year-old Tiger what he wanted for Christmas, after a little hesitation, he said, "How about a one-iron and a two-iron?"

In 1984, Woods won the Junior World Golf Championships for nine-to-ten-year-olds. He was only eight. He then won the tournament in every age group he could enter and became the youngest US Junior Amateur Champion in 1991 at only fifteen years old.

This was likely the time when you may have started to hear about Tiger, or "this kid Tiger" as your dad may have called him. Amateur golf and college golf were likely not on your radar at this point, so his name popped up when *SportsCenter* would make mention of "another win for the amateur golfer, Tiger Woods" in the early '90s. Then he won three US Amateur Junior Championships in a row and the murmurs began to cross over into the mainstream. Not only was there a potential prodigal son in golf to pick up where Jack left off, but he wasn't a white kid from the suburbs; he was black and Asian and exciting and poised beyond his years. He was also relatable.

In a television feature on Woods when he was fourteen, the B-roll showed him wearing a Lakers hat backwards and playing *Zelda* on NES and having a room that looked like your room.

Except he was Tiger Woods.

"Every time I go to a major country club, I can feel it," Woods said at the time about what his life was like. "You can always sense it. People are staring at you. 'What are you doing here? You shouldn't be here.' When I go to Texas or Florida you always feel it because they say, 'Why are you here? You're not supposed to be here.'"

Some of it was his age, of course, but a good portion of the strained reaction was racism. For nearly the entirety of its existence, golf has been an exclusively white sport played by white people on the PGA Tour with almost 100 percent white competitors. Even the Masters in Augusta, Georgia, golf's hallowed ground, was openly racist. The Masters first played in 1934 but didn't invite a black competitor until 1975. They didn't admit their first black member until 1990, when Tiger was already 16. But the day of reckoning was near—Tiger was coming, and he knew what his potential impact could be.

"Since I'm black it might be even bigger than Jack Nicklaus," Woods said. "I might be even bigger than him, to the Blacks. I might be sort of like a Michael Jordan in basketball. Something like that."

Actually, it would be exactly like that.

In 1994, at TPC at Sawgrass, Woods became the youngest ever to win the US Amateur Championship (not "junior") and he'd knock out two more of those. He played in the Masters as an amateur in '95 and was the only non-pro to make the cut (he finished 41st). He won the 1996 NCAA Individual Golf Championship at Stanford and then, finally, he turned pro with two words that would change the face (literally) of golf, forever.

On August 28, 1996, Tiger Woods addressed the media at the Greater Milwaukee Open with a giant Miller Lite logo on a banner over his right shoulder and the GMO logo over his left. Sporting a classic thin-striped '90s golf shirt with a white t-shirt underneath, Woods took the podium, spread out his remarks in front of him, smirked, and began:

"I guess, hello world," he said, grinning. "Yesterday I confirmed that I had decided to become a professional golfer. I did this because I wanted my final round as an amateur to be in the US Amateur Championship."

As the years have gone by, the only two words people remember are "Hello, world" and the gigantic smile that splashed across Tiger's face, but the press conference lasted twenty minutes. Tiger spoke about how he made the decision, who he talked to about it, and what he'd miss about being an amateur—and I can sum it up for you like this: basically, there were no more amateur asses left to kick and it was high time to kick some Grade A professional golf ass.

Also: money.

In the weeks leading up to his press conference, sports agents were guessing what Tiger Woods would be worth as a spokesperson—most believed he'd get around $6 million for his first year. They weren't close. Tiger signed with International Management Group (IMG), and in short order he signed for double that ($12 million worth of endorsement contracts with Nike and Titleist for 1996).

Alistair Johnson, the head of IMG at the time, once told *Golf Digest*, "Do you know how we got so much for Tiger? Because we asked for it. We knew what he was worth to the right people."

In Tiger's first pro performance at the Greater Milwaukee Open, he shot a 67 in the first round, a 69 in the second round, a 73 in the third, and a 68 in the fourth, good for a tie for 60th place and his first paycheck: $2,544.00.

Some of the pros were thinking, $12 million for 60th place? You've gotta be kidding me!

This isn't to say that Tiger Woods should have won his first tournament; but in the run-up to his signing and his premiere on tour, some pros bristled at having to constantly answer questions about an unproven rookie—especially one who was already making more money off the course than they were.

In his second tournament, the Bell Canadian Open, Tiger finished eleventh. In his third, the Quad Cities Open, at TPC Deere Run in Silvis, Illinois, he tied for fifth, shooting a 64 on Friday and a 67 on Saturday. It was his first top-ten finish, and when his father, Earl, was asked about some of the grumbling by the pros about the attention his son was getting, he famously answered, "All those people who think my son was overpaid will realize one day what a bargain he was."

Point: Earl Woods.

At the B.C. Open a few weeks later, uniquely named after the old B.C. newspaper comic strip,[*] Woods continued his movement up the tour's leaderboard by finishing tied for third place. If you're keeping tabs, through four tournaments Woods racked up a 60th, an 11th, a 5th, and a 3rd place finish, good for a combined purse of $140,194. Not bad.

Then, in October of 1996, he broke through.

---

[*] The mind behind the *B.C.* comic strip, Johnny Hart, was born and raised in Endicott, New York, which was the home of the tournament.

o   o   o

Back in 1996, the Las Vegas Invitational was a five-round, 90-hole tournament/tour of Sin City courses that included stops at TPC Summerlin, Desert Inn, and the Las Vegas Country Club. For a time the tournament had the highest purse on the Tour and was one of the most popular stops because golfers love gambling and gamblers love Vegas. Simple. Of course, Tiger Woods was still only twenty years old in '96; too young to gamble or drink (legally). But he didn't care. He wasn't in town to wash down some 3 a.m. Red Bulls and vodka or to learn the finer points of Pai Gow. He was there to rack up birdies.

In round one, he shot a disappointing 70, putting him eight strokes back of the leader, Keith Fergus. And then he caught fire with a blistering 63 in round two, followed by rounds of 68 and 67 heading into the final eighteen for the tournament. His last pairing was with Fergus, who commented, "This was a perfect course for him. There is no rough and a lot of par fives. You knew it was a place he would do well."

As the final round got underway, the other Tour pros glimpsed the future as they noticed that the gallery ebbed and flowed as Tiger moved throughout the course. It was as if he were the moon, pulling the tide of fans wherever he walked and turning some pros into de facto jealous ex-girlfriends.

Hey! Remember me! I play golf too!

The best way to combat it was with humor.

"There were 40 people trailing me all day long," Davis Love III said. "He [Tiger] took 75 percent of the fans and Fred Couples took 20 percent and I think I got 5 percent and we were in the last group."

Yes, Tiger was a curiosity; but he was also hitting the hell out of the ball.

He started the day four shots off the lead.

He finished it with an eight-under-par 64 that put him at the top of the leaderboard.

While Tiger waited in the clubhouse, Davis Love III decided it might not be time just yet to hand over the entire sport to a twenty-year-old who needed a fake ID to buy a Corona. He drove the green on the fifteenth hole and sank his putt for an eagle. Then he birdied the sixteenth hole to put him in a tie with Woods. All he had to do was birdie either the seventeenth or eighteenth holes and the tournament was his. He put himself in position for birdies on both, but missed both attempts, setting up a playoff.

This pitted Love III, 32, a veteran with 10 PGA Tour victories, including the 1992 Players Championship, against Woods, who had joined the tour just six weeks earlier. The playoff began on the eighteenth hole, which had an island tee box surrounded by desert with a long water hazard along the far-left side of the fairway. Love III drove first and hit a beautiful drive right down the middle of the fairway. Woods, wearing black pants and a white shirt (he hadn't started wearing all red on Sundays yet), chose a three wood and hit it about five yards behind Love III.

Tiger stood about 162 yards from the hole after his drive and on his second shot he hit an easy nine-iron, pin high on the green. The crowd ate it up. Love III's second shot drifted left into the bunker, giving Tiger a fifteen-foot birdie putt for the win. After lining up the putt and making excellent contact, the ball ever so slightly drifted to the right of the hole and ran about a foot past.

Ooooohhhhhhhh.

Davis Love III's shot out of the bunker gave him a ten-foot putt. Since the tournament was match play, Tiger took the opportunity to finish out. He calmly sank his putt for par, putting all the pressure on Love III to sink his shot to tie. While we were a few years away from golfers feeling the immense pressure of the "Tiger Slam" version of Tiger, staring them down as they tried to putt with the whole tournament on the line, Love III let the moment get to him and he pulled his putt about two inches to the left, giving Woods the first PGA Tour victory of his career.

The two players shook hands and hugged as the packed house cheered Woods. About thirty seconds after Love III's missed putt, Tiger was in front of the camera being asked, "Did you ever dream your first championship would happen this fast?"

"Kind of," he said, smiling ear to ear. "But it's really hard to describe the feeling because it's been a hard struggle. Had to fight all the way, got lucky and then won in the end. This is a great feeling, it's all I can say."

To make it official, since it was Vegas, Tiger took a photo, happily holding the tournament's trophy while sandwiched between two casino showgirls. This sure beat sneaking in the back door of the Alpine Inn Beer Garden at Stanford on dime draft night.

"We all knew he was going to win sometime. I just didn't want it to be today," Love III joked.

Butch Harmon, Tiger's coach, took it a step further when asked if he was surprised by his star pupil's win.

"Am I surprised?" he laughed. "I'm surprised it didn't come sooner."

Before the Las Vegas tournament, PGA pros and the golf media were wondering if Woods would keep up his hot streak long enough to earn a full-time Tour card for the following season, but the win gave him an immediate two-year exemption.

So much for that.

Two weeks later, wearing his soon-to-be-standard red Sunday shirt, Tiger captured the second win of his nascent pro career at the Walt Disney World/Oldsmobile Classic, setting up the first photo of Tiger and Tigger together on the course. He then finished the season with a 21st place finish at The Tour Championship, wrapping up a remarkable rookie season (half, really) that included eleven events, ten cuts made, five top-ten finishes, two wins, and $790,000 in prize money.

The performance earned him the honor of being named *Sports Illustrated*'s 1996 Sportsman of the Year, feeding into the media machine and creating a little more resentment from some of his PGA Tour brethren.

The kid hasn't won a major yet and he's sportsman of the year? What the hell?

But whatever grumblings the other pros had, they quickly shut up for two reasons. One, Tiger Woods became a near-unstoppable force on the course, winning the Mercedes Championship in early 1997 followed by his King Kong-like demolition of The Masters, where he shot 18-under for his first green jacket.

Two, he was about to make every single golfer on the Tour a richer man.

Tiger drew a sports media-rattling, seismic-audience shift rating of 14.7 on CBS during the Sunday of his Masters win. His current and potential future viewer-drawing power led to a new television contract that increased PGA Tour purses in one year an astonishing 40 percent. If some of the old-timers weren't on board with the Tiger train in '96, they certainly were in '97 because one thing became clear: Tiger not only played golf; he was golf—a fact that has largely continued to this day through his 11 PGA Player of the Year wins, his 15 Majors, and his 82 PGA Tour total wins. Not to mention the billions of dollars and millions of fans he's attracted to the sport.

"I've thanked him profusely," Phil Mickelson has since said, "not only for what he's done for the tour but for the game of golf."

So have we, Phil. So have we.

JETER & THE
YANKEES REVIVAL

THE MOUNTAINEER JOE HUDSON STOOD ON THE
mound for the Red Sox at the old Yankee Stadium. His 6'2", 175-pound,
spindly frame loomed tall, with his right arm dangling loosely at his side,
waiting for the call from Sox catcher Bill Haselman. His brown hair
matted thick against the back of his neck in the warm September air
in the Bronx. The Sox and Yanks were engaged in one of their typical
back-and-forth, commercial-filled, substitution-packed games that lasted
longer than an actual drive between LaGuardia and Logan.

The Red Sox used sixteen position players.

The Yankees used fourteen.

The Red Sox used seven pitchers.

The Yankees used eight.

It was 6 o'clock at night.

The first pitch had been thrown at 1:05 p.m.

Classic Sox/Yanks.

The game was tied 1–1 after four innings until both starters lost
their control and the runs poured in; 5 for the Red Sox in the top of

the 5th, 3 for the Yanks in the bottom; 2 for the Red Sox in the top of the 6th, 3 for the Yanks in the bottom; then 3 runs apiece in the 7th. Mike "Gator" Greenwell was 2–4 for the Sox with a double. Nomar Garciaparra was 2–5 with two RBIs, including a triple and a stolen base. Even Jose Canseco had a 3-run double for Boston.

Yankees leadoff hitter Tim Raines was solid, going 3–6 with two home runs and 2 RBIs. Paul O'Neill was 4–5 and Cecil Fielder hit a 3-run bomb.

Relief pitcher Hudson was summoned to start the bottom of the 10th after the Sox gave up their 1-run lead in the 8th inning and neither team scored in the 9th. It was the third significant lead Boston had given up that day (they'd been up 6–1 in the 5th and then 11–7 in the 7th). They were 12 games back from the Yankees in the loss column but fighting hard for a Wild Card berth. Every win against New York felt like it counted double in September.

Ex-Red Sox great Wade Boggs got things rolling for the Yankees in the 10th, hitting a single to center off Hudson to open the inning. Ruben Rivera sacrificed Boggs to second and then Cecil Fielder was intentionally walked. Hudson got Tino Martinez to fly to center to give him two outs with men on first and second, after which he walked Bernie Williams to load the bases.

This is where we catch up with Hudson, on the mound, sweating, pitching from the stretch, right arm loose at his side, trying to figure out what pitch to throw against Yankees rookie sensation Derek Jeter.

Jeter was riding a 13-game hitting streak and already had two hits on the night. Hudson was ahead on the count. With one ball and two strikes, he pulled the string on a slider away that hung knee-high just long enough for Jeter to flip his bat out to protect the strike zone. It was part lunge, part swing and the ball caught the end of the bat, dunking it straight up the middle—just out of reach of a diving Nomar Garciaparra and good enough to drive Boggs home from third and win the game.

Yes, Derek Jeter's first career walk-off hit was against the Red Sox right past his main rival Nomar Garciaparra in Yankee Stadium—at once giving birth to the "Jeter Sucks" mantra in Boston and foreshadowing every Sox/Yanks showdown until Game 4 of the 2004 American League Championship Series.

"It was a fifteen round, knock down drag-out fight," Red Sox Manager Kevin Kennedy said of the game. "It's what the big leagues are all about."

Tim Raines said the game felt like it lasted two days with all the substitutions and comebacks and pressure.

"It was almost like winning the World Series," he said. "It would have taken some wind out of our sails to lose that one, after we came back. But now, our sails are still up and we're still going."

The win gave the Yankees an 88–66 record and extended their lead in the American League East to 4½ games over the Baltimore Orioles and to 8 games over the Red Sox. With just over a week left in the season, it also tied the Yankees with the most wins they'd had in a decade. Pre-Jeter, the boys from the Bronx were mired in the longest World Series drought in the franchise's history.

From 1923 to 1964, the Yankees never went more than three years without either appearing in a World Series or winning a World Series. They had a ten-year gap between 1965 and 1975 when they didn't make it to the big dance, but then they lost the '76 World Series, only to win in '77, '78, and '81. By 1990, the team had bottomed out with 67 wins and a full decade without post-season success.

By the summer of 1994, the Yankees had finally turned things around. They owned the best record in the American League and had a balanced team, but on August 12 a player's strike shut down the season, sinking the team's World Series hopes. Once the 1996 season rolled around, the Yankees had gone fourteen years without a World Series appearance and the New York City natives and the Steinbrenners were getting restless. That's why a big win against the hated Sox in late September felt momentous. They'd gone a long time without getting those clutch Ws and that newfound confidence was on Jeter's mind during his at bat.

"It got to a point . . . where it was like, we've got to try to win it right now," Jeter said. "It was great to come back. This team feels like it can always win, regardless of the score."

◘   ◘   ◘

"This is our first-round pick?"

It was 1993 and Andy Pettitte, a husky, left-handed pitcher from San Jacinto Junior College, was working his way through the Yankees minor league system when he came across Derek Jeter—the hot-shit prospect from Kalamazoo, Michigan, who hit .530 in high school, who won the '92 High School Player of the Year Award from the American Baseball Coaches Association, and the Gatorade High School Player of the Year Award.

No way this was THE Derek Jeter.

The kid Pettitte saw was tall and skinny, 6'2" at the time and maybe 160 pounds including his uniform, glove, spikes, batting helmet, and Big League Chew. Also, he couldn't buy a hit. In fewer than 50 games, he batted .202 in his first minor league season in the Gulf Coast. When he reached the Greensboro Hornets of the Class A South Atlantic League, his bat stayed on life support (he hit .247) but his glove was dead. He had 9 errors in his first eleven games with the Hornets and then 56 errors the next season for Greensboro.

Pettitte and his new minor league buddy Jorge Posada—a second baseman recently converted to catcher—were unimpressed. This twig did not look like the future face of the Yankees. He didn't even look like the face of the Hornets.

The Yankees used their sixth pick on this?

If it were up to Houston Astros scout Hal Newhouser, the Yankees would have actually been five picks too late. The Astros had the first pick in the 1992 draft and Newhouser had been on team "Draft Jeter" for years, ever since he'd started driving the three-plus hours from his house in Bluefield Hills, Michigan, to Jeter's high school to watch him play. And Newhouser wasn't just some old scout, chomping on cigars and saying he just had a good feeling about the young kid from Kalamazoo. Newhouser knew what the hell he was talking about. He pitched for seventeen years in the big leagues, mostly for the Detroit Tigers, racking up over 200 wins, 7 all-star appearances, 2 MVP awards, 2 ERA titles, a World Series Championship in 1945, and the cherry on top of the sundae: he was in the Hall of Fame.

Newhouser was the kind of guy whose opinion you listened to when it came to ballplayers, and he had more than an opinion on Jeter; he had a vision.

"That kid is something special."

In Buster Olney's book, *The Last Night of the Yankees Dynasty*, he wrote, "Newhouser was taken by the aura that emanated from the teenager, and strongly lobbied the Astros to draft Jeter. There were initially concerns that Jeter—who had been promised a scholarship at the University of Michigan—would hold out for a signing bonus of $1 million or more, a large sum at that time. 'No one is worth $1 million,' Newhouser told his supervisor. 'But if one kid is worth that, it's this kid.'"

When the Astros passed on Jeter and took Phil Nevin instead, Newhouser was hurt. When the Yankees selected him, he was crushed.

Wrote Olney, "If he [Newhouser] couldn't convince the Astros to take Jeter, he figured, then he could never convince them of anything. The former player who had happily driven hours and sat through cold weather to see baseball quit his job and left the game he loved for good."

Despite Jeter's initial struggles, by 1993, the talent that Newhouser had seen in Jeter as a teenager began to bloom. He hit .295 with 75 RBIs and grabbed 18 stolen bases in his second season with the Hornets. In 1994, he leapfrogged up the entire Yankees minor league system in mere months. Starting on June 24, he went from Class-A Tampa to Double-A Albany to a call up to Triple-A Columbus on August 1. In his first 24 games with Columbus, he hit .329 with 7 stolen bases in 85 at-bats.

"He's stepped in here and handled it real well," Columbus manager Stump Merrill said. "He's fit like an old shoe—like he's been here a long time. We have an outstanding individual on our hands."

By the end of the season, Jeter won the Minor League Player of the Year award from *Baseball America*, as well as the same award from *USA Today* and *The Sporting News*. The following season in 1995 he got called up to the major leagues at the end of May but was sent back down to the minors the second week of June, before being called back up again to finish the season. All told, he was officially on the Yankees roster for 15 games.

"I only played in a few games, but it was good to get a small taste of playing, even if it was only for a couple of weeks," Jeter said, looking back on his first major league "cup of coffee." "When I came back at the end of the season, the Yankees were in a playoff race, and they won the Wild Card on the last day of the season. Just being around that and seeing how everyone went about their business every single day—and how every game was so important—was a great learning experience. Getting an opportunity to be around veteran players like Don Mattingly and Wade Boggs that September and for the intense playoff series against Seattle made it so it wasn't foreign when I was on the field in 1996. It helped me get used to that atmosphere."

Spring training of 1996 was all-systems-go for Jeter to take over as the starting shortstop of the New York Yankees and to rightfully assume the mantle of the team's next Mantle.

The front office was ready.

The coaches were ready.

Jeter was ready.

There was only one problem: Yankees owner George Steinbrenner wasn't ready. Despite all of Jeter's minor league success, "The Boss" wasn't convinced that Jeter was really the team's solution at shortstop, so much so that he almost made a disastrous move.

In an attempt to shore up his roster at what he perceived to be weakness at the shortstop spot, Steinbrenner approved a trade that would have netted Felix Fermin, a career .259 hitter from Seattle. All he had to give up was a young closer by the name of Mariano Rivera.

Brian Cashman, then the Yankees' assistant General Manager, and Gene Michael, the Yankees' Vice President of Scouting at the time, pleaded the case for Steinbrenner to let Jeter be the starting shortstop and to keep Rivera.

"We had long hours of discussions about it, and we told him that Derek was going to have growing pains," Cashman said. "We told him [Steinbrenner] Derek was going to make mistakes and that he shouldn't watch until after the All-Star break."

Bullet dodged.

Joe Torre, in his first season as Yankees manager, penciled Jeter in as the team's starting shortstop for 1996.

o   o   o

The snowman wore a beat-up Indians hat with Chief Wahoo grinning above the bill as flurries fell to the ground. His eyes were made of small dark balls and he had no mouth. His head was shaped more like a pineapple than a snowball and his body listed forward, unevenly, as he appeared to guard the Cleveland Indians dugout.

It was April 1, 1996, at Jacob's Field in Cleveland on what was supposed to be Opening Day against the Indians. Instead, three inches of snow fell by the time the first pitch was supposed to be thrown and the game was postponed to the next day. In total, The Cleve got seven inches of snow in what locals hoped was winter's final haymaker before disappearing for six months.

April 2 was a cold, snowless, sunny day (perfect for baseball by Ohio standards), and the Indians were able to get the season underway. Before the game, Jeter was asked if he had any butterflies. He said, "Maybe in New York I'll be a little nervous, but today I feel good."

Yes, he did. In Game 1 of what could be considered the Derek Jeter Era, the twenty-one-year-old rookie turned on a high fastball from Cleveland's forty-two-year-old Dennis Martinez and smoked a rocket of a home run over the left field wall.

"Oh, he got around on that one. That's gone!" legendary Yankees announcer (and player) Phil Rizzuto said on the famous call. "Holy cow! He got around on that inside pitch. A high fastball and he creamed it!"

Privately, Joe Torre had said that he hoped Jeter could hit .240 or .250 his rookie year and that he'd at least play strong defensively. Though the home run wasn't a sign that the team had a new power hitter on their hands (the most homers Jeter ever hit in a season was 24), it did bode well for his comfort level.

"Because of all the questions about me in Spring training, hitting that home run definitely helped, as opposed to going out and having a bad game," he said in an interview for MLB.com. "The media can sort of hang on to something, and if I got off to a bad start, that would have been it. But yeah, I thought it was big because any time you have any level of success, you use that as a building block for your confidence. So I think I used that, and it just sort of snowballed throughout the course of the season."

Jeter was a steady presence in the line-up all year, hitting in the high .270s for much of the first half of the season before turning it on and batting a lights-out .350 after the All-Star break. His final regular season tallies were a .314 average with 10 home runs, 78 RBIs, and a .430 slugging percentage. He also led the Yankees in hits with 157. Unsurprisingly, he won the American League Rookie of the Year Award, earning all 28 first-place votes, only the fifth time in the history of the award that had happened. To be fair, this wasn't exactly a rookie class chock full of hall of famers . . . or even all-stars. If it was a rap record it could have been titled "Journeyman's Delight," with the second and third place finishers in voting—James Baldwin (7 teams) and Tony Clark (6 teams)—playing on nearly half the teams in baseball during their careers while Jeter played for one.

"I must have had some family members voting," Jeter joked, when hearing about the vote totals. "For me to be voted unanimously is something I can't put into words."

Aside from Jeter's individual performance, the 1996 New York Yankees also won the American League East with 92 wins and earned their first division title since 1981. It was a team top-heavy with former stars from other teams, bottom-heavy with future stars from their own farm system, and medium-heavy with New York Mets. Dwight Gooden, Darryl Strawberry, and David Cone, all former all-stars on the famous '80s Mets teams, were on the roster. Former Red Sox perennial all-star Wade Boggs was on the squad, as was longtime Expos all-star Tim Raines, former Detroit Tigers power hitter Cecil Fielder, and three-time all-star for the Texas Rangers Ruben Sierra. Outfielder Paul O'Neill was an all-star with the Reds before coming to New York. Jimmy Key, a two-time all-star with the Blue Jays and Cy Young Award runner-up in 1985, was on the pitching staff.

The locker room was packed with guys who were cornerstones of their former teams and except for Mariano Duncan, the second base-man, all of the men in the everyday starting line-up either were all-stars (Boggs, Raines, Sierra, O'Neill) or would become all-stars, including Joe Girardi, Tino Martinez, Jeter, and Bernie Williams. On the pitching side, reliever John Wetteland would make three All-Star Games, Andy Pettitte would also make three, and Mariano Rivera would become the greatest closer the game has ever seen.

Jeter was very good, there's no doubt about that; but the team was also, as longtime *Boston Globe* columnist Bob Ryan would say, capital S.T.A.C.K.E.D. This is why there's always been a healthy contingent of baseball writers and fans outside of New York who have felt that the mythology built around Jeter by the media in the Big Apple has forever been slightly overblown.

"Jeter was the luckiest man on the face of the earth," Chad Finn, the *Boston Globe* sports media columnist, says. "He was drafted by the Yankees and got in the ideal situation right away in the biggest market right away. The '96 team was absolutely loaded. And so were the other World Series teams. Jeter always had the most of everything around him. This is not to dismiss what he was as a ballplayer, but he was surrounded by other future hall of famers and a tier of guys who were all-stars or almost all-stars. Fox cameras loved him, he got to be on *Saturday Night Live,* and he could just be the guy who was the face of the team. He made the most of every advantage he had, but he got a little too much credit."

In case you want to dismiss this as expected criticism from a Boston writer, Jeter had a few contemporaries who felt the same way, most notably his future teammate, Alex Rodriguez.

"Jeter was blessed with great talent around him," Rodriguez once said in an *Esquire* interview. "He's never had to lead. He can just go and play and have fun. He hits second—that's totally different than third or fourth in a lineup. You go into New York, you wanna stop Bernie and O'Neill. You never say, 'Don't let Derek beat you.' He's never your concern."

Oooof.

This comment would cause some strain when Rodriguez joined the Yankees in 2004. But in 1996, resentment from other players and calls of "overrated" from the media or fans were in the future. At the time, Jeter was just a twenty-two-year-old kid headed to his first postseason with a Yankees team hell bent on ending their World Series drought. And Jeter wanted all the smoke.

He hit .412 in the Division Series against the Rangers, including a mad dash from second base to home plate on an error to score the winning run in Game 2. He followed that up by batting .417 in the American League Championship Series against the Baltimore Orioles, a best-of-seven series the Yankees won in five games. In Game 1, Jeter hit a game-tying (but highly controversial) home run in the 8th inning and the Yankees would eventually win in the 11th.[*] The Yankees scored 19 runs over the final three games and while Jeter was getting on base, Bernie Williams (the MVP of the ALCS), Cecil Fielder, and Darryl Strawberry combined for 8 home runs and over a dozen RBIs to rack up runs and help clinch the series.

And now, after earning the team's first trip to the World Series in fifteen years, what do we have for them, Johnny? A buzz saw! Yes, Johnny! After beating the Texas Rangers and Baltimore Orioles, the Yankees get to face the defending 1995 World Series Champions, featuring a generationally great pitching staff with Greg Maddux, Tom Glavine, and John Smoltz who combined for 7 career Cy Young Awards!!! As a bonus, the Braves offense outscored the St. Louis Cardinals in the last three games of the '96 NLCS 32–1!!!

The storyline leading into the World Series was that the defending champion Atlanta Braves were a forest fire about to burn up baseball for the rest of the millennium. This was their fourth World Series appearance in six years. They had a pitching staff that looked like a future Hall of Fame ballot and a roster of talented hitters like Chipper

---

[*] This was the home run when twelve-year-old Jeffrey Maier reached out of the stands to grab Jeter's ball before the Orioles' right fielder, Tony Tarasco, could get it. The play was not a home run, but because it was Jeter, it was called a home run. Just kidding, but looking back, many people feel that was the beginning of the "Jeter gets lucky" vibe.

Jones, Ryan Klesko, and Fred McGriff to pound in runs. There was a feeling that the Braves, behind manager Bobby Cox, might be positioned to be the team of the end of the 20th century and the team of the beginning of the 21st.

"A lot of us were here for the 100-loss season and losing two World Series," pitcher Tom Glavine said. "That taste of losing is still very fresh in our mouths. Winning one championship hasn't been enough to erase the pain of losing. We have a pride in what we do. People have asked if winning championships ever become blasé. I hope I win enough of them to find out."

The Yankees maintained a posture that they weren't impressed. Particularly their young rookie from Kalamazoo, who had this to say when asked if his team was "in awe" of what the Braves had done.

"No, because we weren't playing them," Jeter said. "They're playing us now. They can beat up on the Cardinals all they want."

Through the first two games of the World Series, it didn't matter who the Braves were playing. They weren't losing.

They won Game 1 by a score of 12–1 and Game 2, 4–0.

That meant they'd won their last five games in the NLCS and World Series by a combined score of 48–3. The pitching was unhittable. The hitting was unstoppable. And worse for the Yankees, they'd been blown out and embarrassed at home in those first two games. With both teams heading down to Atlanta-Fulton County Stadium for games three through five, Braves fans expected to have the Series wrapped up in a couple of days. Printers in Georgia began designing their "Back-to-Back Champions" logos to emblazon on t-shirts throughout the state. The dynasty Atlanta fans had been dreaming about had arrived.

Then . . .

The Braves lost Game 3, 5–2.

No big deal, just a hiccup.

The Braves lost Game 4 in 10 innings, 8–6.

Okay, okay, easy now . . . We just need to settle down and close things out tomorrow night.

Game 5 was a rematch of the Game 1 starters, Andy Pettitte for New York and John Smoltz for Atlanta. Unlike all of the previous games in the Series, this was mano-a-mano, pitcher-versus-pitcher faceoff between Pettitte, playing in his first World Series, and Smoltz, who was 6–0 as a Fall Classic starter so far. Pettitte pitched brilliantly, allowing no runs through the 8th. Smoltz pitched masterfully as well, but allowed 1 run.

The Yankees won, 1–0, and against all odds and momentum, were headed back to Yankee Stadium to either win the World Series at home . . . or lose it. Up three games to two, they had two chances to finish off the mighty Braves.

They'd only need one.

In the third inning of Game 6, Paul O'Neill led off with a double against Maddux and then moved to third after a ground out. A triple by Joe Girardi drove him in and then a single by Jeter drove Girardi in. Jeter then stole second and scored on a single by Bernie Williams.

The 3 runs were all the Yankees needed. Jimmy Key, David Weathers, Graeme Lloyd, Mariano Rivera, and John Wetteland combined to give up only 2 runs and locked in the World Series Championship for the Yankees.

It was Joe Torre's first. It was Pettitte, Rivera, Girardi, Williams, and Jeter's first. It was the dawn of a dynasty that would dominate baseball storylines for the next ten years . . . and would define the future "Captain," Derek Jeter, as well. Jeter's bat cooled off in the Series (he hit only .250), but his defense was solid and he made a few heads-up base running plays, like the stolen base in Game 6.

Looking back on his 1996 season years later, Jeter said, "Everything that I could possibly have imagined happening in my first year happened for me. I can't look back and say, 'Well, I wish this or that happened,' because absolutely everything did happen. It was the perfect picture. There's no other way I would have wanted it to go."

25

THE ROCK

THIRD AND TWELVE ON THEIR OWN 42-YARD LINE,
and West Virginia Quarterback Darren Studstill is trying to call a play
over the roaring, sweat-soaked Orange Bowl crowd in a battle against
the Miami Hurricanes. He takes the snap on the left hash mark and
immediately sprints to his right. Out of the corner of his eye he spots
one of his mammoth O-linemen tangling with a 275-pound bear of a
man, #94 on the Hurricanes. As Studstill reaches the numbers on the
right side of the field, in the scrum, he spots his lineman ripping the
helmet clear off of #94's head!

Just as two defenders collapse on him, he flicks a short pass to an
open receiver about 10 yards downfield. The cornerback, safety, and
middle linebacker converge ahead of the receiver, but from behind, out
of nowhere, a giant lunatic sprints toward the play.

Is that the dude who got his helmet ripped off?

Yes, yes it is.

And he's now barreling toward the receiver, gunning for a tackle even
if it means splitting his skull open. As he closes, the receiver dips down

and the helmetless wonder actually dives at the guy and (luckily) misses him, clearing two of his own teammates and crashing to the ground.

Only after the play is over and he gets up off the ground does Dwayne Johnson look around and think, "I should put my helmet back on."

That's how immersed in football Johnson (Dewey, to his Miami teammates) was. It was his first love, and will be his last. He chose Miami for the swagger, to win championships, and because it was a virtual conveyer belt to get to the NFL. Ed Orgeron, the National Championship-winning coach at Louisiana State University, originally hooked Johnson on the idea of playing for Miami.

"He was a highly recruited kid," Orgeron told ESPN. "We were excited to have him, he came to us ahead of his time. He was developed and extremely quick. He was a hard worker and a humble young man."

Kevin Patrick, a Hurricane teammate and defensive end, said, "At that time in college football I don't think there was any doubt the University of Miami was at the top of their game. If you were on that team and a scholarship player, you were highly recognized. You look at those rosters that Dewey was a part of, they were loaded with talent and he was competitive. I can remember one of the first times he was on campus, it was an official visit. Our D-line coach [Orgeron], who was recruiting him, he was very proud, and he says, 'Look at my new dog.' And you look over and there's this yoked-up kid with muscles everywhere walking around on the field. He got everyone's attention. He was a physical specimen from day 1."

If you'd have asked a twenty-year-old Johnson what his dream was, he'd have said, "I want to play in the NFL and win a Super Bowl with the New York Giants."

Considering that he was playing heavy minutes at "The U" as a freshman on a National Championship-winning team, and that dozens of his teammates were destined to play in the League, his dream wasn't far-fetched. After '91, there was no reason to think that as he got better, he wouldn't climb the depth chart or start for a few years and then—bang, on to the NFL Draft.

There were only two things he wasn't counting on: injuries, which no player can anticipate, and the arrival on campus of a young man who was cockier, stronger, and better at football—Warren Sapp.

"I went down and sat in the D-lineman room," Sapp said in a *Bleacher Report* story about his arrival on campus. "And Dewey walks in and says, 'What are you doing here?' I looked at him and said, 'I'm here for your job, bitch.'"

Johnson summed up how things turned out in a radio interview on *The Dan Patrick Show*. "Like [a] true defensive lineman would do, full of ego, especially down at Miami because we all talked trash, I said, 'Well, you ain't takin' my spot,'" Johnson explained. "Then about six months later he took my spot."

Johnson never won it back. After graduating in 1995 he wasn't drafted by a single NFL team, forcing him to keep his pro football hopes alive by signing with the Calgary Stampeders of the Canadian Football League as a linebacker.

He didn't last three months.

"I had the greatest D-lineman in the history of the game playing in front of me," Johnson said years later while being interviewed by Sapp about their Miami days. "People are always asking me if I regret not making it to the NFL because of my injuries at Miami. Let me be clear: it had nothing to do with my injuries. I didn't make it to the NFL because of one man. That's Warren Sapp. Hands down."

On to Plan B.

�‌   ◌   ◌

The part of the legendary Dwayne Johnson mythology that you may have heard is that after living in a roach-infested motel and sleeping on a mattress he pulled out of a dumpster, Johnson was forced to head home, tail between his legs, with just seven bucks in his pocket (hence the name of his now near-nine-figure multi-platform production company, Seven Bucks Productions). The part you likely didn't know is that upon returning home, he asked his dad to train him to be a wrestler—and was originally turned down.

Johnson's father was Rocky "Soulman" Johnson, a former sparring partner to boxing legends like Muhammad Ali and George Foreman who eventually became a wrestling pioneer as half of the tag-team tandem (along with Tony Atlas) to become the first black men to hold a WWE championship. He wrestled Hulk Hogan, Andre the Giant, Ric Flair, and all the legends of his era, securing his own status as a legend along the way. When Dwayne asked to join the family business (Rocky's father-in-law was "High Chief" Peter Maivia, an American-Samoan professional wrestler), Rocky discouraged him because he knew how difficult it was. After some back-and-forth, Rocky relented and agreed to teach his son, under one condition: he was going to train his son harder than any wrestler he'd ever trained.

"I'll train you, but I'll train you 150 percent," Rocky told his son.

And as Rocky told the world later, "I trained him and the rest is history."

It wasn't as though Johnson's desire to wrestle came out of nowhere. Yes, his dream of making it to the NFL had been crushed; but long before he pictured himself standing at the 50-yard line holding up the Lombardi Trophy, he'd pictured himself as a wrestler.

"He grew up in the wrestling business," Rocky said. "When the VCRs first came out with tapes, he'd set up the camera in his bedroom and he'd do interviews. He'd say, 'I'm Hulk Hogan. I'm Rocky Johnson. I'm Jimmy Snuka.' Every night we'd hear a crash and we'd go into the room and he'd be on the dresser doing back flips from the dresser to the bed, breaking the dresser every night."

Good thing he wasn't practicing The Rock character just yet.

"Dad, do you think you could read me a bedtime story?"

"Sure, I—"

"It doesn't matter what you think!"

But we're getting ahead of ourselves.

After months of training and wrestling at carnivals and side matches in barns for as little as $35 per night, Rocky and longtime wrestling trainer Patrick Patterson set Johnson up with a few small-time matches to work his way into the sport. He appeared in an untelevised event under his real name, Dwayne Johnson, in early 1996, beat the Brooklyn Brawler, and then lost a few matches. After that he wrestled under the name Flex Kavana in Jerry Lawler's United States Wrestling Association. During the summer of '96, Johnson (Kavana) won the tag-team championship with Bart Sawyer in the United States Wrestling Association. After that, he stepped fully into his father's footsteps and signed a WWE contract.

Vince McMahon planned to introduce Johnson as "The Blue Chipper" because of his family lineage in the sport. To further capitalize on the idea, McMahon talked Johnson into combining the names of his father (Rocky Johnson) and his grandfather (Peter Maivia) to form his ring name, Rocky Maivia. Johnson was reluctant, but decided to roll with it.

Typically, wrestlers debuted in the WWE at small venues or after live tapings or at house events, but Johnson's first match (as Maivia) was in the blockbuster pay-per-view event, Survivor Series—at Madison Square Garden. So much for splashing around in the kiddie pool before being allowed in the deep end of the business.

Also, this Maivia character was a far, far, far, far cry from The Rock persona that would one day take over the WWE.

No eyebrow raising.

No sunglasses.

No dagger sideburns or black wrestling gear.

Rocky Maivia came out in an outfit that was supposed to be a nod to his Samoan background but actually looked like an arts and crafts project from a kid's preschool. He wore what can only be described as a giant checkered collar with what look to be plastic white leaves dangling from the edges, interspersed with blue and green and aqua flag-football-type strips of fabric. He had blue elbow pads on each arm and bright blue wrestling shorts. To top off the look he had a curly mop of hair on his head that Johnson, watching the entrance twenty years later, called "a fucking chia pet on my head as a haircut."

Despite the goofy get-up, Maivia found himself as the lone baby face in the ring against two heels, Crush and Goldust. While he stood, two-on-one, in the center of the ring, the 22,000 fans at MSG spontaneously began chanting, "Rocky! Rocky! Rocky!" After being duped into a fake "test of strength" with Crush, where he took a boot to the ribs after locking hands, Maivia pinned Crush, then finished off Goldust with a shoulder breaker bang, winning his first ever match in a huge WWE Pay-Per-View.

The rocket-like ascent was on.

Within a few short months he won the Intercontinental Championship from Triple H and appeared in WrestleMania, but his character and the speed of his success wasn't tracking with fans. The Miz, who claims The Rock as his all-time favorite wrestler and inspiration, had a good idea about why Maivia wasn't hitting the mark at the time.

"When you look at Rocky Maivia, as a fan, it was very cheesy," The Miz says. "The big smile. The hair flapping. You could just tell they were forcing it. They were saying that this was a guy you need to cheer for and it was being shoved in your face. And it wasn't who Dwayne Johnson was. This was an idea from the '80s but by 1996 it was a different period. People wanted things that were more real. MTV's *The Real World* was popular. Jerry Springer was popular. Reality-based shows were coming to fruition. Rocky Maivia wasn't real to people."

It wasn't real to Johnson either, and it showed in his wrestling and in his promos—where he'd regularly get dissed and destroyed in the land of putdowns and mic drops by wrestlers playing characters truer to their nature.

"Rocky would follow the script, but his opponent would go off the script and eat him up," Bruce Prichard, a former manager and writer for the WWF, recalls. "I told him, 'Look, you're getting your ass chewed out right now. The show is live. If you're confident that you can improvise and match him, go for it.'"

By April of the following year, Johnson was regularly hearing chants of "You suck!" from fans. Following a loss to Owen Hart and an injury, when Johnson returned at the end of the summer, he made one of the most important heel turns in WWE's history. He joined the Nation of Domination, embraced the audience hate, began talking shit back, and started to refer to himself as "The Rock," going so far as to pretend the Maivia name didn't exist. Then came the notorious insults and humor and good old-fashioned University of Miami swagger and the catchphrases.

Know your role . . . and shut your mouth!

It doesn't matter what you think!

The Rock says . . .

Finaaaallyyyyyyy . . .

If you smeeeellllllllllll!!! What the Rock! Is! Cooking . . .

Let's also not forget *jabroni*, which was officially added to the dictionary by dictionary.com in 2020 with this definition:

Jabroni (a noun) is slang for "a stupid, foolish, or contemptible person; loser."

"When I was in high school, every Monday we'd race home to watch *Raw* at my house," The Miz says. "We'd be ten-deep in my living room and we'd go absolutely nuts when the superstars came out. It was entertaining. It was captivating. The Rock is my favorite, bar none. He had the whole package. This guy could make you laugh and he could make you believe. You believed in everything he was saying and everything he was doing. If he said he was going after something you believed he was going to get it. I think he and Stone Cold needed each other. They had so many entertaining matches. Those were the big names: Austin vs. Rock. Years later, when I was at WrestleMania, standing where my heroes stood, in front of 90,000 people, I was with those same ten friends, and I looked at them and said, 'We made it.' All because The Rock made me want to be a WWE Superstar."

In an Instagram post on the set of his show, *Ballers*, Johnson wrote about his career path from wannabe NFL player to iconic wrestler to actor and reflected on how his original dream had to die to give his new dreams life.

"It's been quite humbling shooting these scenes amongst NFL teams because for years my #1 real life goal was to play in the NFL," he wrote. "I failed and that dream never came true. But over the years I realized that playing in the NFL was the best thing that never happened for me because after I failed (and after a fun battle with depression) it created a relentless drive that defines who I am today."

And none of it would have happened if Warren Sapp had chosen the University of Florida.

IRON MIKE
PUNCHES OUT

"HURRICANE" PETER MCNEELEY WAS A CROSS between a beefy Happy Gilmore and an East Coast, UMass frat guy version of Jose Canseco. He looked like he could have been a rock breaker on Chuckie's construction crew in *Good Will Hunting*. Or a guy who worked overnight in the warehouse at the old Spag's in Shrewsbury.

What he didn't look like was a man who would knock out Mike Tyson in three rounds, as he'd predicted—even a version of Mike Tyson who hadn't fought in four years due to being in prison on charges of rape.* Even a version of Mike Tyson who was 43 fights deep into his career and was almost thirty. Even a version of Mike Tyson who nobody even saw spar before the fight.

We did, however, hear stories like this one, from his trainer, Rory Holloway.

"I'll tell you when I knew he was a back," Holloway said. "About two weeks into training, he used a big sparring partner. I forget the guy's

---

* McNeeley (or someone on his team) came up with the Tyson nickname, Rusty Mike, as a play on Iron Mike and the fact that he hadn't boxed in a long time.

name, but he was big, about 6'5", 240, 250. He came into the gym and it was clear he had absolutely no respect for Mike Tyson. Well, Mike went after him, and he needed about six or seven stitches in about thirty seconds."

Thirty seconds was an eternity in the boxing ring and many thought McNeeley might not last that long. After all, less than a year before agreeing to square off with Tyson at the MGM Grand Garden Arena in Las Vegas in a fight that would gross more than $96 million around the world (including a record-breaking $63 million in pay-per-view from 1.5 million homes), McNeeley had fought in boxing hotbed Hot Springs, Arkansas, for a clean $190.

Now, on August 19, 1995, he was earning $700,000 for the right to be the first man to face Tyson after his jail sentence. Tyson was a 20–1 favorite with 4–5 odds that McNeeley wouldn't make it out of the first round. When asked what a white Irish heavyweight champion would look like if McNeeley managed to win and keep winning, Don King replied in rhymes as only he could.

"Let your imagination soar because the machines would roar!" he yelled. "Only the internet could handle it. That bet would be too small to call because it would be too big to pay! You're talking about hitting the lottery."

When the lights came on and the fighters were introduced to the crowd, McNeeley looked about as confident as the goat they lowered into the raptor paddock in *Jurassic Park*. He was glistening with sweat, wearing green-and-white-striped shorts and wrapping his gums around a half-green, half-white mouthpiece that looked to be too large. At the pre-fight stare-down in the center of the ring, McNeeley bounced back and forth nervously, while Tyson worked his jaw back and forth, following McNeeley with eyes that looked deadly enough to be registered weapons. Tyson, as always, was in black trunks and black shoes.

When the bell rang, McNeeley bull-rushed Tyson, wildly throwing punches and flailing at him, and after a missed baby hook, Tyson dropped him with a clean right. The fight had been going for about ten seconds. McNeeley instantly bounced up and jogged around the ring, hopped up on adrenaline and foolishness. At about the ninety-second mark, Tyson knocked him down again with an uppercut. This time, the brawler from Boston didn't hop up. He stumbled to his feet with shocked eyes, and his corner had seen enough. They stopped the fight.

McNeeley earned $350,000 per minute of the match.

◘   ◘   ◘

With the "first fight after prison" out of the way, the Mike Tyson comeback tour was about to proceed at warp speed. The goals: the heavyweight belt and gobs of money. The time frame: ASAP. While in prison, he'd missed nearly four full years of his prime as a fighter and earner, and Team Tyson was in catch-up mode. As the years have passed, the timeline has gotten murky. It *feels like* Tyson lost his historic upset to Buster Douglas and then went right to prison, but that wasn't the case. He actually crammed four fights into the window following his loss to Douglas and his incarceration. He beat Henry Tillman in a first-round knockout and then Alex Stewart in a first-round TKO. He then fought Donovan "Razor" Ruddock twice, a mere ninety days apart, winning by TKO in the first fight and by unanimous decision in his second fight.

Then he went to jail.

He was only twenty-five years old.

"Mike Tyson was the face of the heavyweight division," former heavyweight pro boxer, now author, Ed Latimore says. "Whether Tyson was as good as the general public believed, at the end of the day, he was good enough to match the persona that they had built. He was like Allen Iverson in a way. The commonality is street swagger. And there was the video game effect that I don't know if we'll see again. He was great for the popularity of the sport."

To that point, prior to his loss to Douglas, Tyson was 37–0 and the most feared and famous fighter since Muhammad Ali. He was devastating; a destroyer who seemed to truly instill fear in other giant grown men paid to beat on people with their fists. This made him the sport's biggest draw, by far. The purse for his two fights with Razor Ruddock added up to $65 million. The goal now that he was free was to get back to those paydays immediately. To do that, he needed to work his way up from tomato cans like McNeeley to real fighters with actual belts.

A couple of days after squashing the Hurricane, Don King announced that fight number two on Tyson's road to boxing redemption was against Buster Mathis Jr. in mid-December of '95. Mathis Jr. was a 5'11" fire hydrant of a man from Michigan who had almost no name recognition outside of boxing but was 20–0 and held the IBF USBA Heavyweight Title. Unlike the whirling, shot-out-of-a-canon approach McNeeley used to start his fight, Mathis Jr. went with a bobbing and weaving strategy where he bodied Tyson from the opening bell. He clinched him and leaned on him and tried to slip his punches and fight him in a phone booth to keep Iron Mike's punching power at bay.

It worked—briefly. For the first two rounds, Mathis Jr. spent much of his time bent into Tyson, like an oak tree leaning against a brick wall. He had his head and shoulders pressing against Tyson and when he'd get some space, he tried to slide in some quick uppercuts. About two minutes into the third round, Tyson landed his own short uppercut and stunned Mathis, who barely stayed on his feet. A moment later, as they clinched, at the exact moment that Mathis tried to tilt his frame forward and lean into Tyson with his head and shoulders, Tyson skip-stepped to his left and unloaded a grenade of an uppercut that landed square on Mathis's face. As he reeled, Tyson popped him again, sending him to the canvas.

Fight over.

"I expected him to smother me and I'm very familiar with that style of fighting," Tyson said afterward. "I'm the best at that style of fighting. I knew every move he was making. When I did a couple particular moves, he was stunned and didn't expect it. I knew my punches were going to knock him out or hurt him severely because he didn't see the punches coming."

○   ○   ○

The first time Mike Tyson and the pride of England—6'4", 224-pound Frank Bruno—faced off in 1988, it was for the undisputed heavyweight championship of the world. Bruno was 32–2 and at one time had a streak of 21 straight wins by knockout. His punches landed like bazookas and between his 3½" height advantage, his 10-pound weight advantage, and his 11" reach advantage, many fight experts thought Tyson's run of 35 wins could come to an end. At the opening bell, announcer Bob Sheridan made this comparison between the two fighters: "Some say he [Tyson] has the same disadvantage as a lion going against a zebra. And I'd have to agree."

Ten seconds into the fight, Tyson caught Bruno with a right hand that knocked him down to one knee (with a slight assist from a slip on the canvas). Later in the round, Bruno connected with a left hook that wobbled Tyson. It didn't do any lasting damage, but it was significant because it was one of the first times most fans of Iron Mike had seen him catch a punch that hard. He survived until the end of the round and then dominated most of the fight. With a minute left in the fifth round, Tyson was in hunter killer mode, pummeling Bruno.

Hook. Jab. Uppercut. Hook. Hook. Jab. Jab. Right. Right. Right. Left.

Once he got the big man up against the ropes, he teed off on him like he was a slab of meat and the referee had to dive in to stop the fight.

By the time they met up again seven years later, on March 16, 1996, Bruno was thirty-five years old and held the WBC championship belt. He was now a full 27 pounds heavier than Tyson, built like a bodybuilder, and he still hit like a bulldozer. The fight was billed as Tyson vs. Bruno II, and most felt it was the first test of Tyson's post-prison fighting skills. As the main draw, Tyson was guaranteed $30 million and Bruno was guaranteed $6 million—which pissed him off because he was, after all, the fighter with the belt.

"He's getting five times what I am. It hurts a little bit . . . But any way he wants to fight, we'll fight. If he wants a rough fight, we'll fight rough. If he wants to box, we'll box. If he wants to dance, we'll dance... It's the end of Mike Tyson. I'm going to do him a favor. I'm going to wipe him out. He can go on to do other things outside of boxing."

Sure, Frankie. Sure.

"Frank Bruno is the most popular man in England," Don King countered. "But Mike Tyson is the most popular man in the world."

The fight started fast, with Tyson ducking a series of Bruno's punches that were lumbering and deadly but had clearly lost some of the snap since their last fight. After that, the fight was 100 percent Tyson, who attacked like a pit bull off a leash. All Bruno could do was grab hold of his head and shoulders and try to delay the inevitable. In the first minute of round three, Tyson released a barrage of punches on Bruno, hammering him with uppercuts and a lethal combination of back-to-back-to-back hooks from either side.

Pop! Pop! Pop! Pop!

Bruno was out on his feet.

Referee Mills Lane stopped the fight.

"I threw punches in bunches because I knew Bruno couldn't stand up to my power," Tyson said. "I was going for the knockout from the first round. I'm not all the way back, but I'm getting there."

Tyson raised both arms out wide, soaking in the cheers, before dropping to his knees and kneeling on the mat, grateful to once again be a champion of the world. There was a who's who of '90s celebrities in attendance to witness the triumph: George Clooney, Kevin Costner, Jim Carrey, Eddie Murphy, Jack Nicholson, Roseanne, Boyz II Men, Snoop Dogg, and dozens of others. No other fighter of his generation came close to bringing out the stars that Tyson was able to draw. The only question was who he'd pound on next.

"I'll fight whoever Don King puts in front of me," Tyson said afterward.

◘   ◘   ◘

Now we'll really see.

Peter McNeeley was a heavy bag with a pulse.

Buster Mathis Jr. was a lifetime undercard guy.

Frank Bruno was slow and past his prime.

But Bruce Seldon? He was considered legit.

"If he gets by Bruno," boxing Hall of Fame trainer Emanuel Steward said before the Bruno fight, "Tyson won't beat Bruce Seldon."

Seldon, known as The Atlantic City Express, was a hard puncher who started his boxing career with 18 straight victories. He won the WBA title in April of 1995 against Tony Tucker, after the referee stopped the fight in the seventh round because Tucker's eye was swollen shut and Mickey wasn't there to cut him. He had one title defense against "The Boss," Joe Hipp, the first Native American to get a shot at becoming a world champ. Seldon won by TKO in the tenth.

After a behind-the-scenes contractual brawl between HBO, who owned the pay-per-view rights to Lennox Lewis and Riddick Bowe's fights, and Showtime, who owned the rights to Tyson's fights, and the WBC, who had the rights to their belt but no say in who Tyson would fight next, Lennox Lewis was paid $4 million to NOT fight Tyson, so that Tyson could go after the WBA belt that Seldon had and then relinquish his WBC belt.

Yes, boxing's pay-per-view and belt structure has always been as confusing as common core math to those of us who grew up in the '90s, but the reasoning behind this particular gambit by King and Tyson was to unify two of the three main belts, the IBF and the WBA. The only way to do that was to dump the WBC belt after winning the WBA belt against Seldon.

Once Tyson had the WBA belt, he could put it on the line against Evander Holyfield and if he beat Holyfield, he'd have earned his title shot at Michael Moorer, who held the IBF belt. This was boxing in 1996—and to some extent today.

In summation: Tyson has the WBC belt. He wants the WBA and IBF but he can't get it by fighting the WBC guys lined up due to contractual problems. So, he needs to beat a WBA guy, drop the WBC belt, and then go after the IBF to unify two of the three belts.

Got it? Great. There will be a test at the end of this book.

The end result of all this Westeros-level maneuvering is that Tyson agreed to fight Bruce Seldon on September 7, 1996, having already signed a contract in advance to fight Evander Holyfield on November 9. That meant Tyson was on a breakneck pace to fight three times in eight months during '96, including an absurdly small two months between a Seldon and Holyfield fight (assuming he won the former).

"Tyson's people know I'm the only guy who doesn't fear him," Holyfield said before watching the Seldon fight. "In the game of boxing you know you're going to get hit hard and you've seen him hit hard, too. The point is how hard? When he gets hit hard on the chin, it'll affect him the same way it'll affect you. He'll fall just like you may fall. And the chance of him getting up is slim because he's not the kind of person who gets up a lot."

This was what we'll call pre-pre-fight smack talk at its best since Holyfield, at the moment, was about to be a spectator at the MGM like every other fight fan for the night. More than that, he was rooting for Tyson so he could get his monster payday and continue his own ascent back to the top of the sport.

But first, Seldon, who entered the fight against Tyson as a 12–1 underdog.

In the time it's taken you to read the last page and a half, Tyson dispensed of Seldon (who Tyson's camp purposely referred to as "Sheldon" throughout their training).

One minute into the fight, Tyson tagged Seldon with a quick lead hook to the top of the head that brought him to his knees. Ten seconds later, Tyson jammed him with a straight left to the chin and The Atlantic City Express flopped face first onto the canvas. When he stood up, his eyes were glazed, he wobbled, and then he fell back onto the ropes.

Fight over.

There were rumors of a "fix" because the fight lasted less than two minutes and the shots Seldon took didn't appear to be knockout punches; but unlike any counter punches in the fight, Seldon countered the accusations of a fix immediately.

"I came to fight, I came to win," he said. "I did not realize how hard he hits, or how fast he is. He is a destroyer, and I am witness to that. The shot rattled my eyes. And I couldn't see straight."

Maybe. Maybe not. Seldon was certainly dazed, but there was clearly no "fight" in the fighter. After an initial straight to the head in the opening seconds of the fight, Seldon's strategy seemed to boil down to get me the hell out of here. And why not? He made $5 million for ninety seconds of work and then retired afterward.

"I'm punching pretty hard these days," Tyson said. "My mode of operation, once I get a man hurt, is reckless abandon."

The fight was over so quickly and demanded so little effort from Tyson that it was basically a sparring session for his upcoming fight against Holyfield, who he'd already turned his rage and his gaze to at the post-fight media conference.

"You've got something coming, man," Tyson said to Holyfield. "I'm going to like this. I'm going to have a good time this fight."

He was four-for-four with four knockouts since leaving prison and had regained his spot as the most compelling fighter in the world.

"He had a magnetism for being naturally weird," Latimore says. "You could study marketing your whole life and not come up with it. But when you see it, you go, okay, that's perfect. Add in the crazy things he said and his look and you have that lightning in a bottle. Tyson had it."

o   o   o

Evander "The Real Deal" Holyfield was a fighter's fighter. He was tall, thick, and quick. He could go toe-to-toe with any heavyweight in size and strength, but he had the tactical skills and counterpunching ability of a fighter from a lower weight class. This is likely because when Holyfield graduated high school, his nickname could have been "The Real Small Deal." Holyfield says he was 5'8" and 147 pounds when he got his diploma. By the time he turned pro as a Cruiserweight, he'd leveled up to grown-man status, gaining over 4" in height and over fifty pounds in muscle.

In 1988, he defeated Carlos De Leon to go 18–0 and become the first Lineal and WBC champion in that division. Following the fight, he was done screwing around with dudes under 200 pounds. It was time to go whale hunting in the heavyweight division and his Moby Dick was none other than Mike Tyson.

Tyson and Holyfield had known each other since they were teenagers. They trained for the 1984 Los Angeles Summer Olympics together and had been trying to fight each other since 1990. In fact, Tyson had originally planned to use his fight against Buster Douglas as a tune-up for a scheduled fight with Holyfield later that year, but instead, he got tuned up and the plans had to change.

Instead of Tyson fighting Holyfield, the Real Deal fought Buster Douglas in his first title defense and knocked him out in the third round to become the WBA, WBC, and IBF heavyweight champion. Tyson, meanwhile, fought Razor Ruddock, with the idea that after that fight, he'd take on Holyfield; but once again, the fight itself got in the way. Tyson won the bout, but the ending was controversial and triggered an immediate rematch, so the face-off with Holyfield got pushed back.

Again.

After Tyson beat Ruddock a second time, he signed a contract to fight Holyfield on November 18, 1991, but an injury and his conviction on a rape charge wiped that off the books.

Prison. Injuries. Contract clauses. Fight results. It seemed for a long time that the gravity of the twisted boxing universe (and the seriousness of Tyson's legal troubles) was pulling the two fighters apart in their primes. That's why when the fight in 1996 was scheduled, and Tyson actually beat Bruce Seldon, the poster and the theme for the fight conveyed comedy and relief. It simply said: Finally.

The opening odds placed Holyfield as a 25–1 underdog, but by the time fight night arrived, the number shrank down to 5–1. Though many inside boxing still heavily favored Tyson, the public money was coming in heavy on Holyfield.

"There was very little Tyson money," Rob Terry, a race and sports book director, said. "It was actually typical for one of his fights. It's tough for our customers to lay the big lumber on such short odds. They'd rather take a shot at the big odds."

Buster Douglas, who beat Tyson in the most famous boxing upset of modern times—and then got pasted by Holyfield—thought the fight would be close.

"I think it's a tossup," he said. "Both guys are very competitive, so it's a matter of who gets into the flow of the fight the quickest. Mike is the stronger of the two and he throws a great deal more power shots, but Holyfield has power as well. I think Holyfield is underrated in that regard. I think Evander is going to surprise a lot of people."

Everyone could agree that Holyfield had a slight edge over previous opponents who faced Tyson in that his familiarity bred a lack of fear. There would be no "intimidation factor" when it came to Holyfield. He wasn't scared, which seemed to be half the battle against Iron Mike.

"You can't win if you don't hit the guy," Holyfield said. "Everybody knows I'll be trying to hit Mike Tyson. A bully is not used to somebody smashing them. They're not used to feeling something everybody else feels."

Thwaaack!

Bullying or not, less than three seconds after the opening bell of the fight, Holyfield felt Tyson's right fist smash clean into the side of his face and it sent him staggering. For a flutter of a moment, it looked like Tyson might end this fight faster than his microwave popcorn-length Bruce Seldon fight. But Holyfield was a gamer. He balanced against the ropes in his satin purple shorts, clinched Tyson a few times, gathered himself, and soldiered on.

Tyson threw bombs the whole first round, but Holyfield stayed close, leaned in, and countered every chance he got. His wide back and shoulders seemed to help him absorb the blows and when the bell rang to end the first round, he tagged Tyson with a quick left hook after they were separated.

In the second round, Holyfield landed several punishing head shots that slowed Tyson, jamming him against the ropes toward the end of the round as he pounded away. With six minutes gone in the fight, both men realized they weren't scoring a quick knockout and the pace slowed as they settled in for a long, punishing haul. Holyfield was the aggressor in round three. In round four, Tyson looked like the Iron Mike of old, unleashing brutal combinations that Holyfield couldn't keep up with.

Right uppercut to the body.

Left hook to the chin.

Right hook. Right hook. Right hook.

Uppercut. Uppercut. Uppercut.

With one minute and thirty seconds left in the fifth, Tyson popped Holyfield with a short left hook square on the nose and you could hear the squish/smash sound in the upper deck. It was the kind of punch (after a previous barrage of punches) that typically laid out Tyson's opponents, but Holyfield took it, along with a hard right hand that still didn't knock him down.

Holyfield either countered or leaned into Tyson and when he leaned into him, he continuously pressed his forehead into Tyson. The crowd was heavily in Holyfield's favor and the more Tyson pressed, the quieter it got. It was so quiet that you could hear the referee continually tell Holyfield to "watch the head." As it turned out, the Real Deal was dealing mini head butts to Tyson and eventually got a warning after "accidentally" cutting him with one in the sixth round. A minute after the warning for the head butt, Holyfield blasted Tyson with a low blow that wasn't called. The nut shot sparked the crowd and the chants emboldened Holyfield to swing more. At the fifty-second mark in the fifth, with Tyson bleeding from the head butt and wincing from the punch to the family jewels, Holyfield connected on a left hook and put Tyson on his ass for the first time in a long time.

Tyson survived and continued to complain about the cheap shots and head butts. At the end of round seven, Holyfield dropped all pretenses about hiding his dome shots and as Tyson pressed forward for a punch, he ducked his forehead directly into Tyson's face, causing Tyson to scream, wobble, and bleed.

For Holyfield fans, he was doing what needed to be done.

For Tyson fans, Holyfield was fighting dirty.

Either way, Holyfield was ahead on points as the fight moved into the final rounds and Tyson was visibly pissed off. He was frustrated that his powder keg punches weren't blowing Holyfield up and that he was getting hit with Holyfield's head as much as his fists. By round nine, both fighters were sucking wind, but with Holyfield ahead on the cards, Tyson looked to land a kill shot and he got sloppy. Toward the end of the tenth, he tried to land a haymaker. When he missed, Holyfield cracked him and stunned him. Sensing he had an opening, Holyfield pounced and unloaded a series of straights and finishing punches that put Tyson on skates and sent him into the ropes. He somehow stayed on his feet while Holyfield emptied his clip, landing clean blow after clean blow to Tyson's face right up until the bell saved him and he sleepwalked to his corner, out on his feet.

Thirty seconds into the eleventh round, Tyson was no longer protecting himself as Holyfield landed about a dozen punches in a row and the referee stopped the fight.

Holyfield shocked the world.

"I fought competitively, each round, one round at a time," Holyfield said. "I did what it took to win. Tyson fights good inside. My advantage is outside. He throws good, short punches. I threw a right hand and caught him with good, clean shots."

During the post-fight melee, the simmering rage that had been present in Tyson since he first stepped foot out of prison appeared to have been exorcised. He was calm, polite, and respectful.

"I just want to shake your hand," he told Holyfield afterward. "I just want to touch you. You fought a hell of a fight. I have tremendous respect for you."

With the handshake, Tyson's perfect comeback and his air of invincibility, which took a big shot after the loss to Buster Douglas, was knocked down another peg. Losing one time to Douglas could have been written off as a fluke. The second loss meant the bulletproof aura wasn't so bulletproof anymore. He was now just another two-loss heavyweight contender looking for a rematch (though he was still the biggest draw in the sport).

"Don't write Tyson off," Don King said. "We're going to dance again. We're going to see if we can put together the greatest rematch in the history of boxing."

Seven months later, on June 28, 1997, Tyson vs. Holyfield II took place. It has forever been known as "The Bite Fight" because Tyson was disqualified for biting Holyfield's ear in the third round. The two wouldn't fight a third time.

After the bite (fight), Tyson stayed with the sport for a while longer, cashing in huge paydays against a string of nobodies until he got one final chance at the WBC, IBF, and IBO heavyweight belts in a fight with then-champion Lennox Lewis. By this time Tyson was almost thirty-six years old and he was giving up six inches to the much bigger Lewis, who knocked him out in the eighth round, giving Iron Mike a career 49–4 record. He fought three more times, winning once against Clifford Etienne before losing to Danny Williams and Kevin McBride.

The back-to-back losses convinced Tyson to retire and the sport hasn't had an American heavyweight even remotely as exciting since. In a way, Tyson's departure signaled an exit of heavyweight boxing in the American consciousness. The smaller fighters like Floyd Mayweather and the allure of the UFC have stolen much of boxing's thunder. But back in our day, we had Tyson (and *Mike Tyson's PUNCH-OUT!!*), and there was nothing like it. Especially when he seemed to fight on a bi-monthly basis back in '96.

SPACE JAM

THE IDEA STARTED WITH TWO RABBITS: ROGER and Bugs Bunny.

Roger Rabbit, of course, was the title character in the groundbreaking, live-action/animated blockbuster movie *Who Framed Roger Rabbit?* from the summer of 1988. Bugs Bunny needs no introduction—he's the carrot chomping, wise-cracking, Elmer Fudd-foiling legend who made the saying "What's up, Doc?" part of American culture.

The success of Roger's movie proved that a film starring humans and cartoons was not only possible technologically, but done right, could also be a smash hit. And the popularity of Bugs Bunny's early '90s commercials where he co-starred as Hare Jordan alongside Air Jordan himself—Michael Jordan (to promote the Air Jordan VIIIs)—gave Warner Bros. the kernel of the idea they needed to make a movie with their Looney Toons line-ups and real NBA stars.

In a rare move for Hollywood, the studio actually green lit the project and gave it a release date before the script was even written. They had the concept (a Michael Jordan movie with cartoons), the time frame (nineteen months to get it done), and the title (*Space Jam*)—but that was it. They weren't 100 percent sure of the title, which led to this great anecdote from Neil Boyle, the supervising animator on the project.

"One day we got a memo sent around to all of us and it said the new title for the film is *Up In The Air*," Boyle explained. "And I thought, 'Okay, *Up in the Air*, because Michael Jordan's kind of flying through the air and I kind of get that, that's not too bad.' And then about two hours later somebody came around and hastily retracted all these memos, and it had just turned out that one of the secretaries in the meeting said, 'Do we have a new title to put out there?' And one of the producers said, 'Oh man, it's up in the air.' And she had literally thought it's *Up in the Air* and had notified everyone this was the new name of the film!"

The script was famously being written and rewritten during the shoot and the entire studio was under the gun because the star of the film, Michael Jordan, had a hard out when he'd no longer be available: the start of the NBA season.

Not only that, nearly all of the non-animated co-stars except Bill Murray had teams to report to as well: Charles Barkley, Patrick Ewing, Muggsy Bogues, Larry Johnson, and Shawn Bradley. There were also cameos by Larry Bird, Cedric Ceballos, Vlade Divac, Ahmad Rashad, Paul Westphal, and Danny Ainge.

In hindsight, the concept of the movie is kind of brilliant, fictionalizing in real time a version of Michael Jordan's life between his 1993 retirement and his 1995 comeback—including nods to his early days at North Carolina, his father, his dream of playing baseball, and a scene at the end when he's coaxed into a game of three-on-three that presumably leads to his returning to the NBA.

Watching the film twenty-five years later, through the prism of Jordan's second three-peat, books like Roland Lazenby's *Michael Jordan: A Life*, and *The Last Dance*, it's remarkable how the *Space Jam* writers personalized the story to Jordan specifically. That's why the movie resonated so much. It wasn't just a lazy concept of "let's just pair Jordan with Bugs and Daffy and people will watch"; no, there was genuine thought behind Jordan's real-life and fictional backstory and how it matched up with the way audiences would perceive Jordan when the movie hit theaters on November 15, 1996.

Jordan scored 20 points in a blowout home game against Cleveland on the night of the premiere and was confident (but cautious) that the movie would do well.

"I think it's gonna do fine," he said. "But I'm very nervous about it. This is a whole new arena for me, but it's just been a lot of money invested in me, and hopefully I did my part. I tried to do the best I could, and if it's good . . . great. I may do it again. If it's not, certainly I'll know where I stand in that career. I'll stick to the thirty-second commercials."

The movie did more than fine.

It was and still is the highest grossing basketball movie of all time.

It made $90 million in the United States, $230 million worldwide, and the merchandise has brought in an astonishing $1 billion in sales (the film's soundtrack also went platinum six times). The movie was also given a second life via streaming, leading to an entirely new generation of kids who quote the Monstars lines, wonder why Patrick Ewing was so sweaty all the time, and don't understand how cool it was to have Bill Murray in the film. Following its wildly successful theater run, everyone involved was clamoring for a sequel, except the one person critical to getting it done: Jordan.

Writes Roland Lazenby in his book, "David Falk [Jordan's agent] urged him to do another, but by then he had changed his mind and would turn down all offers over the ensuing years."

Almost as famous as the movie itself was the indoor, state-of-the-art basketball court the studio built for Jordan and the pick-up games that took place inside while filming. The court—which was dubbed "The Dome," "The Jordan Dome," or "The Bubble" by the players lucky enough to get an invite—was home to some of the best, most star-studded pick-up games of the entire decade, let alone the summer of 1995. We touched on this earlier in the Magic Johnson chapter, but it bears repeating. This was the #1 run in the United States for NBA guys that summer.

"I was there for about a week," five-time NBA All-Star Tim Hardaway told *Slam Magazine*. "We played every day. You had Chris Mullin, Rod Strickland out there. Gary Payton, of course. Reggie, Pat, Charles [Barkley]. Charles needed it because you know, he's always getting heavy during the course of the summer. He really needed to be in shape and ready to go. He loved it. Charles would be going at people. We had to go double team him because basically when he got it down low, nobody could stop him. If you didn't want to lose, you had to go down there and double team."

It wasn't unusual to have celebrities hanging out on the sidelines, taking in a veritable free NBA All-Star Game. On any given day you could have Kevin Costner, Queen Latifah, Arnold Schwarzenegger, LL Cool J, and Halle Berry watching Barkley maul people and Reggie talk shit.

In addition to the NBA stars, a few college standouts were invited and the occasional member of the *Space Jam* production, including Joe Pytka, the film's director, were allowed to play. Pytka gives the best description of what it would be like for an average dude to play pick-up against Michael Jordan.

"I only played up there three or four times," Pytka told *Slam*. " . . . Michael was a beast. The most memorable experience I had up there was, Michael was coming down on a break and I was going to take a charge right in the middle of the key. Mike was coming right at me and he never went left or right, he went right through me and dunked over me. I'm gonna tell you something and you're not going to believe this, I didn't feel anything. I don't know if he went over me, I'm 6'5" and weigh about 230. It was magic. It was like a ghost went through me and dunked. I don't know whether he jumped completely over me. I wasn't crouching down, I was standing straight up to take the charge. He just dunked it and it was like a ghost. I'll never forget that."

One day we'll find out if LeBron James gave the director of *Space Jam II* the same courtesy.

THERE'S SOMETHING
ABOUT FAVRE

BRETT FAVRE STEPPED HESITANTLY TO THE podium on May 14, 1996, with his coach, Mike Holmgren, over his left shoulder and his soon-to-be wife, Deanna, over his right. Favre was a beat-up jeans, old t-shirt, and sweat-stained baseball hat type of guy, but for this press conference he'd cleaned up. Dark pants. Light sports coat. White shirt buttoned all the way to the collar. The ensemble was a red flag and the reporters in the room immediately knew something was wrong.

Favre then began to talk in a stilted, forced voice, shifting from foot to foot. He sounded more uncomfortable than his outfit. As he spoke, he paused often with his tongue in the corner of his mouth to gather himself. His eyes were downcast, and he had a puffy look to him.

"Throughout the last couple of years, in playing with pain and injuries and suffering numerous surgeries, I possibly became dependent on medication," Favre said. "And the last surgery, being ankle surgery, I suffered a seizure in the hospital a couple of months back. Because of that I've sought help through the NFL . . . It's not an easy thing.

I'm going to admit into a treatment facility for however long it takes to get better."

Unspoken in the statement, but confirmed by ESPN's Chris Mortensen at the time, at least part of the reason Favre entered a rehab facility was for alcohol issues. He originally wanted to go to the world-renowned Betty Ford Clinic, but it wasn't a sanctioned facility by the NFL at the time, so he wound up at the Menninger Clinic in Topeka, Kansas.

The news ricocheted around the sports world. Favre was the face of a signature NFL franchise; a torchbearer to the legacy of Bart Starr and Vince Lombardi; a future superstar in the league and its reigning MVP. Also, the news came out of absolutely nowhere.

Brett Favre has a drug problem? What the hell? He just won the MVP!

Seeing as Favre was THE role model in Green Bay, the *La Crosse Tribune* reached out to their younger readers to get a sense of what they were feeling after the announcement

"He was brave to come out and tell the world," fourteen-year-old Matt Knebes said. "Maybe other NFL players have a problem and haven't said anything."

"He's Green Bay's hero and I feel let down," twelve-year-old Jesse Smith responded. "I feel sorry for him."

"He used painkillers so he could play and help the team," Adam Millen, twelve, said. "That's different than illegal drugs."

The kids were unaware of the alcohol part of the problem, and they didn't understand the magnitude of abuse Favre was putting himself through with the pills he was taking. We'd also learn much later that Favre actually attended rehab three times to beat his painkiller and alcohol addiction.

"Oh, I remember that week," Favre told Peter King on a phone call years later about the '96 press conference. "You thought, 'Man, this guy's high on life.' You didn't know there was a reason for it. It is really amazing, as I think back, when I woke up in the morning, my first thought was, 'I gotta get more pills.' I took fourteen Vicodin, yes, one time. I was getting an hour or two of sleep many nights. Maybe thirty minutes of quality sleep. I was the MVP on a pain-pill buzz. The crazy thing was, I'm not a night owl. Without the pills I'd fall asleep at 9:30. But with the pills I could get so much done, I just figured, 'This is awesome.' Little did I know Deanna would be finding some of my pills and when she did, she'd flush them down the toilet."

Favre spent a month and a half in rehab at Menninger. When he reappeared in front of the press early in training camp, he looked younger and refreshed. The blood was back in his face. His voice sounded stronger. He looked fit and comfortable.

"You know, I'm going to beat this thing," he said. "I'm going to win a Super Bowl. And all I can tell people if they don't believe me is, 'Just bet against me.'"

◘   ◘   ◘

Hey, Atlanta Falcons Head Coach Jerry Glanville, how do you feel about the Brett Favre kid your team drafted out of Southern Mississippi?

Glanville: "It would take a plane crash for me to put Favre into the game."

Ooooohhh kayyy, then.

From the minute the Falcons selected Favre with the 33rd overall pick in the 1991 NFL Draft, Glanville pretty much hated him. He hated how cocky he was. He hated how undisciplined he was. He hated how he stayed out late and took naps during meetings. He hated how he broke his four rules, which went like this, according to *the Atlanta Journal Constitution*:

1. Be on time.
2. Prepare all week to play.
3. Spill your guts on the field.
4. Only accept victory.

"If he'd have got to three and four, he'd have been fine," Glanville told the paper.

"But he never got past one and two."

Glanville disliked Favre so much that he refused to even make him the backup to starting QB Chris Miller. And so, after drafting Favre, the Falcons had to trade for Billy Joe Tolliver to take over the role. All in all, Favre ended up throwing four passes for the Falcons. He was intercepted half the time (his first pass as an NFL quarterback was actually a pick to the house).

"I'm sure I didn't help my cause by trying to drink up Atlanta," Favre once said about his time with the Falcons.

As fate would have it, that time would be short thanks to Green Bay Packers General Manager Ron Wolf. Wolf had been on Favre's scent since an assistant at Southern Mississippi, Thomas Coleman, asked him to come check out Favre in 1990. At the time Wolf was a scout with the Oakland Raiders. A year later, he'd moved to the New York Jets front office and in preparation for the 1991 NFL Draft, Wolf had Favre as the number-one pick on his draft board. The Jets didn't have a first rounder that year, so all they could do was hope that Favre fell to them with the 34th overall pick. They came close. Atlanta nabbed him one spot earlier and the Jets went with Browning Nagle from the University of Louisville.

Toward the end of 1991, Wolf was hired as the General Manager of the Green Bay Packers and he began plotting to get Brett Favre before he even picked out his office chair.

Wolf knew the situation in Atlanta was untenable and that Glanville would rather douse his eyes with Tabasco sauce than deal with his insufferable, young QB—so Wolf figured that rather than deal with him, maybe they'd deal him.

One quick note: years later, Glanville denied that he despised Favre, telling ESPN, "Favre was a young guy in a big city, and I went to all the bars where he went and I asked them to quit giving him drinks. I flew his mom and dad into my office. Does that sound like a guy who didn't like him? I paid to fly in his mom and dad to help me talk to him. They said nobody cared more about him than me. But was I ever happy with him there? He hadn't grown up yet. But we've all been there. Guess what? If I was that age, I'd probably be the same guy."

Regardless of which version you believe, when Wolf approached Glanville and the Falcons with an offer for Favre, they listened. When he offered the Packers' first round pick, they accepted. A short time later, Favre was in the kitchen at his mom's house when the phone rang. It was June Jones, the Falcons' offensive coordinator.

"In some ways I'm excited for you, and in other ways I'm disappointed," Jones told Favre on the call. "We traded you to Green Bay. I enjoyed working with you. I hope you have a great career. This is a great opportunity for you."

Favre put the phone down to tell his mom the news and then the phone rang again. This time it was Ron Wolf.

"Look, I'm the GM in Green Bay and we just traded for you," Wolf said. "And I want you to know that we're very excited about having you lead our team."

After the call, the Packers arranged for Favre's travel and sent a young assistant by the name of Jon Gruden to pick him up at the airport.

The Green Bay franchise that Favre was joining had fallen on hard times. Their last playoff win had come over twenty years earlier, in the 1967 Super Bowl under iconic coach Vince Lombardi. From 1968 to 1992, the Packers made the playoffs twice and only had a handful of seasons above .500. For the '70s and '80s and early '90s, the Packers were feeder fish, mere appetizers for the 49ers, Cowboys, Giants, and Redskins, all of whom had won multiple Super Bowls since the last time Green Bay won the trophy that was named after their own coach.

With Favre on the roster and new coach Mike Holmgren already in place, Wolf believed he had the coach/QB tandem his franchise needed to stop messing with the minnows and start swimming with the sharks again. At the time, the Packers' starting quarterback was Don Majkowski, a 6'2" field general out of the University of Virginia who had one solid season in 1989 and then missed games due to injury and poor play over the next few years. He opened '92 number one on the quarterback depth chart but started 0–2. In the Packers' second game against Tampa Bay, Holmgren benched him at halftime after falling behind 0–17. Favre didn't lead the team to a miraculous comeback, but he did enough to earn the starting job the next week against the Cincinnati Bengals. To Packers fans, this QB shuffle felt all too familiar. A sort of here we go again moment.

Wrote Mark Beech in his book *The People's Team*, "On Sunday morning, the marquee outside Motor Parts West, in Ashwaubenon, just a few blocks southeast of Lambeau Field, read, Go Pack. Beat Someone. Anyone. Please."

Things started off poorly, for Favre. Through three quarters he'd fumbled four times (losing the ball twice) and blew two snaps as the holder for field goals, causing kicker Chris Jacke to whiff on two of his three attempts. The Packers were down 17–3 to start the fourth, and then the guy most fans still called fav-ray became FAVRE. He led the team on three scoring drives in the final fifteen minutes that culminated in the first touchdown pass of his career, the first fourth-quarter comeback of his career, the first game-winning touchdown throw of his career, and his first win as a starting quarterback in the NFL.

"Favre threw that pass," Wolf said. "And everything changed."

The Packers went 8–5 under Favre in 1992 and he threw for 3,227 yards and 18 touchdowns (against 13 interceptions), good enough for his first Pro Bowl selection. In 1993 he inched the team a little further to respectability with a 9–7 record. His passing yards and touchdown numbers were nearly identical to the year before, but he threw a league-leading 24 interceptions. Still, he made his second Pro Bowl. Favre's true breakout year was 1994, when he threw for 33 touchdowns and just over 3,800 yards. The team finished 9–7, but the table was set for '95. Favre was ready to start feasting.

Utilizing Pro Bowl tight end Mark Chmura, running backs Dorsey Levens and Edgar Bennett, and wide receiver Robert Brooks (who caught 102 passes and 13 touchdowns), Favre scorched the NFL's defenses. He threw for a league-leading 4,413 yards, a league-leading 38 touchdowns, and he won his first NFL MVP award. The Packers were 11–5 in the regular season and in a bit of poetic justice, they dusted the Atlanta Falcons 37–20 in the NFL Wild Card game. They followed that up by beating the San Francisco 49ers in the Divisional Round, 27–17, before falling to the Cowboys in the NFC Championship Game, 27–38.

That's why Favre's press conference in the spring of 1996 was such a monstrous deal. This wasn't just some NFL starter—or even a star linebacker or running back from a fringe franchise—announcing he needed rehab. This was the league's MVP quarterback from one of its headline teams, coming off a conference championship game, saying he had a drug problem. Favre, while brilliant in 1995, and the Packers, while excellent as well, were still in the "promise unfulfilled" stage of their ascent, having fallen short of the Super Bowl. Favre's drug problem put the entire trajectory of the franchise in limbo.

There was also the commercial impact to consider. Outside of the NFL, Favre had become a blue-chip advertiser with major national brands. His style of play (cue John Madden's, "He's like a kid out there!") along with his public persona of a relaxed country boy (constant stubble, ripped t-shirts, stories about mowing his lawn) had advertisers lining up to sign him. Over time he'd have national spokesman deals with Nike, Snapper lawnmowers, Sears, Sensodyne toothpaste, Mastercard, and Wrangler jeans, which often showed advertisements with Favre playing pick-up football in the mud wearing a pair of jeans—something nobody would ever actually do.

All of this was up in the air as the Packers opened up the 1996 regular season against the Tampa Bay Bucs.

Would he be rusty? Could he handle the pressure and pain without the pills? Was he focused?

Unfortunately for the Bucs, Favre was radiant, not rusty. And he scoffed at the pressure, rather than succumbed to it. And his focus was never better. Over the course of four humid quarters, to paraphrase LL Cool J's "Mama Said Knock You Out," Favre sliced and diced and made the competition pay the price. He was an extremely efficient 20–27 passing with 4 touchdown passes (three of them to Keith Jackson) and no interceptions. The Packers won 34–3 and Favre was pulled midway through the fourth. Ex-Chicago Bears legend Jim McMahon came in for mop-up duty.

When reporters approached Favre after the game to ask if he felt that he'd answered any questions from the concerning off-season, Favre, ever the jokester, said, "There were questions? I think that question's answered. I had no doubts about myself. I told you guys a long time ago to bet against me. I don't know where your money is . . . "

In weeks two and three of the season the Packers hung 39 on the Philadelphia Eagles and 42 on the San Diego Chargers. They lost a close game to the Vikings in week four, but then resumed their Brett Favre "Bet Against Me" tour, beating the Seahawks and Bears by a combined score of 67–16.

Their next game was a Monday Night Football matchup against the 49ers. On a chilly night at Lambeau Field, 60,176 people witnessed one of the oddest games of the season for Favre and the Packers. On the positive side, he threw for 395 yards on a ridiculous 61 attempts, hitting Don Beebe for 11 catches, 220 yards, and a touchdown.

On the negative side, that would be the only touchdown pass of the game for Favre (despite all those yards) and he'd throw 2 interceptions. The Packers had no rushing touchdowns and their scoring per quarter was a rare 6–0–8–6. But it was just enough to force overtime, where Favre was an awful 1–6 on his pass attempts.

But the "one" got kicker Chris Jacke close enough to hit a 53-yard game winner. Bizarre.

"Those were some of the most zany things I've ever seen in a game," San Francisco's head coach, George Seifert, said, summing up the contest.

Next, the Packers beat the Bucs (again) and the Detroit Lions to push their record to 8–1, but then they surprisingly lost two games in a row, one to the Chiefs and the other to the Cowboys. Deion Sanders and company stymied Favre for four quarters, holding him under 200 yards for the first time all season. The offense managed just 6 points.

It was a disaster on multiple levels.

One, they didn't avenge their loss from the previous year's playoff meeting and two, there was a decent chance the road to the Super Bowl would run through the Cowboys again. The Packers were hoping to even the score against them, rather than go into that match-up with a two-game losing streak. The only silver lining was that the Packers' defense was stout all night, holding Troy Aikman, Emmitt Smith, and Michael Irvin without a touchdown.

"Who'd have thought we could hold them without a touchdown and lose?" Favre asked rhetorically afterward. "But I knew coming in it would be a tough game."

The loss dropped the Cowboys to 8–3 at a critical point in the season as teams geared up for the playoffs and tried to earn home-field advantage.

"That took the wind out of our sails," Coach Holmgren said. "For the most part, I wasn't particularly happy with the way we played."

Holmgren wouldn't be unhappy for long.

The dud in Dallas was his team's last loss. The Packers bounced back with a 24–9 win against the Rams, then a 28–17 win against the Bears. The Broncos and their number-one ranked defense in the NFL loomed next. No matter. Favre picked them apart for 280 yards, 4 touchdowns, and 41 points before posting 31 points against Detroit (win #12) and 38 against the Vikings (win #13). By the end of the 13–3 season, Favre had thrown for 39 touchdowns, then the third-most in NFL history, as well as 3,899 yards, good enough for his second straight MVP award.

As a team, the Packers finished the season on a molten hot streak, scoring 110 points over their last 12 quarters and setting up a Division Playoff home game against the 12–4 San Francisco 49ers at Lambeau Field.

o   o   o

Nine degrees.

That was what the temperature felt like at kickoff of the 12:30 p.m. playoff game between the Packers and the 49ers. The real temperature hovered just above freezing, but add in the twenty-mile-per-hour winds whipping around the stadium and the wind chill was pushed into the single digits. It also poured the entire game, making the conditions a bit like playing in a breezy meat locker with the sprinklers on.

The Packers jumped out to a 14–0 lead on a meager 9 yards of total offense thanks to a 70-yard punt return by Desmond Howard for a touchdown, and then a 46-yard punt return by Howard into the red zone that set up a 4-yard touchdown pass to Andre Rison.

At the start of the second quarter Favre hit Edgar Bennett for a 10-yard pass and then handed off to him for a 2-yard touchdown run. The Packers were up 21–0, but the 49ers scored before the end of the first half and then again to start the third quarter, cutting the lead to 21–14. That was the closest they'd get.

As the frigid winds pounded the stadium, the Packers handed the ball off over 30 times to running backs Bennett and Dorsey Levens, who combined for 124 yards and 2 touchdowns. Favre only threw the ball 15 times the whole game. He completed 11 passes to 7 receivers for a grand total of 79 yards, the lowest of his career up to that point. The Packers won 35–14.

"Every once in a while, the elements take a star player and don't allow him to do what he does best," Mike Holmgren said afterward.

In a display of frostbitten fortitude, toward the end of the game, the loony and loyal Lambeau faithful chanted, "We want Dallas! We want Dallas!"

They wanted vengeance for the playoff loss. They wanted vengeance for the mid-season loss. But most of all, to quote Ric Flair, in order to be the man, they wanted to beat the man . . . and the "man" in this case was the mighty Dallas Cowboys.

That was the fans' perspective.

The Green Bay Packers players were indifferent about who they'd face.

"We don't care about Dallas," Antonio Freeman said. "We want whoever wins that game."

"That game" being the afternoon match-up between the Dallas Cowboys and the upstart Carolina Panthers under head coach Dom Capers.

"Nobody feels invincible," Freeman continued. "But we're a football team on a mission. Invincible is a big word. We like our chances. I think that says it best."

Ultimately, Green Bay never got the chance to vanquish Troy Aikman and the rest of the star-studded crew. The Panthers beat the Cowboys 26–17 that afternoon, setting up a game in Wisconsin in January, where the average temperature without wind chill factored in was 22 degrees.

When game day came around, twenty-two degrees would have felt like an afternoon on the beach in Key Largo compared to the inhospitable, hypothermia-inducing conditions the players were faced with.

Three degrees on the thermometer.

Twenty-mile-per-hour winds

-16-degree wind chill factor.

It was weather meant for the Iditarod, not a football game, and Favre started horribly. He fumbled. He threw an interception. He freelanced too much.

Sensing that his star quarterback was letting his excitement get the best of him and veering too far from the game plan, Holmgren put a governor on Favre's engine, throttling back the play calls a bit and keeping it simple. The Packers scored in the second quarter on a 29-yard pass from Favre to Dorsey Levens and then again on a touchdown pass to Antonio Freeman. Favre was erratic all game, but came through when his team needed him.

"The guy still makes plays when he has to," Panthers defensive tackle Greg Kragen said. "Just when you think you've got him, he somehow gets the pass off."

After the Freeman touchdown, the rest of the Packers' offense came from the kicking game (Jacke hit 3 field goals) and the running game. Bennett and Levens tallied 187 yards on 35 carries and 1 touchdown and the Packers won 30–13.

They were finally headed back to the Super Bowl.

"I think we're a really good football team," Favre said. "Everyone expected us to win today and we did. I'm assuming everyone is picking us to win the Super Bowl, but anything can happen."

Favre was right; the Packers were 14-point favorites against their AFC opponents, the New England Patriots. The Patriots were 11–5 on the regular season and manhandled the Pittsburgh Steelers in the Divisional Game 28–3, then easily beat the Jacksonville Jaguars 20–6. They were coached by living legend Bill Parcells and led by cannon-armed quarterback Drew Bledsoe.

And the Pats had been picked by just about nobody to be in the Super Bowl.

In the two-week media circus leading up to Super Bowl XXXI in New Orleans, the biggest story wasn't whether the Packers defense could stop the Bledsoe-to-Ben Coates combination; rather it was, "Is Bill Parcells leaving to coach the Jets after the game?" The rumors were a constant distraction for the Patriots.

In Michael Holley's book, *Patriot Reign*, then-Patriots assistant (and now iconic coach in his own right) Bill Belichick said, "Yeah, I'd say it was a little bit of a distraction all the way around. I can tell you firsthand, there was a lot of stuff going on prior to the game. I mean, him talking to other teams. He was trying to make up his mind about what he was going to do. Which, honestly, I felt [was] totally inappropriate. How many chances do you get to play for the Super Bowl? Tell them to get back to you in a couple of days. I'm not saying it was disrespectful to me, but it was in terms of the overall commitment to the team."

Distracted or not, the Patriots had a game to play and they got behind early. With 11:54 remaining in the first, Favre called the kind of audible quarterbacks dream about, changing the entire play at the line of scrimmage. After the ball was snapped, Favre dropped straight back along the hash marks, looked the defense off to his left, and then threw a bomb down the seam, hitting Andre Rison, who'd blown through the entire secondary. It was a 54-yard touchdown and when Rison crossed into the end zone, Favre took off his helmet and sprinted off the field holding it up like they won the game. A few minutes later

Jacke hit a field goal to put the Packers up 10–0, but the Patriots were unfazed and answered with their own two scores, a Bledsoe to Keith Byars touchdown and then a Bledsoe to Coates touchdown. When the first quarter ended, the Patriots were surprisingly up 14–10 and had all the momentum.

Less than a minute into the second quarter, Favre called another audible and hit Antonio Freeman for a then-Super Bowl record 81-yard touchdown pass and the Packers grabbed the lead for good. After another Jacke field goal and a 2-yard rushing touchdown by Favre, the score was 27–14 Packers at halftime.

Side note: If you don't remember the halftime show for this game, you probably blocked it out. It was a show titled "Blues Brothers Bash" performed by Dan Aykroyd, John Goodman, and Jim Belushi—which probably seemed like a good idea in a pitch meeting but likely got somebody fired after the game.

Following fifty Blues Brothers-dressed performers in suits, the second half of the game kicked off and the Patriots defense held the Packers on their first two possessions. With six minutes left in the third quarter, the Patriots offense got rolling. Bledsoe hit Ben Coates for a 13-yard pass. Then he hit Shawn Jefferson for 9 yards to get the Patriots inside Green Bay's 30-yard line. Curtis Martin took a handoff 8 yards and then on second down, he busted right up the middle of the NFL's number-one ranked defense for an 18-yard touchdown to cut the Packers' lead down to 27–21.

The Patriots had survived two quick touchdowns and were back on their feet, cobwebs cleared, ready to knuckle up for the championship. They'd stalled the Packers offense and found a few blocking schemes to get their own Pro Bowler, Curtis Martin, running downhill. Amazingly, the Pats had momentum heading into the last twenty minutes of the game.

"When they came back and scored, you're thinking, man, this is going to be one of those games that goes right down to the wire. That's the feeling I had," Mike Holmgren said.

Then Adam Vinatieri kicked off to Desmond Howard.

It was a high, beautiful kick that Howard caught on the Packers' 1-yard line and immediately took straight up the field. He raced to the 20-yard line untouched, like there was a force field around him. At about the 25-yard line, he took a shot from his right side but bounced off and scampered away at top speed, breaking left of the hash and dropping the hammer, blasting past Vinatieri and dashing straight down the numbers for a Super Bowl record-breaking 99-yard touchdown.

Patriots' momentum: gone.

Packers' emotion: sky high.

The fourth quarter was a defensive stalemate, where both teams held the other's offense in check, and Howard's touchdown turned out to be the last score of the game.

The Green Bay Packers won the Super Bowl, 35–21. The Vince Lombardi Trophy was finally going back home thanks to the kid from Kiln, Mississippi. The "Bet Against Me" tour that had begun at the awkward press conference in May of '96 and continued with his return press conference at the start of pre-season had reached its final destination.

"I did everything I possibly can," Favre said, downright giddy after the game. "I hope too many people didn't bet against me, because they're broke right now."

JERRY MAGUIRE

I'M RUNNING GASSERS IN 92-DEGREE MIAMI HEAT
on a beat-up high-school football field with Jerry Maguire running right
beside me.

Ten-yard line and back.

Fifteen-yard line and back.

Twenty-yard line and back.

Waterfalls of sweat dump off our heads as we push through air so
thick with moisture you could drink it.

Fifty-yard line and back.

Forty-five-yard line and back.

Forty-yard line and back.

We're not wheezing, but we're close. We're not puking either, but
again, we're close. We're pushing each other until finally, thankfully, we
cross the goal line and drop to our knees.

"What's more productive? Running gassers out here with my clients, or
taking them to a crowded bar somewhere? When we're pushing through
a workout together, they see that when I say that I work hard, I mean it."

Full disclosure: The man speaking isn't Jerry Maguire exactly. It's super-agent Drew Rosenhaus, who was one half of the two agents *Jerry Maguire*'s writer/director Cameron Crowe very loosely pulled some traits from for the character of Jerry Maguire. The other was Rosenhaus's sports agent rival, Leigh Steinberg—though Crowe has made it very clear that Jerry Maguire is nearly 100 percent fictional. In fact, the original inspiration for the movie was based on a photo that didn't include Rosenhaus or Steinberg.

"It started with a photograph," Crowe told *Deadline.com* in a retrospective on the piece. "James L. Brooks handed me this photo from *New York Magazine* of a sports agent, Gary Wichard, and the Boz, Brian Bosworth, who was then a hot property in the NFL. It was just a fun picture of these two guys; one clearly the business, and the other, the brawn. He said, look at this relationship between these guys. What do you think about that kind of a story in this world?"

I, your humble author, was running sprints with Rosenhaus for a feature in *Muscle & Fitness Magazine* that explored how Rosenhaus's agency used weightlifting and training to stay in shape and attract clients. Rosenhaus had a cameo in *Jerry Maguire*, and it seemed like every write-up done about him mentioned Maguire. Having spent the day with him, I could see why. He had the same energy; smarts hidden with a smile that seemed to be able to turn into a sneer instantly. He dressed the part, with the slick hair and the suits and the omnipresent phone (he did wind sprints holding his phone).

And he talked like Maguire, too.

"I've been through some brutal workouts with my clients," Rosenhaus told me. "Terrell Owens. Jeremy Shockey. They were hard on me. But the toughest workout I ever did with a client was with Sean Taylor. He was a tremendous athlete and person. We did a set of 24 110-yard sprints on this field and I was throwing up afterward. It was the toughest workout I've ever been through."

You can easily imagine T.O. shouting about "the Quan" to Rosenhaus during sprints, channeling Rod Tidwell.

*It means love, respect, community . . . the dollars, too. The entire package. The
Quan!*

"Jerry came from a lot of different fictional places, but we got elements and spice from guys like Leigh Steinberg. He helped me a lot, and
opened a lot of doors," Crowe said. "Another guy was . . . Rosenhaus.
He was kind of like a Bob Sugar, but the whole idea of putting a focus
on personal attention to your clients, that came from conversations with
Jim Brooks. We talked about what would be the most embarrassing
thing that could happen to a shark in the middle of the night, drilled
on coffee and bad pizza, and finding a conscience he didn't know he
had? What would he say that would really get him in trouble? And
that's where we came up with the more personal attention thing. Fewer
clients. Less money."

In an alternate universe, the *Jerry Maguire* you know and love didn't
star its iconic actors. The movie was written partly for Tom Hanks,
not Tom Cruise. For a while, Jamie Foxx was the front-runner for Rod
Tidwell, not Cuba Gooding Jr. And Gwyneth Paltrow and Mira Sorvino
both had excellent reads for the part of Dorothy Boyd before Crowe
decided that Renee Zellweger was the one

Imagine a version of *Jerry Maguire* starring Hanks, Foxx, and Paltrow.
That's likely still an awesome movie—but a very different one.

Cameron Crowe spent five years working on the script with the
help of writer/producer James L. Brooks, and by the time the movie
hit theaters on December 13, 1996, the buzz surrounding the film had
reached ludicrous heights. It was billed as *the movie to see*, complete with
an original song for the soundtrack from Bruce Springsteen. Cruise was
coming off the worldwide blockbuster success of *Mission: Impossible*
and Cuba was ready to showcase his next great performance after a
few misses following *Boyz n the Hood*.

By Monday morning, December 16, 1996, water coolers the business world over were already spreading the word.

You have to see Jerry Maguire*!*

Quotes from the movie became a part of pop culture at a staggering pace. By January 1, 1997, with the movie well on its way to earning $153 million in the United States and $273 million worldwide, the catchphrases seemed to be everywhere.

Show me the money!

Help me help you!

You complete me.

The human head weighs eight pounds.

You had me at hello.

Ya know! Ya know!

The fuckin' zoo's closed, Ray.

Twenty-five years later, these lines, those performances, and this movie are as popular as ever. And to think, we owe it all to a picture of Brian Bosworth.

What better way to wrap up 1996 than with an iconic sports movie inspired by a true '80s icon, The Boz?

ACKNOWLEDGMENTS

IT'S LIKE I'VE ALWAYS SAID, "THERE IS NO BETTER time to write a book on the greatest year in sports than the one year in the history of modern sports when sports completely stopped."

I've had the idea for a project celebrating the 25th anniversary of the 1996 sports year for a long time, but little did I know that when the publishing stars would finally align to kick off the book, it would happen at the exact moment when sports would be taken away from us.

The NBA season would stop short.

The NHL season would stop short.

March Madness would be cancelled.

Baseball would push back and truncate their season.

The Masters would move to the fall.

For a brief moment in sports time, there was nothing.

Well . . . nothing new.

We did have the one thing that, in some ways, is stronger even than live sports: nostalgia. I graduated high school in 1996, which is why the idea for this book was so important to me. In many ways, our collective love of sports crystallizes around this time period in our lives. For one, it's the last time that we're younger than all of the professional athletes that we follow. Once you hit college, you're no longer a kid watching pros; you're a grown man or woman watching peers. That is a seismic shift in your sports brain. It also solidifies some things.

Since you're only a child once, you can only have one set of childhood heroes. In many ways, for those of us who graduated high school anywhere in the '90s, these are our athletes. Sure, some of them like Jordan and Magic belong to the '80s as well, but for the most part, the athletes and teams covered in this book came of age in the '90s and then influenced every athlete after them, as we've read about.

In a way, 1996 is a line of demarcation.

There's before '96 and after '96.

Before '96, we lived in a pre-Kobe, pre-Iverson, pre-Tiger, pre-Tyson vs. Holyfield, pre-Jordan comeback, pre-Venus and Serena, pre-*Jerry Maguire* and *Happy Gilmore*, pre-MLS, and pre-WNBA world.

Is this a world you can even picture? No Iverson? No Williams Sisters or Tiger? No Kobe Bryant and the impact his life had on so many athletes? No *Space Jam*? No *Last Dance*?

I can't picture it either.

If you're reading this far, then we're in the same boat and I hope you've had a blast taking this trip down memory lane with me.

I wrote this book for much of 2020, stuck at home like all of you, with my kids doing virtual learning the entire time; with a new rescue dog in the house; with the world being turned upside down outside of the house; and through a move from Dallas, Texas, to South Florida.

No coffee shops were open to write in. No bookstores or Barnes & Nobles were letting writers like myself linger and read and research. Libraries were closed, so I couldn't stack a ton of books on a desk and pore over them as I wrote.

Everything in 2020 was strange and different, which is why escaping back to 1996 was so much fun for me—and I hope for you.

It was the best sports year.

The dopest sports year.

The year that influenced all the years after it the most.

In short, it was the big bang of modern sports.

Thanks for reliving it with me.

I'd like to thank my agent, Joe Perry, for believing in every version of this book long before it was even a book, and for sticking with me through a myriad of proposals and ideas that eventually became the pages you have in your hands. Thanks also to Keith Wallman from Diversion Books for "getting" this idea from the jump. It's a simple idea but a huge concept to execute that covers a lot of ground, and not every publisher would have the vision to see it through and to understand the massive audience lying in wait.

I also have to thank all of the people who took the time to speak with me to help put the incredible year that was 1996 in context: Ray Allen, Jamal Crawford, Warrick Dunn, Chad Finn, Steve Grad, Bobby Jones, Ed Latimore, Rebecca Lobo, The Miz, Gary Payton, Steve Rushin, Nate Robinson, Brandon "Scoop B" Robinson, Isaiah Thomas, Danny Wuerffel, and so many more.

I need to also take the time to thank all of my high school and college buddies who I shared endless little nuggets of '96 information with as I wrote this book. The little wormholes, nostalgia hits, side conversations about the Yankees and basketball and Tyson, and a zillion other things with Eddie Coblentz, Sean Carrigan, and Seth Weidner kept things fun while writing late into the night.

And of course, my brother, Craig, who received more screen shots and texts and videos of mid-'90s awesomeness than one man should possibly have to endure, but he took it like a champ.

I have to also thank my wife, Steph, and my kids, Reese and Grant, and my dog Lyla, for their unending support and patience as I knocked this manuscript out.

My wife went to Miami with a true '96 all-star, The Rock, but somehow never really got into his WWE performances, so getting to relive all of the late '90s, "It doesn't matter what you think!" joy with her and the kids has been a blast. And to Reese and Grant, who watched *Space*

Jam and *Happy Gilmore* with me a dozen times and can now quote them as well as I can, I'm so proud of both of you (for the people you're becoming—and for memorizing the quotes).

And no, I won't get you a glass of "shut the hell up." Ha!

And as always, thank you, the reader. I paraphrase Jay-Z at this spot in all of my books because I mean it. You could have picked up any book to read in the world, and you chose this one. I appreciate that and I am forever grateful.

— Jon (Class of '96)

SELECTED REFERENCES

1   Spurrier vs. Bowden vs. Osborne

FiestaBowl.org. "25th Annual Game, 1996." Jan. 2, 2002, https://www.fiestabowl.org
/sports/psfb/roster/25th-annual-game-1996/56.

Hambleton, Ken. "Champs! NU swamps Gators 62–24, caps 12–0 year." *Lincoln Journal
Star*, Jan. 3, 1996, https://www.newspapers.com/image/?clipping_id=49950702
&fcfToken=eyJhbGciOiJIUzI1NiIsInR5cCI6IkpXVCJ9.eyJmcmVlLXZpZXctaW
QiOjI5NzU0ODQ4NSwiaWF0IjoxNjA5Nzc2Nzc3LCJleHAiOjE2MDk4NjMx
Nzd9.-9n8qUThZ2UZEzRwdpdb6nqhQ3TPRjSLq88b6AnqOjw.

Huskers.com. "1996 Fiesta Bowl." Jan. 2, 2002, https://huskers.com/news/2002/1
/10/168.aspx.

Layden, Tim. "Runaway!! Nebraska Left Florida in the Fiesta Bowl Dust and Won a
Second Consecutive National Title." *Sports Illustrated*, Jan. 8, 1996, https://vault.
si.com/vault/1996/01/08/runaway-nebraska-left-florida-in-the
-fiesta-bowl-dust-and-won-a-second-consecutive-national-title.

McMullen, Paul. "Florida states its case, 52–20; No. 1 FSU no match in rematch, as
Gators roll to Sugar Bowl win; Florida eyes national title; Wuerffel leads way with
three TD passes." *The Baltimore Sun*, Jan. 3, 1997, https://www.baltimoresun.com
/news/bs-xpm-1997-01-03-1997003136-story.html.

2   The Triplets and Deion

DallasCowboys.com. "Throwback Thursday: Troy Aikman Remembers His Draft Day."
https://www.dallascowboys.com/video/throwback-thursday-troy-aikman
-remembers-his-draft-day-374561.

DallasCowboys.com. "Throwback Thursday: Michael Irvin On Being Drafted By
Cowboys." https://www.dallascowboys.com/video/throwback-thursday
-michael-irvin-on-being-drafted-by-cowboys-374956.

Ruiz, Steven. "Deion Sanders recalls the time he savagely snubbed the Giants at the 1989
combine." *USA TODAY*, Mar. 6, 2017, https://ftw.usatoday.com/2017/03
/deion-sanders-recalls-the-time-he-savagely-snubbed-the-giants-at
-the-1989-combine.

YouTube.com. "Deion Sanders 1989 Draft Day Layaway Quote." Apr. 15, 2019,
https://www.youtube.com/watch?v=Uarox4j3tG4.

YouTube.com. "Super Bowl 30 – Cowboys vs Steelers." July 6, 2019, https://www
.youtube.com/watch?v=VaREL8LSN-s.

4 Griffey in '96
Groeschen, Tom. "At Moeller, Griffey Jr. was main attraction." *The* (Cincinnati) *Enquirer*, July 22, 2016, https://www.cincinnati.com/story/sports/2016/07/22 /high-school-griffey-jr-main-attraction/87429400/.

Snyder, Mark. "Ken. Griffey Jr. could have gone to Michigan for football." *Detroit Free Press*, Mar. 28, 2017, https://www.freep.com/story/sports/college/university -michigan/wolverines/2017/03/28/michigan-football-ken-griffey/99738970/.

6 The Answer
Casey, Tim. "The Brief, Brilliant Football Career of Allen Iverson." Vice.com, Sept. 9, 2016, https://www.vice.com/en/article/wnmxam/the-brief-brilliant-football -career-of-allen-iverson.

Cervantes, Joseph. "Michael Jordan's first 5 words to Allen Iverson when they met." ClutchPoints.com, May 17, 2020, https://clutchpoints.com/nba-news -michael-jordan-first-5-words-to-allen-iverson-when-they-met/.

DePaula, Nick. "The Rise Of Allen Iverson And Reebok Basketball // An Oral History." NiceKicks.com, June 7, 2015, https://www.nicekicks.com /rise-allen-iverson-reebok-basketball-oral-history/.

KicksOnFire.com. "NCAA Kicks Retro: Allen Iverson Runs Georgetown In The Air Jordan ll 'Concord.'" Apr. 9, 2015, https://www.kicksonfire.com/ncaa-kicks -retro-allen-iverson-runs-georgetown-in-the-air-jordan-11-concord/.

Teel, David. "May 2, 1996: Iverson leaves Georgetown, says he'll turn pro." (Virginia) *Daily Press*, Jan. 19, 2011, https://www.dailypress.com/sports/dp-spt-gt -turning-pro-20110119-story.html.

YouTube. "Allen Iverson Remembers Crossing Over The Legendary Michael Jordan | The Fat Joe Show." Sept. 5, 2020, https://www.youtube.com/watch?v =tLrOZbIYw2I&feature=emb_logo.

7 Pitino's Bombinos
Schreiber, Harlan. "Rick Pitino and the Knicks: A Portrait in Dysfunction." HoopsAnalyst.com, Oct. 5, 2017, https://hoopsanalyst.com/?p=1743.

TheRinger.com. "The Pioneer of the 3-Point Shot." Feb. 2, 2017, https://www .theringer.com/2017/2/2/16042862/ringer-nba-show-stu-jackson-rick -pitino-providence-final-four-aa8ed4d025e3.

Tramel, Berry. "Billy Donovan: How Rick Pitino's NBA experience launched 3-point revolution." *The Oklahoman*, Mar. 18, 2016, https://oklahoman.com/article /5485798/billy-donovan-how-rick-pitinos-nba-experience-launched-3-point -revolution.

8 Eric Wynalda Kickstarts the MLS
Butler, Dylan. "Eric Wynalda reminisces about first MLS game, his first goal." MLSSoccer.com, Apr. 5, 2020, https://www.mlssoccer.com/post/2020/04/05 /eric-wynalda-reminisces-about-first-mls-game-his-first-league-goal.

Froh, Tim. "A league is born: An oral history of the inaugural MLS match." MLSSoccer.com, Apr. 5, 2020, https://www.mlssoccer.com/post/2016/04/06/

league-born-oral-history-inaugural-mls-match#:~:text=And%20witness%20to%20 all%20this,sell%2Dout%20crowd%20of%2031%2C683.

9   We Got Next

Knight-Ridder. "NBA forming women's pro league." Apr. 25, 1996, https://www .newspapers.com/image/200559714/?terms=WNBA&match=1.

10   Stone Cold

New.com/au. "Stone Cold Steve Austin reveals the key battle that defined him." May 16, 2017, https://www.news.com.au/sport/more-sports/stone-cold-steve-austin -reveals-the-key-battle-that-defined-him/news-story/2472ca164b548f7794c6eb5c e27f2294.

Pena, Daniel. "Steve Austin's Ex-Wife Talks Coming Up With 'Stone Cold', Past Drug Addiction, WCW." SEScoops.com, May 13, 2015, https://www.sescoops.com /steve-austins-ex-wife-talks-coming-up-with-stone-cold-past-drug-addiction-wcw/.

11   How Jordan's Bulls Lost Ten Games

Schmitz, Brian. "Jordan, Bulls motivated by Magic to go 72–10." *Orlando Sentinel*, Apr. 6, 2016, https://www.orlandosentinel.com/sports/orlando-magic/os-bulls-nba -record-brian-schmitz-0407-20160406-column.html.

12   Into the Shaq-verse

Corry, Joel. "The inside story: How the Magic let the Lakers steal Shaquille O'Neal." CBSSports.com, July 21, 2016, https://www.cbssports.com/nba/news /the-inside-story-how-the-orlando-magic-let-the-lakers-steal-shaquille-oneal/.

Diaz, George. "A Penny Could Be Worth Millions." *Orlando Sentinel*, Mar. 18, 1993, https://www.orlandosentinel.com/news/os-xpm -1993-03-18-9303180125-story.html.

Fromal, Adam. "Shaq Says He 'Would've Stayed' in Orlando If He Had a Mulligan." BleacherReport.com, Mar. 22, 2015, https://bleacherreport.com/articles/24120 12-shaq-says-he-wouldve-stayed-in-orlando-if-he-had-a-mulligan.

Glasspiegel, Ryan. "A Look Back at Those Great Lil' Penny Commercials with Chris Rock." *Sports Illustrated*, Nov. 8, 2013, https://www.si.com/extra-mustard/2013/11 /08/a-look-back-at-those-great-lil-penny-commercials-with-chris-rock.

Heisler, Mark. "Lakers Hit The Shaqpot." *Los Angeles Times*, July 19, 1996, https://www .latimes.com/archives/la-xpm-1996-07-19-sp-25797-story.html.

Joshi, Maitreyee. "'I knew it was over': Former Teammate Reveals How Departure of Shaquille O'Neal Doomed Orlando Magic." EssentiallySports.com, May 15, 2020, https://www.essentiallysports.com/nba-news-i-knew-it-was-over-former-teammate -reveals-how-departure-of-shaquille-oneal-doomed-orlando-magic/.

14   Kobe's Draft Class

The Associated Press. "76ers make Iverson No. 1 pick." June 27, 1996, https://www .newspapers.com/image/342960308.

The Associated Press. "Timberwolves' trade pleases Marbury." (Madison) *Wisconsin State Journal*, June 27, 1996, https://www.newspapers.com/image/398432581/?terms =Stephon%2Bmarbury%2BMinnesota.

Bonnell, Rick. "Kobe Bryant was almost never traded to Lakers. Hornets tried to break deal, GM says." *The Charlotte Observer*, Jan. 29, 2020, https://www.charlotteobserver.com/sports/charlotte-hornets/article239760573.html.

McDonald, Archie. "Jackson got the player, and person, he wanted." *The Vancouver Sun*, June 27, 1996, newspapers.com/image/496390250/?terms=Vancouver%2BSun%2BNBA%2BDraft.

May, Peter. "Walker goes to the Celtics with the 6th pick." *The Boston Globe*, https://www.newspapers.com/image/441015694.

Reischel, Rob. "Allen confident he'll help." (Madison) *Wisconsin State Journal*, June 27, 1996, https://www.newspapers.com/image/398432581/?terms=Stephon%2Bmarbury%2BMinnesota.

Ryan, Bob. "Bird has word: This draft pick is a real keeper." *The Boston Globe*, https://www.newspapers.com/image/441015694.

The Washington Post. "Iverson the smallest No. 1 draft pick." June 27, 1996, newspapers.com/image/496390250/?terms=Vancouver%2BSun%2BNBA%2BDraft.

Wimbish, Jasmyn. "Kobe Bryant death: Hornets GM says trade that sent NBA legend to Lakers in 1996 draft almost never happened." CBSSports.com, Jan. 29, 2020, https://www.cbssports.com/nba/news/kobe-bryant-death-hornets-gm-says-trade-that-sent-nba-legend-to-lakers-in-1996-draft-almost-never-happened/.

Woelfel, Gery. "Bucks wheel, deal for Allen." *The* (Racine, Wisconsin) *Journal Times*, June 27, 1996, https://www.newspapers.com/image/342960308.

Woelfel, Gery. "Ugliest moment in Bucks' history." *The* (Racine, Wisconsin) *Journal Times*, June 27, 1996, https://www.newspapers.com/image/342960308.

15 Madison Square Gretzky
The Associated Press. "Busch Stadium rolls out the grass." Feb. 14, 1998, https://news.google.com/newspapers?id=sMQfAAAAIBAJ&sjid=h9gEAAAAIBAJ&pg=4456%2C5874912.

Hertzel, Bob. "Busch Stadium holds the heat." *The Pittsburgh Press*, Aug. 3, 1987, https://news.google.com/newspapers?id=LakcAAAAIBAJ&sjid=OWMEAAAAIBAJ&pg=5646%2C2336703.

Gordon, Jeff. "Hot Wings Spice Up Crowd, Give Blues A Case of Heartburn." *St. Louis Post-Dispatch*, May 6, 1996, https://www.newspapers.com/image/142527977#.

Luecking, Dave. "Twist Has A Fight With . . . His Conscience." *St. Louis Post-Dispatch*, May 6, 1996, https://www.newspapers.com/image/142527977#.

Miklasz, Bernie. "Blues Showed No Talent, No Work, No Class." *St. Louis Post-Dispatch*, May 6, 1996, https://www.newspapers.com/image/142527953.

16 Venus Meets Steffi
The Associated Press. "It's a struggle, but Graf prevails over Williams at Acura." Aug. 15, 1996, https://www.newspapers.com/image/246810173/?terms=venus%20williams&match=1.

The Associated Press. "Serena Tops Venus, Passes Graf, Reclaims No. 1 with 23rd Singles Slam." Jan. 27, 2017, https://www.tennis.com/pro-game/2017/01/marta-kostyuk-wins-australian-open-junior-girls-title/63779/.

Dohrmann, George. "Williams' Best Shot Falls Short." *Los Angeles Times*, Aug. 15, 1996, https://www.latimes.com/archives/la-xpm-1996-08-15-sp-34365-story.html.

Wiedeman, Reeves. "Child's Play." *The New Yorker*, May 26, 2014, https://www.newyorker.com/magazine/2014/06/02/childs-play-6.

17   Ali Ignites Atlanta

Gajanan, Mahita. "The Story Behind the Iconic Image of Muhammad Ali and the Olympic Flame." *Vanity Fair*, June 4, 2016, https://www.vanityfair.com /news/2016/06/the-story-behind-the-iconic-image-of-muhammad-ali-and-the -olympic-flame.

Ourand, John. "An Ebersol moment: Ali and the '96 flame." *Sports Business Journal*, May 18, 2015, https://www.sportsbusinessdaily.com/Journal/Issues/2015/05/18 /Sports-Business-Awards/Ebersol-Ali.aspx?ana=register_free_form_2_filled.

YouTube. "Gold Medal Moments: Muhammad Ali @ Atlanta 1996 Games Opening Ceremony." June 28, 2012, https://www.youtube.com/watch?v=QEhNDUwksvU.

18   Michael Johnson's Golden Feet

The Associated Press. "Barnes puts away gold; Johnson takes his time." July 27, 1996, https://www.newspapers.com/image/135998098/?terms=Michael%20 Johnson%20nike&match=1.

BleacherReport.com. "Michael Johnson and the Night the Shoes Went Golden." Aug. 9, 2016, https://bleacherreport.com/articles/2656561-michael-johnson-and-the -night-the-shoes-went-golden.

Groves, Peter. "Michael Johnson Atlanta 1996 Gold 400m/200m." YouTube.com, July 6, 2016, https://www.youtube.com/watch?v=hJAeyMfMhnI.

Schwartz, Larry. "Johnson doubled the difficulty." ESPN.com, https://www.espn.com /sportscentury/features/00016046.html.

19   Dream Team III

Miklasz, Bernie. "Dream Realized, But Thrill Is Gone." *St. Louis Post-Dispatch*, Aug. 4, 1996, https://www.newspapers.com/image/142530665/?terms=august%20 3rd%20muhammad%20ali%20medal%20barkley&match=1.

NBCSports.com. "Why Michael Jordan didn't return for 1996 Atlanta Olympics." May 1, 2020, https://olympics.nbcsports.com/2020/05/01/michael -jordan-atlanta-1996-olympics-dream-team/

Smith, Sam. "Dream Team Opens by Beating Argentina." *Chicago Tribune*, July 21, 1996, https://www.chicagotribune.com/news/ct-xpm-1996-07-21-9607210264-story .html.

(Fort Worth) *Star-Telegram*. "Dream Team avoids upset." July 7, 1996, https:// www.newspapers.com/image/645651879/?terms=team%20usa%20 basketball&match=1.

21   Agassi Reinvented

Elmore, Charles. "Agassi's greatest hit: pure gold." *The Atlanta Journal-Constitution*, Aug. 4, 1996, https://www.newspapers.com/image/403357436/?terms=Andre%20 Agassi&match=1.

Vafidis, Jen. "Andre Agassi: Remembering Tennis Legend's Golden Olympic Moment." *Rolling Stone*, July 27, 2016, https://www.rollingstone.com/culture/culture-sports/andre-agassi-remembering-tennis-legends-golden-olympic-moment-248765/.

23 Tiger's First Roar

Cash, Meredith. "Videos of Tiger Woods golfing as a kid show he's always been destined for greatness." Business Insider, Apr. 14, 2019, https://www.businessinsider.com/tiger-woods-childhood-golfing-videos-2018-9.

Dohrmann, George. "Tiger Woods wins his first PGA tourney." *Los Angeles Times*, Oct. 7, 1996, https://www.newspapers.com/image/144965739/?terms=Tiger%20Woods&match=1.

Sirak, Ron. "Golf's first Billion-Dollar Man." *Golf Digest*, February 2006, https://web.archive.org/web/20070513225510/http://www.golfdigest.com/features/index.ssf?%2Ffeatures%2Fgd200602top50.html.

Steinemann, Sean. "The Ultimate Tiger Woods Career Timeline." *Golf*, Dec. 1, 2016, https://golf.com/news/tournaments/the-ultimate-tiger-woods-career-timeline/.

24 Jeter & the Yankees Revival

Antonen, Mel. "For Yanks quartet, winning a fifth title would add to a legacy." USATODAY.com, Oct. 6, 2009, https://usatoday30.usatoday.com/sports/baseball/al/yankees/2009-10-06-yankees-quartet_N.htm.

Edes, Gordon. "Jeter fits in Yankees' near future." *Fort Lauderdale Sun-Sentinel*, Aug. 28, 1994, https://news.google.com/newspapers?id=V91HAAAAIBAJ&pg=3679,4921919&dq=derek-jeter+albany&hl=en.

Harper, John. "Jeter single in 10th caps wild rally over Red Sox." (New York) *Daily News*, Sept. 22, 1996, https://www.newspapers.com/image/492052390/?terms=derek%20jeter&match=1.

Kiesel, Connor. "Looking back: Jeter's milestone Opening Day in Cleveland." FoxSports.com, July 9, 2014, https://www.foxsports.com/ohio/story/new-york-yankees-derek-jeter-first-home-run-cleveland-indians-opening-day-1996-070914.

(Mansfield, Ohio) *News-Journal*. "Opener snowed under." Apr. 2, 1996, https://www.newspapers.com/image/296187564/?terms=cleveland%20indians%20opening%20day&match=1.

Santasierre III, Alfred. "Yankees Magazine: Toast of the town." MLB.com, Sept. 13, 2016, https://www.mlb.com/news/derek-jeter-recalls-1996-yankees-world-series-c201153426.

YouTube.com. "Derek Jeter delivers first career walk-off hit in 1996." Feb. 12, 2014, https://www.youtube.com/watch?v=LWfzOitXDeI.

YouTube.com. "Watch Derek Jeter's first career home run in 1996." Sept. 24, 2014, https://www.youtube.com/watch?v=2k935zu2xE4.

Walker, Ben and Tom Withers. "Braves have experience; N.Y. has home field edge." The Associated Press, Oct. 19, 1996, https://www.newspapers.com/image/240465619/?terms=Yankees&match=1

25   The Rock

Charendoff, Taylor. "The Rock Reflects on Failing at His Original Dream of Playing in the NFL." ScreenRant.com, June 12, 2019, https://screenrant.com/rock-failed-nfl-dream-reflection/.

Friedell, Dan. "How good was The Rock at football?" ESPN.com, Dec. 11, 2012, https://www.espn.com/blog/playbook/fandom/post/_/id/15186/how-good-was-the-rock-at-football.

Johnson, Richard. "Warren Sapp says he told The Rock at Miami: 'I'm here for your job, b---h.'" SBNation.com, May 1, 2018, https://www.sbnation.com/college-football/2018/5/1/17305438/warren-sapp-dwayne-the-rock-johnson-miami-teammates.

Mooneyham, Mike. "Pro Wrestling's 'Soulman' Rocky Johnson, The Rock's dad, fought the odds and won." *The Post and Courier* (Charleston, South Carolina), Sept. 14, 2020, https://www.postandcourier.com/sports/wrestling/pro-wrestling-s-soulman-rocky-johnson-the-rocks-dad-fought-the-odds-and-won/article_7fb7858c-3eb9-11ea-b901-87147a515cc8.html.

Morgan, Kaya. "Dwyane Johnson—How The Rock Transformed from Pro Wrestler to Bankable Movie Star." IslandConnections.com, Aug. 29, 2017, https://web.archive.org/web/20170829034426/http://www.islandconnections.com/edit/dwayne_johnson.htm.

Stern, Macklin. "How Dwyane Johnson's Forgotten Football Career Prepared Him for Superstardom." BleacherReport.com, May 1, 2018, https://bleacherreport.com/articles/2773531-how-dwyane-johnsons-forgotten-football-career-prepared-him-for-superstardom?utm_source=twitter.com&utm_medium=referral&utm_campaign=programming-national.

YouTube.com. "Rocky Johnson Opens Up About Training His son The Rock." Oct. 7, 2019, https://www.youtube.com/watch?v=2CHDP9GOOa4.

26   Iron Mike Punches Out

Borges, Ron. "Holyfield given a fighting chance." *The Boston Globe*, Nov. 9, 1996, https://www.newspapers.com/image/441074351/?terms=Mike%20tyson&match=1.

Cloud, Bob. "Holyfield win has sports books crying blues." *Las Vegas Sun*, Nov. 11, 1996, https://lasvegassun.com/news/1996/nov/11/holyfield-win-has-sports-books-crying-blues/.

Katz, Michael. "IBF challenger may shun Tyson." (New York) *Daily News*, Mar. 17, 1996, https://www.newspapers.com/image/475618721/?terms=Mike%20Tyson&match=1.

Murray, Jim. "This One Was Over Before It Even Began." *Los Angeles Times*, Sept. 8, 1996, https://www.newspapers.com/image/158754123/?terms=mike%20tyson&match=1.

Ryan, Bob. "Tyson has good mind to keep on fighting." *The Boston Globe*, Aug. 19, 1995, https://www.newspapers.com/image/440864762.

Springer, Steve. "After Belting Bruno, Tyson Gets a Belt Back." *Los Angeles Times*, Mar. 17, 1996, https://www.newspapers.com/image/159269848/?terms=mike%20tyson&match=1.

27 *Space Jam*

Failes, Ian. "The Oral History of 'Space Jam': Part 1 – Launching the Movie." CartoonBrew.com, Nov. 15, 2016, https://www.cartoonbrew.com/feature-film/oral-history-space-jam-part-1-launching-movie-144935.html.

Squadron, Alex. "An Oral History of Michael Jordan's Legendary 'Space Jam' Pickup Runs." SlamOnLine.com, May 11, 2020, https://www.slamonline.com/the-magazine/space-jam-pickup-runs-michael-jordan/.

28 There's Something About Favre

The Associated Press. "Favre admits addiction." May 15, 1996, https://www.newspapers.com/image/513766757/?terms=Brett%20Favre&match=1.

Beech, Mark. "Reflecting on Brett Favre's First Victory with the Green Bay Packers." *Sports Illustrated*, Nov. 13, 2019, https://www.si.com/nfl/2019/11/13/brett-favre-debut-book-excerpt-mark-beech-the-peoples-team-green-bay-packers#:~:text=In%20an%20excerpt%20from%20his,started%20the%20season%200%2D2.

Carlson, Chuck. "Favre erases doubts, looks like old self." *The* (Madison, Wisconsin) *Capital Times*, Sept. 2, 1996, https://www.newspapers.com/image/522279937.

D'Amato, Gary. "Seasons of Greatness: Top 10/No. 4: Brett Favre, 1996." (Milwaukee) *Journal Sentinel*, Feb. 24, 2012, https://archive.jsonline.com/sports/140383503.html/#:~:text=SHARE-,Brett%20Favre%2C%201996,NFL%20most%20valuable%20player%20awards.

Demovsky, Rob. "The Great Favre Gamble." ESPN.com, Aug. 4, 2016, http://www.espn.com/espn/feature/story/_/id/17211520/how-brett-favre-landed-green-bay-packers-made-happen.

Dougherty, Pete and John Morton. "Agent: Progress made on Favre pact." *Green Bay Press-Gazette*, Jan. 5, 1997, https://www.newspapers.com/image/190445271/?terms=Brett%20Favre&match=1.

Greenberg, Alan. "Closer Look at Parcells' Departure from Patriots." *Hartford Courant*, Sept. 26, 2004, https://www.courant.com/news/connecticut/hc-xpm-2004-09-26-0409260284-story.html.

Meyer, Angie. "Brett Favre: Is This the End?" BleacherReport.com, Aug. 4, 2010, https://bleacherreport.com/articles/429734-brett-favre-is-this-the-end.

Silverstein, Tom. "Trading places: Wolf hits the jackpot in deal for Favre." (Milwaukee) *Journal Sentinel*, Sept. 24, 2005, https://web.archive.org/web/20060113071715/http://www.jsonline.com/packer/news/sep05/358097.asp.

29 *Jerry Maguire*

Fleming Jr., Mike. "Tom Hanks, Jamie Foxx, Billy Wilder & Gwyneth Paltrow? Cameron Crowe Reflects On His 'Jerry Maguire' Journey." Deadline.com, Jan. 2, 2017, https://deadline.com/2017/01/jerry-maguire-cameron-crowe-tom-cruise-james-l-brooks-cuba-gooding-glenn-frey-leigh-steinberg-drew-rosenhaus-20th-anniversary-1201877503/.

INDEX

ABOUT THE AUTHOR

JON FINKEL IS THE AWARD-WINNING AUTHOR of *Hoops Heist, The Life of Dad, The Athlete, Heart Over Height,* "*Mean" Joe Greene,* The "Greatest Stars of the NBA" Series, and other books about sports, fatherhood, fitness, and more. His work has been endorsed by Spike Lee, Tony Dungy, Jerry Jones, Mark Cuban, and Chef Robert Irvine. He is the co-host of the *Life of Dad Show* podcast and Lunch Break Facebook Live Show with more than one thousand viewers. He has written for *GQ, Men's Health,* Yahoo! Sports, the *New York Times,* and dozens of other national publications. He lives in South Florida with his wife, two kids, and their rescue dog Lyla.